Creating and Digitizing Language Corpora
Volume 1: Synchronic Databases

Also by the editors

CREATING AND DIGITIZING LANGUAGE CORPORA
Volume 2: Diachronic Databases

Creating and Digitizing Language Corpora

Volume 1: Synchronic Databases

Edited by

Joan C. Beal
Sheffield University

Karen P. Corrigan and Hermann L. Moisl
Newcastle University

Foreword by Shana Poplack
University of Ottawa

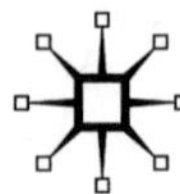

First published 2007 by
PALGRAVE MACMILLAN
Houndmills, Basingstoke, Hampshire RG21 6XS and
175 Fifth Avenue, New York, N.Y. 10010
Companies and representatives throughout the world

PALGRAVE MACMILLAN is the global academic imprint of the Palgrave Macmillan division of St. Martin's Press, LLC and of Palgrave Macmillan Ltd. Macmillan® is a registered trademark in the United States, United Kingdom and other countries. Palgrave is a registered trademark in the European Union and other countries.

ISBN 13: 978–1–4039–4366–8
ISBN 10: 1–4039–4366–4

This book is printed on paper suitable for recycling and made from fully managed and sustained forest sources. Logging, pulping and manufacturing processes are expected to conform to the environmental regulations of the country of origin.

A catalogue record for this book is available from the British Library.

Library of Congress Cataloging-in-Publication Data
Creating and digitizing/language corpora/ edited by Joan C. Beal, Karen P. Corrigan, Herman L. Moisl; foreword Shana Poplack.
p. cm.
Includes bibliographical references and index.
Contents: v. 1. Synchronic databases – v. 2. Diachronic databases.
ISBN 1–4039–4366–4 (cloth)
1. Computational linguistics. I. Beal, Joan C. II. Corrigan, Karen P., 1961–
P98.C73 2007 2006049407
410.285–dc22

10 9 8 7 6 5 4 3 2 1
16 15 14 13 12 11 10 09 08 07

Printed and bound in Great Britain by
Antony Rowe Ltd, Chippenham and Eastbourne

Contents

List of Tables

List of Figures

Foreword

Only two or three decades ago, those of us who had the patience and the wherewithal to construct a computerized corpus of recorded speech, however clunky, were the envy of our colleagues. In those days, linguists interested in quantitative analysis simply slogged through their audio-tapes, extracting unfathomable quantities of data by hand. Cedergren, to name but one notable example, analyzed 53,038(!) tokens of phonological variables, culled individually from her tapes, in her 1973 analysis of Panamanian Spanish.

The gold standard for transcribed corpora at the time was the concordance, possessed by a fortunate few, and coveted by all who were doomed to manual extraction. Of course the vintage concordance was largely limited to lexically-based retrieval, but at least it was searchable. The papers that Joan Beal, Karen Corrigan and Hermann Moisl have assembled in these companion volumes are eloquent testimony to how far the field of corpus linguistics – now rife with electronic corpora – has come in so short a time.

Building a corpus arguably involves a greater investment in time, resources and energy than any other type of linguistic activity. Decisions are legion at every stage of the process: sampling, ensuring representativeness, collecting data, transcribing them, correcting, standardizing the transcription, correcting, tagging and markup, correcting, and facilitating retrieval. Adding to the challenge is the fact that at the outset of the project the researcher is often not even familiar enough with the materials to make the best decisions, and changing midstream is costly and time-consuming. What could possibly make such a huge front-end investment worthwhile? Dealing with corpora at every stage of development, from fledgling endeavours to large-scale, heavily exploited enterprises, these reports offer a state-of-the-art synthesis of the problems researchers have encountered and the solutions they have adopted to deal with them.

The focus of these volumes is on *unconventional* corpora, like the non-standard, regional and dialectal varieties of speech, creole texts and child language discussed in Volume 1. Each poses problems hardly imaginable to the early builders of more orthodox corpora based on written or standard materials. The unifying question is how to 'tame' them, in the editors' terminology. Taming, as understood here, is largely a question of representation: How to represent forms for which there is no standard orthography, what to represent, how much to annotate, how much analysis to impose on the materials, how to represent ambiguities and indeterminacies, how to represent the finished product to the end-user. Noting the diversity, not only in the models underlying different corpora but also in their methods of encoding and analysis, the editors, themselves seasoned corpus builders, question whether it is reasonable or even feasible to aim for standardized protocols of the kind employed in traditional corpora for the collection, transcription, annotation and preservation of their less conventional counterparts.

Perhaps the first to grapple with the problem of taming unconventional data were the Sankoff-Cedergren team, whose *Montreal French Corpus* (Sankoff and Sankoff 1973) was built to elucidate a stigmatized variety previously widely believed to be an incorrect version of European French. Their goal was to show that the 'deviant' forms were part of a complex sociolinguistic structure, by tapping into different sources of speech variation: inter-individual, intra-individual and intra-linguistic. Chief among the problems inherent in such an endeavour was the issue of representativeness: How to guarantee representativeness of all the possible diversity in speech, while maintaining randomness in the selection of informants? They achieved this by implementing a detailed sampling frame, which, in contrast to their material procedures, has not yet been superseded. Their problems and solutions hark back to a simpler time, especially as compared with those corpus linguists face today. The transcription protocol – standard orthography – was dictated by the number of symbols on the punch keyboard for the IBM computer cards they used. Correction was effected by removing the card containing the error and inserting a correctly punched card in its place. The 100,000 cards containing the transcriptions then had to be converted into reams of computer printouts – and all without dropping a single card! In an era in which an entire corpus can be carried around on a memory stick or an iPod, it is worth noting that the print concordance of the 3.5 million-word *Ottawa-Hull French Corpus* (Poplack 1989), for example, occupies an entire wall – floor to ceiling – of the Ottawa Sociolinguistics Lab. The technology was primitive.

Since then, striking advances, not only in terms of hardware, but also in the area of annotation systems, have revolutionized corpus linguistics. No protocol has yet emerged as standard, though – as observed by the editors in initiating this project. So it's no surprise that the issue of annotation enjoys pride of place in these volumes, with researchers weighing in on what to annotate, how much detail to include, and whether it is preferable to replicate markup schemes of other corpora or tailor them to one's own. It is clear that the old problem of finding the right balance of quantity, recoverability and faithfulness is still with us. Faithfulness at every linguistic level to data with much inherent variability (i.e. all speech, and many older and/or nonstandard written texts) inevitably results in diminished recoverability and less quantity. Without sufficient quantity, statistical significance is impossible to establish and full cross-cutting conditioning yields mostly empty cells. Optimum recoverability comes at the expense of less faithfulness to the many variant realizations of what is underlyingly a single form.

Each of the contributors to these volumes grapples with these problems in their own way. Some prefer to abandon one or more of the principles, others respond with complicated interfaces. As a result, the corpora described in this collection illustrate the full gamut of possibilities, from an annotation system so rich and complex that it already incorporates a good deal of the linguistic analysis, at one extreme, to virtually no markup whatsoever at the other. Linkage of transcripts to (audio and video) recordings and syntactic parsing will no doubt be the wave of the future.

The projected use of the corpus, as *end-product* or *tool*, is clearly the determining factor. Those for whom the corpus is a tool tend to advocate minimal annotation. These researchers are able to tolerate more indeterminacy and ambiguity, either because they have determined that it will not affect what they're looking for (e.g. a number of the corpora described here provide no detail on phonetic form or discourse processes), or because the sheer volume of data available allows them to omit the ambiguous cases or neutralize errors through large-scale quantitative analysis. Others, for whom the corpus is the end-product, tend to aim for consistency with guidelines for existing corpora, even if these do not seem immediately relevant to the proposed research. So what is the best annotation system? The amalgamated wisdom to be gleaned from these contributions: the one that works for you. At the moment, then, the answer to the editors' query regarding the feasibility of standardizing transcription protocols seems to be a qualified 'no'.

Comparatively less emphasis is placed on the issue of *representativeness,* the extent to which the sample of observations drawn from the corpus corresponds to the parent population. Achieving representativeness for (socio)linguistic purposes involves identifying the major sources of variation in the population (of speakers and utterances) and taking them into account while constructing the sample. Few corpora in these volumes, by necessity or design, claim to be representative in the sense of Sankoff (1988). Rather, in most of these contributions, (as in much social science research more generally), the sample is opportunistic. This is an issue that every corpus must come to terms with, since even large numbers of observations cannot compensate for a sample frame from which the major sources of variation are missing. To the extent that the sample does not span the variant answers to the research question, pursuit of that question via that corpus can only be spurious.

Whether representativeness or annotation is more fundamental to the eventual utility of the corpus is a moot point. It is worth noting, however, that the awkward, and for some, simplistic, transcription protocols of early unconventional corpora did nothing to diminish their interest, value and current relevance. Hundreds of studies have been, and continue to be, based on them, perhaps because the research questions they were constructed to answer are still burning ones. The same is of course true of a number of the established corpora described in these volumes, and no doubt will be of many of the more incipient ones as well. The good news is that these repositories have an enduring value that far transcends our automated treatment and handling of them.

I end this foreword by returning to the question I posed at the beginning. What could possibly make the huge front-end investment required to build a corpus worthwhile? Obvious answers include the enormously enhanced speed of data collection, enabling consideration of ever greater quantities of data with relatively little extra effort. This in turn increases the chances of locating rare tokens, achieving statistical significance and determining which factors condition the choice between alternating forms. All of these are inestimable boons for quantitative analysis, but they pale in comparison to what for me remains the most exciting aspect of corpus work: the opportunity it affords to serendipitously discover what one wasn't looking for, to characterize the patterned nature of linguistic heterogeneity, and in particular the hidden, unsuspected or 'irrational' constraints that are simply inaccessible to introspection or casual perusal.

How much closer are we to the goal of agreeing on a standardized annotation? Well, we aren't there yet, though only time will tell. In the interim, anyone who has ever considered building a corpus or is engaged in doing so now will want to have a copy of this book close at hand. The wide variety of contributions convey much of the excitement of this burgeoning field. Despite inevitable differences in methods and projected end uses, the common thread is the shared goal of finding and implementing the best practices in corpus construction and preservation. These companion volumes, examining both synchronic and diachronic corpora, serve as a model for how to achieve them. For this, we can only be grateful to the editors, who encouraged such stimulating dialogue.

SHANA POPLACK

References

Cedergren, Henrietta. 1973. 'Interplay of social and linguistic factors in Panama'. PhD dissertation, Cornell University.

Poplack, Shana. 1989. 'The care and handling of a mega-corpus'. *Language Variation and Change* (Current Issues in Linguistic Theory, 52), ed. by R. Fasold and D. Schiffrin, pp. 411-451. Philadelphia: John Benjamins.

Sankoff, David. 1988. 'Problems of representativeness'. *Sociolinguistics. An International Handbook of the Science of Language and Society*, Vol. 2, ed. by U. Ammon, N. Dittmar and K. J. Mattheier, pp. 899-903. Berlin: Walter de Gruyter.

Sankoff, David and Sankoff, Gillian. 1973. 'Sample survey methods and computer-assisted analysis in the study of grammatical variation'. *Canadian Languages in their Social Context,* ed. by R. Darnell, pp. 7-63. Edmonton: Linguistic Research Inc.

Notes on the Contributors

Jean Anderson is the Resource Development Officer for the School of English and Scottish Language and Literature at the University of Glasgow. She lectures in Literary and Linguistic Computing and has been involved in digital projects since 1987 (her most recent being the Scottish Corpus of Texts and Speech (SCOTS) begun in 2001 and still ongoing).

Lieselotte Anderwald is Assistant Professor of English Linguistics at Freiburg University, Germany. She has published *Negation in Non-Standard British Dialects: Gaps, Regularizations, Asymmetries* (2002).

Sjef Barbiers was Lecturer in Dutch Linguistics at Leiden University. He is currently Special Researcher at the Meertens Institute, Amsterdam and Professor of Variationist Linguistics at Utrecht University. He was leader of the Syntactic Atlas of the Dutch Dialects (SAND) project and is co-author of *SAND*, Volume 1 (2005). He is currently leader of the ESF-funded project European Dialect Syntax.

Joan C. Beal was Senior Lecturer in English Language at Newcastle University until moving to the University of Sheffield in 2001. She was Co-investigator on the AHRC-funded Newcastle Electronic Corpus of Tyneside English (NECTE) project at Newcastle and is currently Professor of English Language and Director of the National Centre for English Cultural Tradition. Recent publications include *English in Modern Times* (2004) and *Language and Region* (2006).

Dave Beavan is Computing Manager for the Scottish Corpus of Texts and Speech at the University of Glasgow. His prime areas of expertise are in data management and internet delivery of content. He is a strong advocate of open source, standards-based computing solutions.

Leonie Cornips is Senior Researcher of Syntax and Sociolinguistics and Head of Department at the Meertens Institute, Amsterdam. She was responsible for designing the methodolology underpinning the Syntactic Atlas of Dutch Dialects project. Her recent publications focus on syntactic variation (with Karen Corrigan), syntactic elicitation methodology (with Cecilia Poletto) and L1/L2 acquisition (with Aafke Hulk).

Karen P. Corrigan has held lectureships at University College, Dublin and the universities of Edinburgh and York (UK). She was Principal Investigator on the NECTE project and is currently a Reader in Linguistics and English Language at Newcastle University. She was awarded a Leverhulme Trust Research Fellowship (2000–02) and has recently published *Syntax and Variation* (2005) (with Leonie Cornips).

Susan Dray completed her doctorate on non-standard writing practices in Jamaica at Lancaster University in 2004 with funding from an ESRC studentship. She is an Honorary Research Fellow in the Department of Linguistics and English Language at Lancaster, and was Co-investigator on a recent ESRC-funded project, Language and Literacies of Young Caribbeans in Manchester.

Penelope Gardner-Chloros is Lecturer in the School of Languages, Linguistics and Culture at Birkbeck, University of London. Her books include *Language Selection and Switching in Strasbourg* (1991) and *Code-switching* (forthcoming). She is a founding member of the LIPPS/LIDES Group, which is setting up an electronic bilingual database. She also works on French Sociolinguistics, especially Terms of Address.

Jeffrey Kallen is Fellow of Trinity College Dublin, where he is a Senior Lecturer in Linguistics and Phonetics. A former president of the Irish Association for Applied Linguistics, he has published widely on the English language in Ireland, discourse analysis, semiotics, and socio-linguistic perspectives on linguistic pluralism.

Christian Kay is Honorary Professorial Research Fellow in English Language at the University of Glasgow and Convener of Scottish Language Dictionaries Ltd, which has taken on responsibility for the future development of the *Dictionary of the Older Scottish Tongue (DOST)* and the *Scottish National Dictionary (SND)*. She is joint author of *A Thesaurus of Old English* (2000) and a director of the Historical Thesaurus of English and SCOTS corpus projects at Glasgow.

John Kirk is Senior Lecturer in English and Scottish Language at Queen's University Belfast. With Jeffrey Kallen, he is a co-director of the International Corpus of English: Ireland project. With Dónall Ó Baoill, he is a general editor of *Belfast Studies in Language, Culture and Politics*.

Jan Pieter Kunst worked on the *Bibliography of Dutch Language and Literature (BNTL)* which was published by the Netherlands Institute for Scientific Information Services (NIWI-KNAW). He currently works as a software developer at the Meertens Institute, Amsterdam where he uses open source to build web applications, among which DynaSAND is his most recent project.

Brian MacWhinney, Professor of Psychology and Modern Languages at Carnegie Mellon University, has developed the CHILDES Project for the computational study of child language transcript data and the TalkBank system for the study of conversational interactions. He has also developed a model of first- and second-language acquisition and processing called the 'Competition Model'.

Hermann L. Moisl is Senior Lecturer in Computational Linguistics at Newcastle University and he was Co-investigator on the NECTE project. His interests and publications are in natural language processing, neural modelling of language and multivariate analysis of corpora.

Melissa Moyer is Associate Professor of English Linguistics at the Universitat Autónoma de Barcelona. Her publications and research interests include code-switching in Gibraltar, language contact phenomena in bilingual communities, and the role of English as a global language in new migrant contexts in the city of Barcelona. Her most recent book (in collaboration with Li Wei) is the *Guide to Research Methods in Bilingualism and Multilingualism* (forthcoming).

Mark Sebba is Reader in Sociolinguistics and Language Contact in the Department of Linguistics and English Language at Lancaster University. His interests include pidgin and creole languages, bilingualism, and the sociolinguistics of orthography. His research into the language of young African-Caribbeans in London is reported in his book *London Jamaican* (1993).

Sali A. Tagliamonte is Associate Professor in the Linguistics Department of the University of Toronto, Canada. Her expertise is in language variation and change in synchronic corpora. She has published on African American English as well as on the English dialects of the British Isles, teen language and the impact of television on dialect change. Her ongoing research focuses on morphosyntactic change using cross-variety and apparent time comparisons.

Susanne Wagner is currently doing research on English in Newfoundland. She received her PhD in English Linguistics from the University of Freiburg in 2003, where she has also lectured. Her research focus is on morphosyntactic variation in dialects of Great Britain in general and the South-west of England in particular.

List of Abbreviations

BC	British Creole
BE	Bank of English
BNC	British National Corpus
CA	Conversation analysis
CHAT	Codes for the human analysis of transcripts
CHILDES	Child Language Data Exchange System
CLAN	Computerized language analysis
CS	Code-switching
CSD	*Concise Scots Dictionary*
CSS	Cascading Style Sheets
CUD	*Concise Ulster Dictionary*
CWBC	Corpus of Written British Creole
CWJC	Corpus of Written Jamaican Creole
DAT	Digital audio tape
DOST	*Dictionary of the Older Scottish Tongue*
DV	Digital video
EDD	*English Dialect Dictionary*
FRED	Freiburg English Dialect Corpus
HTML	Hyper Text Markup Language
HUD	Department of Housing and Urban Development
ICE	International Corpus of English
IPA	International Phonetic Alphabet
LDC	Linguistic Data Consortium
LIDES	Language Interaction Data Exchange System
LIPPS	Language Interaction in Plurilingual and Plurilectal Speakers
NECTE	Newcastle Electronic Corpus of Tyneside English
OCR	Optical character recognition
OED	*Oxford English Dictionary*
ONZE	Origins of New Zealand English
PHP	PHP: Hypertext Preprocessor
SAND	Syntactic Atlas of the Dutch Dialects
SBCSAE	Santa Barbara Corpus of Spoken American English
SCOTS	Scottish Corpus of Texts and Speech
SE	Standard English
SED	*Survey of English Dialects*

SJE	Standard Jamaican English
SLD	Scottish Language Dictionaries
SND	*Scottish National Dictionary*
SQL	Structured Query Language
SS15	Fifteenth Sociolinguistics Symposium
SVG	Scalable Vector Graphics
TEI	Text Encoding Initiative
UG	Universal Grammar
VITC	Vertical Interval Time Code
XHTML	Extensible HyperText Markup Language
XML	Extensible Markup Language
YCOE	York Corpus of Old English

1
Taming Digital Voices and Texts: Models and Methods for Handling Unconventional Synchronic Corpora

Joan C. Beal, Karen P. Corrigan and Hermann L. Moisl

1 Stimulus for the volume and its overarching aim

Six of the contributions to Volume 1 (Anderson *et al.*; Anderwald and Wagner; Barbiers *et al.*; Sebba and Dray; Kallen and Kirk; Tagliamonte) arose from invited presentations at the workshop on 'Models and Methods in the Handling of Unconventional Digital Corpora' organized by the editors of the present volume that was held in April 2004 during the Fifteenth Sociolinguistics Symposium (SS15) at the University of Newcastle. The book project then evolved by inviting further contributions from key corpus creators so that the companion volumes would contain treatments outlining the models and methods underpinning a variety of digitized diachronic and synchronic corpora with a view to highlighting synergies and points of contrast between them. The overarching aim of the project is to establish whether or not annotation standards and guidelines of the kind already employed in the creation of more conventional corpora on standard spoken and written Englishes, such as the British National Corpus (http://info.ox.ac.uk/bnc) and the Bank of English (http://titania.cobuild.collins.co.uk/boe_info.html), should be extended to less conventional corpora so that they too might be 'tamed' in similar ways.

Since the development of the Brown corpus in the 1960s (see Francis and Kučera, 1964), the variety of electronic corpora now available to the linguistics community and the analytical tools developed to successfully mine this data have gone hand in hand with improvements in standards and guidelines for corpus creation and encoding. Contemporary spoken and written regional English corpora, as well as those containing bilingual and child language data of the kinds described in this volume, pose an array of additional problems as regards standards, since the creation of such databases often requires the encoder to come to the task *ab initio*. As such, while the resultant corpora are clearly high quality resources in their own right (and extremely valuable research tools within the discipline to which they relate), there is considerable variation in the models and methods used in the collection of these digital corpora and in their subsequent encoding and analysis, largely because the underlying theoretical goals and assumptions of the researchers are quite distinctive (cf. Ochs, 1999; McEnery and Wilson, 2001, section 2.2; Milroy and Gordon, 2003, p. 143). There are marked differences, for instance, in the nature of the data contained therein and they also vary in: (i) the levels of phonetic, lexical, grammatical and semantic annotation that they encode; (ii) the means by which information is accessed/retrieved by the end-user and the means by which it is displayed (whether or not the written/spoken word or multilingual texts are aligned, for example).

Advances in technology, from the ability to digitize historical manuscript materials and field recordings to the dramatic improvements in computer hardware, software, storage facilities and analytical tools, have enabled the collection and organization of such data sets into a growing number of user-friendly electronic corpora. The latter have the potential to offer new insights into linguistic universals, for instance, since they allow, for the first time, rapid, systematic and efficient comparisons to be made between first and second languages/dialects across genres as well as social and geographical space. In addition, these corpora should be utilizable by researchers from a range of disciplines so that they are potentially as accessible to the socio-syntactician as they are to the conversation analyst or child language specialist in keeping with the aspirations of the Linguistic Data Consortium and Oxford Text Archive, inter alia.

These companion volumes are unique, since public output to date has primarily concentrated on describing and assessing the models and methods which underpin conventional corpora and the annotation standards/analytical tools developed specifically for them.[1]

2 Outline of contributions and their methodologies

The chapter by Anderson, Beavan and Kay provides an account of a corpus which consists of data from a wide range of sources and in a number of formats: written text, audio and video. The SCOTS corpus is intended eventually to include data from all the languages spoken in Scotland, but at present consists of material in Scots and Scottish

English. The authors here acknowledge that these two varieties are best thought of as a continuum with 'broad Scots' at one end and (Standard) Scottish English at the other. As such, the SCOTS corpus fills the gap left by the lack of a Scottish component for the ICE corpus to match the ICE-Ireland corpus described by Kallen and Kirk in this volume.

The upsurge of interest in Scottish language and culture surrounding the devolution of political power from London to Edinburgh meant that the compilers of the SCOTS corpus had a very positive response to their initial call for material. At the time of writing, the corpus consisted of some 600,000 words, but, as a monitor corpus, it is updated whenever significant amounts of new data are available. The involvement of the public, and the open-ended nature of this corpus, meant that legal/ethical issues of copyright, along with practical considerations of record-keeping, are probably more critical than those which apply to many of the corpora in these volumes (though see Sebba and Dray, as well as Kallen and Kirk). The administration system developed in response to these challenges is described and illustrated here, providing a useful model for teams embarking on similarly complex projects.

Like the compilers of many other corpora described in this volume, the SCOTS corpus team were confronted with the challenge of developing standards for transcribing texts for which standardized spelling conventions have not been developed. Indeed, they found that writers of some Scots texts submitted were not consistent in their spelling, even within the same text (the same issues were, of course, faced by the compilers of many of the diachronic corpora described in Volume 2). Since SCOTS is a searchable corpus, variability of spelling is also an issue for search-words: the team are, therefore, working with Scottish Language Dictionaries to devise headwords and a sophisticated enough spelling system.

Since the SCOTS corpus is intended to be publicly available to a wide variety of end-users, the website has been designed with accessibility in mind, using XHTML for the main website, but with provision for viewing and downloading plain text. The intention is to make TEI-compliant XML data sets available in future, in the manner of Allen *et al.*, Volume 2.

Finally, there is some discussion of the desirability of 'balance' in a corpus, but, as for most of the corpora described in these volumes, any attempt on the part of the SCOTS team to produce a corpus satisfying, for example, the British National Corpus (BNC) criteria for 'balance' and 'representativeness' would be futile, since, as the authors explain here, it is not yet known what proportion of writing in Scots is found in the various genres.

Lieselotte Anderwald and Susanne Wagner describe a corpus (the Freiburg English Dialect Corpus or FRED) which was compiled from data already collected by oral historians and, in that sense, there is an obvious relationship between it and NECTE (Allen *et al.*, Volume 2), though it does not share the latter's diachronic concerns. Consisting as it does of material recorded from older speakers in the 1960s and 1970s, FRED provides data which are comparable with those collected by the *Survey of English Dialects* (Orton, 1962), in that it represents the traditional dialect of speakers who reached adulthood before the Second World War, had minimal education and little or no mobility, and were mostly male. As such, FRED was designed to be regionally, rather than socially, representative.

The use of oral history data in a corpus digitized for linguistic purposes is novel, but, just as the diachronic corpora described in Volume 2 have proved of interest to historians, so linguists might well make more use of historical corpora.[2] Anderwald and Wagner discuss the drawbacks of using material compiled by non-linguists: transcription is often unsatisfactory, either 'normalizing' the text so that regional morphology disappears, or, conversely, using 'eye-dialect' in an attempt to convey the 'flavour' of the dialect. However, where audiotapes are also available, this can be corrected. A more serious drawback is the predominance of past over other tense forms, so that the corpus would not be useful for a study of present or future forms. Since the interviews are monologic, the FRED corpus would not be suitable either for the study of discourse features, but the same could be said of much interview data.

Reports on preliminary investigations using the FRED data which close this chapter demonstrate that corpus-based studies of regional variation in the morphology and syntax of English are overdue: for instance, the view put forward by Wakelin (1975) that the dialect of West Cornwall is more 'Standard' than that of the rest of the South-West is contradicted by Wagner's study of gendered pronouns, which, in the FRED corpus, are, in fact, most common in this region.

The third chapter in this volume by Barbiers, Cornips and Kunst describes at length the 'taming' of a larger-scale dialect syntax project relying on more recent data, namely, the Syntactic Atlas of the Dutch Dialects (SAND). The survey was conducted in the Netherlands and

Flanders and it aimed to create both a traditional printed atlas and an electronic searchable version that used specially created cartographic software for generating maps of particular morphosyntactic features online.

The data upon which both atlases are based are drawn from a range of sources: oral interviews conducted at various sites and followed up by telephone as well as the more traditional postal survey method (though at 156,000 question–answer pairs, the SAND version of the latter is considerably more extensive than most[3]).

The chapter relates in considerable detail the methodologies that underpin this mammoth venture outlining the typical social characteristics of SAND informants as well as the specialized techniques used to elicit responses from them (and the advantages and disadvantages of these more generally).

Praat (a transcription tool originally developed for phonetic data) was used to create the electronic versions of the corpus as it allowed alignment between orthographic transcription and speech signal and also made it possible to signal different levels in the transcription (an often problematic issue with transcribed spoken corpora, which is naturally, therefore, addressed by other authors in Volume 1, such as Gardner-Chloros *et al.*, as well as Allen *et al.* in Volume 2). The Barbiers *et al.* chapter also outlines the transcription protocol adopted, which, essentially, amounted to a normalization of the data into Standard Dutch orthography as far as practicably possible.[4] This was necessary for several reasons, most critical of which are: (i) it permits a certain amount of automatic lemmatization and pre-tagging and (ii) it has the added benefit that spelling across dialects is made uniform. The second of these is clearly an important consideration when you are developing online search and cartographic tools for a range of variables drawn from over 260 quite divergent dialects.

In contrast to most of the other linguistic corpora referred to in these volumes, SAND, like aspects of the SCOTS corpus described above, takes the form of a relational database. This permits more flexibility for the updating of the corpus in various ways over time and thus obviates the multiple versions issue that can arise when electronic corpora consist merely of collections of tagged text files. As already mentioned, the main function of SAND is to serve as a dynamic syntactic atlas and setting the corpus up as a relational database also facilitates its end-use as such in important ways. Users can perform database queries that can (both automatically and manually) create the input for maps that show the spatial distribution of syntactic variables across Flanders and The

Netherlands. Moreover, users can perform their own analyses by combining syntactic variables in one map so as to ascertain the extent to which their distribution coincides geographically. No doubt this unique corpus, which rests on meticulous methodological considerations, will live up to the aspirations of its creators, namely, to further research into syntactic microvariation from theoretical, typological, geolinguistic, historical and quantitative perspectives.

The next chapter, by Penelope Gardner-Chloros, Melissa Moyer and Mark Sebba, focuses on the Language Interaction Data Exchange System (LIDES) which is affiliated with the CHILDES enterprise, described below and in more detail in its creator's own chapter elsewhere in Volume 1 (see MacWhinney). The main goal of LIDES is to establish a network of scholars, working on the language interactions of adult multilingual speakers, who are committed to the same objectives with respect to developing coding schemes and guidelines for the electronic databases they produce.

Gardner-Chloros *et al.* in their chapter focus on the rationale behind the choice of the CHAT coding scheme and the CLAN tools in CHILDES for this purpose, noting that, despite some drawbacks, their adoption was encouraged by the fact that they are so open to further elaboration and updating and because: (i) there is a user-friendly interface already in place between CHAT and XML formats; (ii) CLAN programs recognize Unicode which is proving to be important for research on linguistic (including phonetic) data because it allows researchers to use their computer keyboard to represent a character from any language that has different script types;[5] and (iii) CLAN will eventually be fully able to support Praat which, as our discussion of the SAND project demonstrated, is increasingly becoming a standard tool for aligning and splicing real-time speech alongside written transcriptions of it.

In addition to facilitating the exchange and comparison of data sets created using these standards and tools, there are further benefits of LIDES, including the fact that the CLAN programs can be used to easily search very large data sets for patterns (of code-switching, for instance) or to provide quantitative analyses of various types.

A particular concern of the chapter is one shared by many contributors to these volumes, namely, the theoretical and practical problems encountered when transcribing spoken data. Indeed, Gardner-Chloros *et al.* clearly demonstrate that the difficulties described by our other authors whose corpora are composed of monolingual discourse are considerably exacerbated when transcribing *plurilingual* data. It is not surprising, therefore, that a considerable amount of discussion in the chapter revolves around the nature of the problems and the strategies which the LIDES team have found to be effective in resolving them. Critical to this dialogue is the working through of problematic cases using genuine data, a process which is concluded by presenting a step-by-step outline of the CHAT transcription scheme. The latter will clearly be invaluable to readers wishing to use the system to code their own multilingual data sets, as will the concluding section of the chapter in which applications (searches and frequency counts, for example) of CHAT-coded data are demonstrated.

Jeffrey Kallen and John Kirk, whose ICE-Ireland project has already been mentioned as sharing certain similarities with the SCOTS corpus in particular, provide the next chapter. It begins, naturally enough, with a brief history of the International Corpus of English (ICE) and its goals, and then turns to the specific application of these guidelines in an Irish context. At its most basic level, an ICE corpus must contain 300 spoken texts and 200 that are written, all of which are transcribed using the ICE coding system so that they can be compared with one another in a similar manner to that advocated in other international collaborative corpus projects featured in these volumes, such as CHILDES, LIDES and YCOE (see Taylor, Volume 2).

Although the criteria for creating the ICE corpora seem straightforward enough, a number of issues have had to be resolved by the ICE-Ireland team in their creation of an Irish version. An overriding issue (not faced by ICE-GB because of its southern-centric English bias but clearly also a consideration for other ICE collections, such as those in the Caribbean) was the definition of state boundaries, which Kallen and Kirk term the 'national context issue' (p. 123). Simply put, their concern is connected with the incongruity between more recent political and legal divisions of Ireland and its natural island geography as well as its more long-standing linguistic and social history, which do not necessarily match. The solution has been to eschew the production of two separate corpora (dictated by national boundaries) in favour of a single corpus that transcends these. This choice permits, for example, the inclusion of conversations between speakers both north and south of the technically separate state borders and a corpus content, which is split equally between Northern Ireland and the Republic. Although this distorts actual population distributions between the two jurisdictions, it is in keeping with practices adopted in the ICE programme more generally.

The collection and digitization of the ICE-Ireland corpus was begun in 1990 and has quickened in pace from 1999 onwards thanks to the receipt of research council and other awards. While additional material outwith the 1990–94 timescale of the ICE corpora more generally had to be collected in 2002 and 2003 to reach the target number of conversations and texts, the project is now complete and this chapter presents a wide-ranging account of the particular hurdles that had to be overcome in order to accomplish this. Of particular concern is the fact that access to certain kinds of data (such as recordings of courtroom proceedings and telephone conversations with male informants) normally found in ICE was impossible because of legal prohibitions and other culture-specific restrictions. Kallen and Kirk relate their attempts to fill these lacunae and the extent to which these were successful.

The constraints imposed by the transcription and annotation protocols of ICE meant that decisions with regard, for instance, to orthographic representation (a recurrent theme of chapters in each of these volumes) were considerably more straightforward for Kallen and Kirk, though they were also not without their own challenges (on account of having to encode certain unique aspects of Irish English in the digitized corpus).

Since so much of ICE-Ireland is prescribed in this way, the main focus of this chapter is on the kinds of analysis that can be performed on the finished product and therefore the sorts of research question it can be used to address. Given the nature of the corpus, these centre primarily on the extent to which Irish English is standardized (and thus similar to other regional standards digitized during the ICE programme) and the degree to which it retains regional dialect features (lexical and morphosyntactic) particular to the languages (Irish and English) of Ireland. Although their answers to these questions are naturally tentative at this stage in the research, ICE-Ireland offers intriguing data for the discussion of wider questions, such as the means whereby standard languages are also subject to structured patterns of variation and change more typically thought of as characteristic of non-standard dialects.

MacWhinney describes the current state and projected developments of the TalkBank project, 'a new system that will lead to a qualitative improvement in social science research on communicative interactions' (p. 179). He begins with the observation that phenomenal growth in the power and connectivity of computers and associated software developments have led to dramatic advances in the methodology of 'hard' science and engineering, but that the behavioural and social sciences have not shared fully in these advances due, in large part, to the complexity of human interactional behaviour and of the difficulty of representing this complexity in ways suitable for scientific analysis. TalkBank is a National Science Foundation-funded project whose goal 'is to support data-sharing and direct, community-wide access to naturalistic recordings and transcripts of human and animal communication' (p. 164), and which will address seven needs: (1) guidelines for ethical sharing of data, (2) metadata and infrastructure for identifying available data, (3) common, well-specified formats for text, audio and video, (4) tools for time-aligned transcription and annotation, (5) a common interchange format for annotations, (6) a network-based infrastructure to support efficient (real-time) collaboration, and (7) education of researchers to the existence of shared data, tools, standards and best practices.

The discussion looks at several issues in human behaviour and communications data analysis from a TalkBank point of view. The first issue is transcription of the 'complex pattern of linguistic, motoric, and autonomic behaviour' so as to 'capture the raw behaviour in terms of patterns of words and other codes' (p. 165). This has historically been difficult for three reasons: (1) lack of coding standards, (2) indeterminacy, that is, subjectivity and the possibility of error in representing what is observed, and (3) tedium, the labour-intensive nature of transcription and, again, the consequent probability of error. As a solution, TalkBank proposes digitization of the recording media and subsequent use of computational tools that provide time-aligned linkage of transcripts and codes with the original audio or video recordings. This relieves the transcriber of the need to represent as much of the original recordings as possible, since the analyst can check and where necessary augment the transcription.

The second issue is collaborative commentary. In text-based disciplines such as literary criticism and historical analysis, provision of an object of study and discussion of alternative views of that object have historically been the norm, and have now been made even easier via electronic text and communication media. Provision and discussion of spoken discourse have, until recently, been more cumbersome; MacWhinney and his co-workers have been developing an XML-based schema for making the CHILDES and TalkBank corpora available for collaborative commentary via the Web.

The third and final issue is 'community of disciplines': 'TalkBank seeks to provide a common framework for data-sharing and analysis of each of the many disciplines that studies conversational interactions' (p. 171). The data requirements of the following research areas are discussed: classroom discourse, animal communication, field linguistics, conversational analysis, gesture and sign, second language learning and bilingualism, aphasia, first language acquisition, cultural anthropology, psychiatry, conflict resolution, and human–computer interaction.

The discussion concludes with an outline of proposed further developments in TalkBank:

- Creation of a qualitative data analysis tool called Coder, which 'will allow the user to create and modify a coding framework which can then be applied to various segments of the transcript' (p. 177).
- Creation of new and flexible ways of displaying data.
- Development of more user-accessible ways of framing profiles and queries for data filtering.
- Provision of teaching tools that 'directly introduce students to the study of language behaviour and analysis' (p. 178).
- Transfer of control over the construction of TalkBank and associated data from the current few individuals to the relevant research community.

The next chapter, by Mark Sebba and Susan Dray, relates their experiences of developing two digital Creole corpora at Lancaster University, namely the Corpus of Written British Creole (CWBC) and its sister corpus the Corpus of Written Jamaican Creole (CWJC). Since each of these was created for a slightly different purpose, their annotation schemes are dissimilar in certain respects, though the basic principles behind them both are fundamentally the same. Their contribution addresses specific issues regarding the selection and annotation of English Creole texts, but it also draws out more general issues which are echoed in other chapters across both volumes that engage with 'unconventional' written texts. Their particular concern is the extent to which visual and graphological features contained in the originals need to be retained in the computerized versions.

The chapter opens by usefully defining and contextualizing the two kinds of Creole that were used in the creation of these corpora. As such, we are introduced to the very particular socio-historical circumstances that allowed British and Jamaican Creoles to develop and the exact relationship between them. A short history of writing in these varieties is also given, noting that the increased prestige of Jamaican Creole has impacted upon the range and number of written works in which it can be found. While British Creole does not benefit to the same extent from this increased acceptability, the number of public texts produced in this variety has grown from negligible in the 1980s to 'analysable' in the 1990s. As such, developing the CWBC provided an opportunity for researching the creation and exploitation of a very new form of unstandardized writing in English. The goal of the CWJC was to permit analyses of the distinctive non-standard writing strategies employed by Jamaicans so as to contribute to ethnographic research into this community's literary practices.

Given the contemporary nature of the written resources (published and unpublished) that comprise the CWJC and the CWBC, issues of copyright which beleaguered other corpus creators in this volume (SCOTS and ICE-Ireland especially) also applied. Since this project's financial resources were rather more meagre than that of the SCOTS corpus, for example, this restricted the size and composition of the CWJC and CWBC in various ways, as they were unable to develop a similar database system for pursuing permissions. By adapting a solution rather like that of Raumolin-Brunberg and Nevalainen (Volume 2) in relation to their Corpus of Early English Correspondence, Sebba and Dray were, nevertheless, able to produce, within a reasonable timescale, digital corpora containing various written genres of British and Jamaican Creole suitable for certain kinds of linguistic analysis.[6]

In order to facilitate investigations of various kinds, the corpora have been manually annotated using a set of contrastive tags marking differences in graphology and lexis as well as discoursal and grammatical structure between Standard English and the two types of Creole texts. Metadata of various types are also tagged with both geographical provenance and visual cues contained in the originals being preserved in this manner.

After a discussion of similar issues to those addressed by other authors in these volumes who have worked with 'texts' as opposed to 'voices' (the preservation of non-verbal meaning and the complex type–token relationship, in particular), the authors close by presenting some applications of the corpora. Although the relatively diminutive size of these corpora by comparison to SCOTS, SAND and ICE-Ireland, for instance, delimit the nature of linguistic investigations that can be performed on them, the CWBC has already been used for a small-scale study of future modality (Facchinetti, 1998) and for a study of orthographic practices (Sebba, 1998a, 1998b) which was able to discriminate genuine 'Creole' from 'non-Creole' texts. In the longer term, as a monitor corpus, the CWBC will become invaluable to socio-historical linguists for whom it will present a rare opportunity to document an unstandardized language developing written forms and functions.

The final chapter in Volume 1, by Sali A. Tagliamonte, focuses on what she considers to be 'tried and true procedures' (p. 241) for the creation and annotation of electronic corpora derived from vernacular speech. The chapter draws on Tagliamonte's own previous experience since the late 1980s of various corpus-building enterprises in order to illustrate the models which she advocates for the maximally efficient management and analysis of spoken data collected via the sociolinguistic interview method.

Tagliamonte's particular contribution in this regard is the very careful account that she gives of the importance of establishing strict protocols for orthographic transcription at the outset of any annotation programme. She argues that representing the non-standard phonologies and morphosyntactic features prevalent amongst speakers of distinctive social and regional varieties can be particularly problematic. It is therefore crucial that conventions regarding the kinds of information to encode are based on best practice and are strictly adhered to across the entire data set to allow maximum comparison between speakers across regional, social and temporal space.

In this regard, Tagliamonte is another advocate of the normalization of spelling and punctuation when digitizing corpora, though in this case her rationale is not primarily to facilitate database searches as it was for Barbiers and the SAND project team, but to enhance both readability and the speed of transcription (particularly key considerations when dealing with smaller-scale private corpus-building enterprises of this kind). Crucial too, of course, is the creation of orthographic protocols that do not normalize blindly, but incorporate specific unplanned aspects of speech as well as certain variant realizations that are so meaningful to your particular research questions that they are worth the extra effort to encode. Tagliamonte uses extracts from various corpora that she has been associated with to illustrate exactly what these might be and the manner in which they have been encoded for her particular purposes.

Again, as we have seen with all the corpora referred to in these two volumes, the data collection and annotation processes described in Tagliamonte's contribution go hand in hand with the creation of metadata of one sort or another (in her case a relational database created using the FileMaker program). This allows processing and searching of the data in various ways alongside the use of other software that can be applied to the text files themselves (such as Concorder), producing frequency counts per social category of speaker and so on. This then facilitates the transfer of the data to statistical packages that add further levels of encoding relating to the testing of research hypotheses of various kinds (GoldVarb is the one usually advocated in the kind of variationist research that Tagliamonte is associated with). The chapter concludes with a demonstration of these stages using genuine corpus data alongside a critical evaluation of the methods themselves.

Although the electronic corpora which Tagliamonte describes in this chapter are, like Dray's CWJC, 'private' in the sense of Bauer (2004), the discussion still has much to offer with regard to the principles of database management and the mechanics of corpus-building for all kinds of linguistic data sets.

3 Acknowledgements

The editors would like to close by acknowledging the financial support provided to various phases of this project by: (i) the School of English Literature, Language and Linguistics, Newcastle University; (ii) Newcastle Institute for the Arts, Humanities and Social Sciences; (iii) Palgrave Macmillan; (iv) the Arts and Humanities Research Council (grant no. RE11776) and (v) the British Academy (grant no. BCG-37408).

We would also like to express our deeply felt gratitude to our authors who have gracefully endured our cajoling and actively engaged with us in pursuing a research agenda in corpus linguistics, the ultimate goal of which is to foster 'international standards for metadata', and articulate 'best practices for the collection, preservation, and annotation of corpus data for language archives' (Kretzschmar *et al.*, 2005, 2006).

There are also a number of other people who deserve special thanks, including: Jill Lake, the commissioning editor responsible for these companion volumes, for her helpful feedback from inception to completion; the staff at Palgrave Macmillan for their patience with our many technical queries; Tina Fry, Alison Furness, Kaycey Ihemere, Adam Mearns and Naglaa Thabet for their assistance with formatting and indexing; the organizing and scientific committees of SS15 and our anonymous reviewers who submitted the SS15 Workshop papers and the chapters in these volumes to critical, stylistic and formal scrutiny. Finally, we are indebted to Shana Poplack for writing the foreword to this volume and for the many discussions we have had with her regarding the shape that these volumes should take since the idea for this project was first mooted back in 2002. Any remaining shortcomings are, as usual, our own.

Notes

1. See, for instance, Francis and Kučera (1964); Johansson *et al.* (1978); Aarts and Meijs (1984); Garside (1987); Garside *et al.* (1987); Leech (1992); Hughes and Lee (1994); Burnard (1995); Haslerud and Stenstrom (1995); Sampson (1995); Knowles *et al.* (1996); Aston and Burnard (1998); Biber *et al.* (1998); Condron *et al.* (2000), inter alia.
2. For a discussion of the advantages and disadvantages of using such resources as tools for linguistic analysis more generally, see Corrigan (1997).
3. Compare, for example, the relatively recent *Dictionary of American Regional English* (Cassidy and Hall, 1985–), http://polyglot.lss.wisc.edu/dare/dare.html, which was based on just over 1,800 questions (see Wolfram and Schilling-Estes, 2005, p. 126).
4. For instance, clitic clusters, for obvious reasons, were handled rather differently.
5. This is why Unicode was also preferred by the NECTE team (see Allen *et al.*, Volume 2).
6. The type of analysis being restricted largely by the small sizes of the corpora (CWBC= 28,000 words and CWJC = 70,000 words), which presents issues of representativeness.

References

Aarts, Jan and Willem Meijs (eds). 1984. *Corpus Linguistics*. Amsterdam: Rodopi.

Aston, Guy and Lou Burnard. 1998. *The BNC Handbook*. Edinburgh: Edinburgh University Press.

Bauer, Laurie. 2004. 'Inferring variation and change from public corpora'. *Handbook of Language Variation and Change*, ed. by Jack K. Chambers, Peter Trudgill and Natalie Schilling-Estes, pp. 97–114. Oxford: Blackwell.

Biber, Douglas, Susan Conrad and Randi Reppen. 1998. *Corpus Linguistics: Investigating Language Structure and Use*. Cambridge: Cambridge University Press.

Burnard, Lou. 1995. *Users' Reference Guide to the British National Corpus*. Oxford: Oxford University Computing Services.

Cassidy, Frederic G. and Joan H. Hall (eds). 1985–. *Dictionary of American Regional English*, 4 vols. Cambridge, Mass.: Harvard University Press.

Condron, Frances, Michael Fraser and Stuart Sutherland. 2000. *Guide to Digital Resources in the Humanities*. Oxford: Humanities Computing Unit, Oxford University.

Corrigan, K. P. 1997. 'The syntax of South Armagh English in its socio-historical perspective'. Unpublished doctoral thesis, National University of Ireland at University College Dublin.

Facchinetti, R. 1998. 'Expressions of futurity in British Caribbean Creole'. *ICAME Journal* 22:7–22.

Francis, W. Nelson and Henry Kučera. 1964. *Manual of Information to Accompany a Standard Corpus of Present-Day Edited American English, for Use with Digital Computers*. Providence, RI: Dept. of Linguistics, Brown University.

Garside, Roger. 1987. 'The CLAWS word-tagging system'. *The Computational Analysis of English: A Corpus-Based Approach*, ed. by Roger Garside, Geoffrey Leech and Geoffrey Sampson, pp. 30–41. London: Longman.

Garside, Roger, Geoffrey Leech and Geoffrey Sampson (eds). 1987. *The Computational Analysis of English: A Corpus-Based Approach*. London: Longman.

Haslerud, Vibecke and Anna-Britta Stenstrom. 1995. 'The Bergen London Teenage Corpus (COLT)'. *Spoken English on Computer*, ed. by Geoffrey N. Leech, Greg Myers and Jenny Thomas, pp. 235–42. London: Longman.

Hughes, Lorna and Stuart Lee. (eds). 1994. *CTI Centre for Textual Studies Resources Guide 1994*. Oxford: CTI Centre for Textual Studies.

Johansson, Stig, Geoffrey N. Leech and Helen Goodluck. 1978. *Manual of Information to Accompany the Lancaster–Oslo/Bergen Corpus of British English, for Use with Digital Computers*. Dept. of English, University of Oslo.

Knowles, Gerry, Briony Williams and Lolita Taylor. 1996. *A Corpus of Formal British English Speech*. London: Longman.

Kretzschmar, William A., Jean Anderson, Joan C. Beal, Karen P. Corrigan, Lisa-Lena Opas-Hänninen and Bartek Plichta. 2005. 'Collaboration on corpora for regional and social analysis'. Paper presented at AACL 6/ICAME 26, University of Michigan, Ann Arbor, 12–15 May 2005.

Kretzschmar, William A., Jean Anderson, Joan C. Beal, Karen P. Corrigan, Lisa-Lena Opas-Hänninen and Bartek Plichta. (2006). 'Collaboration on corpora for regional and social analysis'. Special Issue of *Journal of English Linguistics* 34:172–205.

Leech, Geoffrey N. 1992. '100 million words of English: the British National Corpus'. *Language Research* 28(1):1–13.

McEnery, Tony and Andrew Wilson. 2001. *Corpus Linguistics*, 2nd edn. Edinburgh: Edinburgh University Press.

Milroy, Lesley and Matthew Gordon. 2003. *Sociolinguistics: Method and Interpretation*. Oxford: Blackwell.

Ochs, Elinor. 1999. 'Transcription as theory'. *The Discourse Reader*, ed. by Adam Jaworski and Nikolas Coupland, pp. 167–82. London: Routledge.

Orton, Harold 1962. *Survey of English Dialects: Introduction*. Leeds: Arnold.

Sampson, Geoffrey. 1995. *English for the Computer: The SUSANNE Corpus and Analytic Scheme*. Oxford: Clarendon.

Sebba, Mark 1998a. 'Meaningful choices in Creole orthography: "experts" and users'. *Making Meaningful Choices in English: On Dimensions, Perspectives, Methodology and Evidence*, ed. by R. Schulze, pp. 223–34. Tübingen: Gunter Narr.

Sebba, Mark 1998b. 'Phonology meets ideology: the meaning of orthographic practices in British Creole'. *Language Problems and Language Planning* 22(1):19–47.

Wakelin, Martyn F. 1975. *Language and History in Cornwall*. Leicester: Leicester University Press.

Wolfram, Walt and Natalie Schilling-Estes. 2005. *American English: Dialects and Variation*, 2nd edn. Oxford: Blackwell.

Websites

Bank of English: http://titania.cobuild.collins.co.uk/boe_info.html
British National Corpus: http://info.ox.ac.uk/bnc
Dictionary of American Regional English: http://polyglot.lss.wisc.edu/dare/dare.html

2
SCOTS: Scottish Corpus of Texts and Speech

Jean Anderson, Dave Beavan and Christian Kay

1 Introduction

Scotland contains a rich variety of languages. A recent survey of 300 respondents revealed that over 30 different languages are regularly spoken at home and at work (Institute for the Languages of Scotland (ILS) Report, 2003). In addition to the Scottish English spoken by the majority, there are substantial numbers of speakers of the other indigenous languages, with an estimated 58,650 Scottish Gaelic speakers at the 2001 Census, and about half the population claiming knowledge of Scots (Macafee, 2000).[1] Non-indigenous languages include Arabic, Bengali, Cantonese, Dutch, Hindi, Italian, Kurdish, Polish, Panjabi, Romany and Urdu. British Sign Language has a flourishing Scottish variety.

The Scottish Corpus of Texts and Speech (SCOTS) was set up in 2001 to begin the task of making a corpus to represent and monitor the languages of Scotland.[2] Such a corpus is long overdue. Major British corpora, such as the British National Corpus (BNC) and the Bank of English (BE), contain Scottish material but did not collect it comprehensively. The International Corpus of English (ICE) could not find a partner to deal with Scotland in its collection of major varieties of World English. The SCOTS project will thus supply a gap in research materials. Initially we are concentrating on the two most accessible varieties, Scots and Scottish English, but our long-term intention is to sample the languages of Scotland in their totality, thus providing a snapshot of the linguistic situation in one particular geographical area. Our primary interest is sociolinguistic, matching linguistic patterns to social and demographic categories. Our current chronological cut-off point is 1940, though earlier materials may be included if they are of special interest or contribute to filling gaps. Our informants are not limited to native speakers, since anyone who has lived in Scotland for a substantial period of time may well have been influenced by Scots or Scottish English. Information on place of birth and residence is available in the corpus metadata.

Even our starting point presents the analyst with problems. Information is lacking on how extensively and in what contexts Broad Scots is used, while the range of features characterizing Scottish English is not fully defined. Indeed, many of its speakers are unaware that their usage differs in anything but accent from that of speakers of so-called Standard English. Speakers employ features of Broad Scots and Scottish Standard English to different degrees, often depending on context, so that, rather than regarding them as two distinct varieties, it is more accurate to talk about a linguistic continuum running from Scottish English at one end to Broad Scots at the other.[3] At the Scots end there is the further complication of considerable regional diversity, with, for example, marked differences in the speech of the north-east, Glasgow or the Northern Isles. Such diversity is compounded by the fact that there is no agreed spelling system for transcribing these variations. These and other problems will be discussed as the chapter progresses.

2 Data collection

SCOTS was launched in the wake of the devolution of political power from the British Government in London to Scotland.[4] This situation, and especially the reopening of the Scottish Parliament after a gap of nearly three hundred years, markedly increased public interest in the language and culture of the country. The initial response to our call for data was swift and positive. Offers came from 113 people, and 355 units were identified as suitable. These were processed along with other texts and added to the system to provide a test corpus of around 400,000 words. They included written, spoken and visual materials from a range of genres such as conversation, interviews, correspondence, poetry, fiction and prose. A sub-project was started to collect spoken, written and visual data from the Scottish Parliamentary elections in May 2003. This exercise was repeated for the European elections in June 2004. The materials overall show an expected imbalance, with much of the Scots material being poetry or literary prose (see section 7). Each document in the database is accompanied by an extensive set of searchable metadata comprising textual and demographic information and indicating whether the necessary permissions have been received to enable the text to be made public. Such information is currently collected on paper forms, but we expect to develop downloadable versions. The sociolinguistic and administrative data together occupy over 500 fields in the database.

2.1 Types of data

All documents in the corpus are of one or more of the following types:

Text:	document originally conceived as written work
Audio footage:	recording of live speech
Audio transcription:	transcription of speech
Video footage:	recording of live speech with visuals
Video transcription:	transcription of video

In addition, we have comprehensive information about the individuals involved:

Author:	author of a document
Participant:	person appearing in audio or video

We also hold associated administrative information, used, for example, in tracking documents from initial contact with the contributor to full copyright clearance, including clearance of third-party copyright.

An example of this complicated document structure is given below. This scenario is based upon a lecture to a group of people and clearly demonstrates the complex requirements of even a common type of document. The example shows the data collected and the way in which the different elements of the document are mapped to the database under the four major categories described above. Considerable discussion and comparison with other projects went into the development of the subcategories, but they are not immutable and may be refined further.

The original lecture notes prepared in advance of the talk are identified as a text, that is, a written document. This necessitates compiling the following information.

Text

- Text audience (e.g. age, gender, number of people)
- Text details (e.g. date by decade, mode of composition)
- Text medium (method of transmission, e.g. book, email)
- Text performance/broadcast details
- Text publication details
- Text setting (domains such as Education, Journalism)

- Text type, with a large number of subtypes:
  - Advertisement (e.g. junk mail)
  - Announcement (e.g. notice)
  - Article (in newspaper, journal, etc.)
  - Correspondence/letters
  - Diary
  - Essay
  - Instructions (e.g. manual, recipe)
  - Invoice/bill/receipt
  - Novel
  - Poem/song/ballad
  - Prepared text (e.g. lecture/talk, sermon, public address/speech)
  - Prose: fiction
  - Prose: non-fiction
  - Report
  - Review
  - Script (film, play, radio, TV, etc.)
  - Short story
  - Written record of speech (e.g. Hansard, legal proceedings, minutes of meetings)

Video footage

Since a recording of the lecture was made, the data are also classified as video footage, requiring information on:

- Audience (e.g. age, gender, number of people)
- Awareness and spontaneity (Did the participants know they were being recorded or might be recorded? Was the event scripted to any extent?)
- Footage information (date, person recording, etc.)
- Footage publication details
- Footage series/collection information (i.e. if it is part of a series)
- Medium (e.g. cinema, radio, telephone)
- Setting (domains such as Education, Journalism, plus location, e.g. in a classroom, in Inverness)
- Relationship between recorder/interviewer and speakers (family, friend, professional, etc.)
- Speaker relationships (Did they know one another prior to the recording, and if so, how?)
- There is a further range of types appropriate to this medium:
  - Advertisement
  - Announcement (e.g. news)

- Commentary
- Consultation (e.g. medical, legal, business)
- Conversation
- Debate/discussion
- Documentary
- Dramatic performance
- Instruction (e.g. demonstration)
- Interview
- Lecture/talk, sermon, public address/speech
- Lesson/seminar
- Meeting
- Poetry reading/song/ballad performance
- Press conference
- Prose reading
- Story telling

Video transcription

A transcription was made of the above recording, which necessitates video transcription details:

- Transcription publication details
- Transcription information
  - Title of original
  - Transcriber identity number in database
  - Conventions
  - Year of transcription
  - Year material recorded
  - Word count

Author

We also require details of the author of the original text:

- Author details
  - Author identity number in database
  - Name
  - Gender
  - Decade of birth
  - Highest educational attainment
  - Age left school
  - Upbringing (cultural/religious affiliation either now or in the past)
  - Occupation

  - Place of birth
  - Region of birth
  - Birthplace *CSD* dialect area (the dialect areas from the *Concise Scots Dictionary* listing)[5]
  - Country of birth
  - Place of residence
  - Region of residence
  - Residence *CSD* dialect area
  - Country of residence
  - Father occupation
  - Father place of birth
  - Father region of birth
  - Father birthplace *CSD* dialect area
  - Father country of birth
  - Mother occupation
  - Mother place of birth
  - Mother region of birth
  - Mother birthplace *CSD* dialect area
  - Mother country of birth
- Languages
  - Name of language known and whether spoken, read, written or understood
  - Circumstances where language is used (e.g. at home or work).

  A checklist of languages is given, but the contributor may list others.

Participant(s)

Similar details are collected for participants, for example someone taking part in a discussion, introducing the speaker or presenting a talk of which they are not the author.

As can be seen, describing a document is not necessarily as straightforward as it may at first appear since any of these subtypes can in theory be applied in many combinations. Using the *Concise Scots Dictionary* (*CSD*) dialect areas enables us to connect our information to a generally recognized classification. All documents, regardless of their type, are treated and manipulated in the same way inside the administrative database (see section 4). We also have a series of forms to ensure that data protection and copyright legislation are observed. These involved much consultation with the university lawyers and the team learned a great deal as a result.[6]

3 Formats

3.1 Text

We accept document submissions in as many formats as feasible, with a preference for electronic formats wherever possible to reduce processing time. The corpus administration system accepts documents in plain text, maintaining sentence and paragraph breaks only. Plain text was chosen as, for linguistic research, the document content is more important than its presentation; we are also restricted by time and resources. Where a submission is handwritten we take a digital copy of the page. Although we do not currently allow this to be accessed directly by end-users, access is allowed by request; we hope this may prove useful to future researchers. The handwritten document is then keyed following strict guidelines and proofread. For typed or printed documents we use optical character recognition (OCR) software to generate text. This method is normally faster than rekeying, but the lack of a Scots dictionary for the software means that it can generate wrong presumptions about words and the result requires careful proofreading. For example, scanning of a page of text from a story written in the Doric (north-eastern) variety produced <bait> for <hait> 'hot', <oat> for <oot> 'out', and <0> (zero) for <o'> 'of'. The Scots past tense verb ending <-it> was separated from its stem, producing <pump it> rather than the correct <pumpit> 'pumped'. We have also found that writers of Scots texts are not always consistent in their spelling, even within a single text.

3.2 Audio and transcription

When we record data ourselves, we use digital audio tape (DAT) wherever possible. Given the diversity of data we are offered, we must also have the capability to accept source recordings from a number of consumer formats such as tape, CD, minidisc and computer files. These are immediately converted onto DAT. As it is a high quality digital format we can duplicate and edit DAT material with no quality loss. DAT tapes are thus digitized into the computer with no degradation of quality. Once the information is in computer format we can easily provide members of the team, such as transcribers, with copies of the recording in their format of choice, such as CD or minidisc. The recording must also be edited before its inclusion in the corpus. Typical tasks include trimming the segment (to neaten up the beginning and end of the piece) and noise reduction to combat hiss and background noise.

In the early days of the project, we investigated ways of making these recordings available on the internet. The principal goals were to support a broad user base and to provide flexibility in our own computing requirements. Apple QuickTime was chosen, which gives both PC and Mac users access to the recordings. The server software is open source and free, running on Linux, Unix or Mac. QuickTime will also allow for streaming of the resource: the end-user does not have to wait for the entire piece to download, and can easily jump to any point in the source for near-instant playback. To enable everyone to get the most out of the resource we chose to implement two profiles: one for low-bandwidth users (modem) and a higher quality version for high-bandwidth users (broadband, academic institutions). Transcription is orthographic only, but we aim to provide high enough quality to enable phonetic or phonemic transcriptions to be made by individual researchers.

The transcription guidelines are being refined as our experience grows. Broad Scots raises interesting transcription issues as a language with a range of spoken dialects, and a substantial written record dating back to the fourteenth century, but no accepted standard written form. This presents problems for corpus-building, notably in transcribing spoken data, in identifying specifically Scottish forms, and in lemmatizing variant lexical and grammatical forms under search-words. In tackling these issues, we are working with Scottish Language Dictionaries (SLD), which is responsible for the two major Scots dictionaries, the *Scottish National Dictionary* (*SND*) and the *Dictionary of the Older Scottish Tongue* (*DOST*), which together form the digitized *Dictionary of the Scots Language* (http://www.dsl.ac.uk/). They supply us with headword listings and are developing a spelling system based on frequency of occurrence of forms.[7]

Examples of transcribed material can be seen in Figure 2.3 and on our website. The current guidelines for SCOTS read:

> The *Scottish Corpus of Texts and Speech* is intended to be of use to as wide a range of disciplines as possible, for example to lexicographers, grammarians of Scots/Scottish English, authors and linguists, teachers and pupils. For this reason, the initial unparsed/unannotated orthographic transcription of spoken language should be flexible, in order to encompass all foreseeable uses of the corpus. Conventional orthography can obscure the presence of spoken language phenomena. This problem is encountered where corpora of spoken English are concerned, but is even more of a concern where spoken Scots and

Scottish English is to be adequately represented. Many of the definitive features of Scots and Scottish English are not preserved in English orthography.

Since no phonemic transcription of spoken material collected for the *Scottish Corpus of Texts and Speech* is planned at this stage, it is desirable that the initial orthographic transcription reflects certain important aspects of Scots and Scottish English pronunciation as closely as possible. Scots words should be transcribed using the orthographic representation of each word, as it is found in the *Scottish National Dictionary*. Where there are several options for the spelling of a Scots word, the form that is closest to the pronunciation used by the informant should be selected. At this stage, no Scots spelling conventions have been decided upon, so spellings might have to be normalized at a later date.

The primary orthographic transcription is intended to represent Scots words and Scots/Scottish English forms of pronunciation as closely as possible, by adapting Standard English (henceforth SE) orthography and by making use of existing Scots spelling systems. The transcriber should try to stick to standard English orthography, except where the transcription guidelines indicate otherwise, or where they feel it would enrich the corpus to distinguish between the Scottish pronunciation and the standard English orthographic representation of the word. Examples might be <a> for SE <all> and <doun/doon> for SE <down>, etc.

3.3 Video

The project team has access to a digital video (DV) camera which we use for all our own data collection. If submissions are of other formats (such as VHS) we use Glasgow University Media Services to assist us in digitization. Following the same procedures as with audio documents, we initially digitize the source. With DV recordings this is done at zero quality loss as the source is already digital. The computer file is not preserved past the end of processing because of the major storage requirements of the format (2.1 gigabytes per ten minutes of footage). Certain editing tasks are performed to neaten up the recording, such as noise reduction and enhancements to the visual presentation. When we have attained the best results, we create an intermediate file for the video compression software to use as its source.

Again as with the audio footage, we use Apple QuickTime to compress the video to suitable sizes for modem and broadband users. The quality is much reduced compared to the original, but this is necessary for delivery to users over the internet. QuickTime provides streaming access so users can jump to any point in the file for playback.

4 Administration system

Our requirements were for a system that could give access to the entire data set, including the document contents, from one interface. Tight controls on validation and other rules regarding the integrity of the data must be possible. The system must allow access and updates to the data from different people, at different places, possibly at the same time. For the future, when we begin to collect data from non-indigenous minority languages, the system must be capable of supporting more than just the Latin character set. In addition to these requirements, it must be capable of integrating with other administrative functions such as mail merges, report writing, generation of form letters, and so on. The user interface we provide to all project staff must be easy to use. This is particularly important to reduce training time for casual staff, such as students assisting with data entry.

For storing the raw data a relational database product suits the project very well. To give us the greatest degree of flexibility in the future, and in order not to tie us down to any particular computing platform, an open source, free solution was preferred. After trialling potentially suitable products we chose PostgreSQL. The user interface is implemented in Microsoft Access (see Figure 2.1 on page 27), which provides an easy transition for users of other Windows software. Reports can be generated and ad hoc queries made by any user via a visual interface. Integration with the rest of the Microsoft Office suite provides a mail merge facility in Word for numerous correspondence tasks.

There are comprehensive tracking options to record the status of each submission and document. These can be used to ensure we have the correct permissions before public release of the document. Status reports can be generated so that we can identify situations where more investigation or follow-ups are required, for example when a contributor fails to return the necessary metadata forms within a specified period of time.

5 Website

The sole deployment of the project is our website. The conditions of our initial EPSRC grant, and now the AHRC grant, require that access be completely free of charge to all users. We expect these users to have

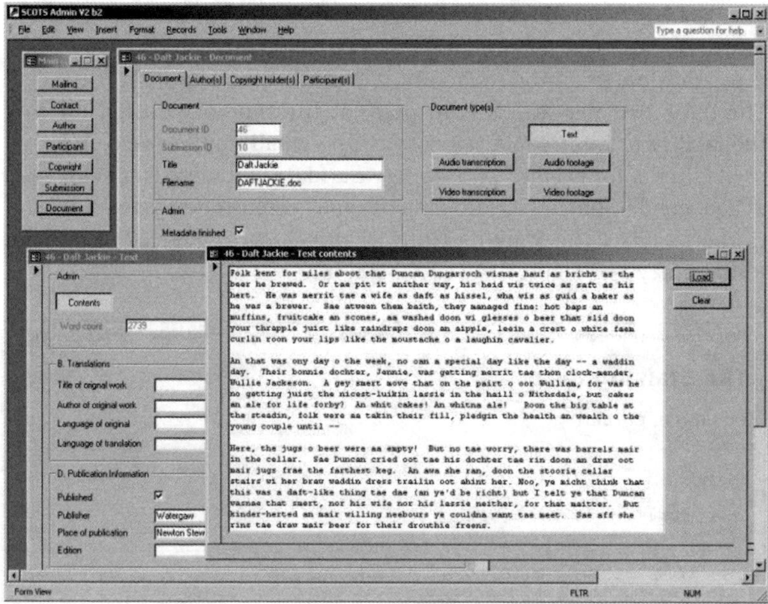

Figure 2.1 Administration system in MS Access

Word/phrase	lang syne
Author	
Name/id	
Gender	- All
Birth/reside region	- All
Document	
Type	Spoken ☑ Written ☑
Include poetry	☑
Title	
Year composed	From ___ to ___
Reset	Find texts

Figure 2.2 Basic search options

a wide variety of interests and to include schoolchildren and teachers, businesses and the general public as well as academics.

In addition to a browse facility, a two-tier search system is needed. The basic first-tier search is in place at the time of writing, offering the facility to interrogate the corpus by a small number of commonly used criteria, for example word/phrase and certain metadata fields such as age, gender, birthplace, document type, as illustrated below for John Corbett's talk, 'The Stalking Cure'. Figure 2.2 (on page 27) shows an initial query and Figure 2.3 a successful hit.

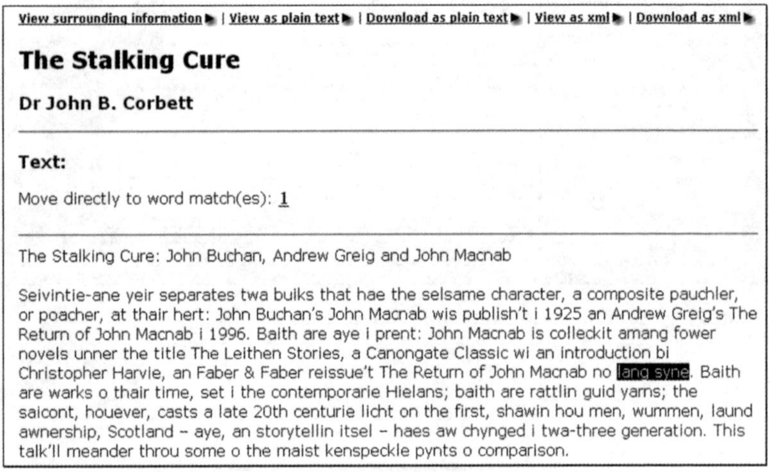

View surrounding information ▶ | View as plain text ▶ | Download as plain text ▶ | View as xml ▶ | Download as xml ▶

The Stalking Cure

Dr John B. Corbett

Text:

Move directly to word match(es): 1

The Stalking Cure: John Buchan, Andrew Greig and John Macnab

Seivintie-ane yeir separates twa buiks that hae the selsame character, a composite pauchler, or poacher, at thair hert: John Buchan's John Macnab wis publish't i 1925 an Andrew Greig's The Return of John Macnab i 1996. Baith are aye i prent: John Macnab is colleckit amang fower novels unner the title The Leithen Stories, a Canongate Classic wi an introduction bi Christopher Harvie, an Faber & Faber reissue't The Return of John Macnab no lang syne. Baith are warks o thair time, set i the contemporarie Hielans; baith are rattlin guid yarns; the saicont, houever, casts a late 20th centurie licht on the first, shawin hou men, wummen, laund awnership, Scotland – aye, an storytellin itsel – haes aw chynged i twa-three generation. This talk'll meander throu some o the maist kenspeckle pynts o comparison.

Figure 2.3 Search result with phrase highlighted

A far more advanced search facility will be developed, to include the facility to use any number of the metadata fields concerning the document, author and participants, as shown in Figure 2.4. A visual query builder-style interface will allow users to combine their criteria before submitting their search. A list of documents matching the criteria is displayed so that users may select those they wish to view in more detail.

For designing the website we have used Extensible HyperText Markup Language (XHTML) and Cascading Style Sheets (CSS) to provide the greatest accessibility, not only to browsers but also other user agents such as screen readers. For the visually impaired we have a 'high contrast' option which disables any unnecessary graphics and enhances clarity and text size. Documents are viewed by default directly inside the website as HyperText Markup Language (HTML). Provision is also

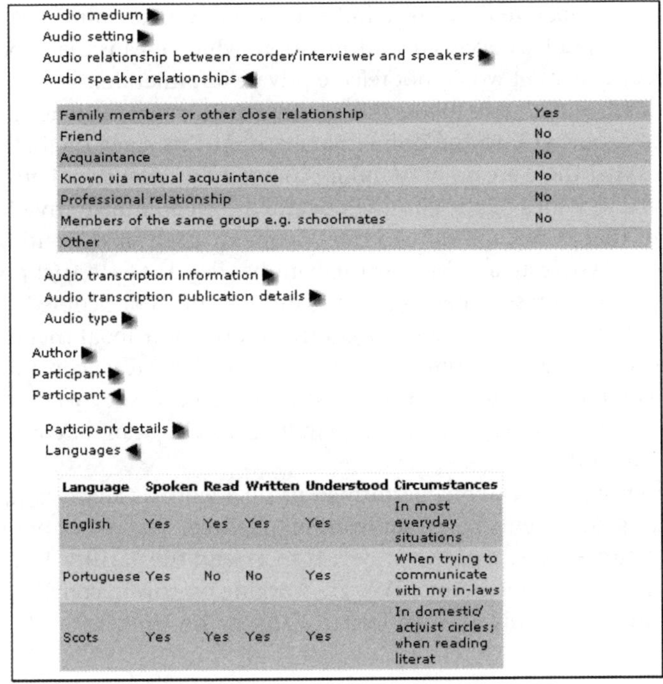

Audio medium ▶
Audio setting ▶
Audio relationship between recorder/interviewer and speakers ▶
Audio speaker relationships ◀

Family members or other close relationship	Yes
Friend	No
Acquaintance	No
Known via mutual acquaintance	No
Professional relationship	No
Members of the same group e.g. schoolmates	No
Other	

Audio transcription information ▶
Audio transcription publication details ▶
Audio type ▶

Author ▶
Participant ▶
Participant ◀

Participant details ▶
Languages ◀

Language	Spoken	Read	Written	Understood	Circumstances
English	Yes	Yes	Yes	Yes	In most everyday situations
Portuguese	Yes	No	No	Yes	When trying to communicate with my in-laws
Scots	Yes	Yes	Yes	Yes	In domestic/ activist circles; when reading literat

Figure 2.4 Viewing surrounding information (metadata)

made for viewing and downloading the plain text. In the future, Text Encoding Initiative (TEI) compliant Extensible Markup Language (XML) data sets will also be available. If a search was performed using a word or phrase as a criterion this is highlighted, along with a list to jump quickly to each occurrence of the word or phrase in the document. Access to 'surrounding information' or metadata is given for each document. The different categories as described in section 2.1 can be expanded and contracted at will to reveal the information that the user requires. A list of all recently viewed documents is kept at the bottom of the page to provide quick and easy return access.

We use a relational database (again PostgreSQL) to provide the storage and search facility for the website. All dynamic pages are constructed using templates and processed using PHP: Hypertext Preprocessor (PHP) scripts. PostgreSQL enables us to make use of built-in advanced text indexing, and we also have the capacity to extend or modify the way this facility works, possibly using word stemming, and so on. For security reasons, and to allow more flexibility in the future, the online database is separate from the administrative one. The online database holds only publicly accessible information, which means that a potential security exploit would not release private information.

On a scheduled basis all documents that are marked ready for public use are exported into the online database. At this stage the database ensures that there are no outstanding copyright or intellectual property rights (IPR) issues relating to the document. All administrative information that is not relevant to the document itself or the authors is removed. Where an author or participant has decided to restrict private information to researchers only this information is not copied. Since contributors can give as much or as little information about themselves as they choose when submitting material, they have total control over what is publicly or privately known about them. If they wish public recognition, as most of the creative writers do, they can, of course, be named as authors.

Currently, if a search is performed using a word as a criterion, any matching documents have that word highlighted. One of our priorities for the current phase of the project is to extend this facility and offer users an online concordance. We are working on this in collaboration with the Computing Science Department at the University of Oulu, Finland.

6 Preservation and backup

All correspondence is kept, either in digital form (emails and similar things) or paper (documents sent and received from contributors, authors and so on). If at all possible we keep the original copies of the source documents. If contributors request that these be returned, an archive-quality digital image is made for storage. While processing is in progress, all paper documents are held in secure storage and computer files are accessible by project staff only. Once all the documents relating to a particular submission are fully entered into the administrative system, and processing is finalized, the original documents are passed over to University Archive Services for appropriate storage. Researchers or interested parties may contact Archive Services to be granted access to this material. Any interim revisions of the document are removed once processing is completed, leaving us with the original submission, noting any changes, such as replacement of names which might identify a third party, and the corpus-ready version.

All computer files relating to the corpus are stored on a network drive administered by University Arts IT Support; this storage has a nightly backup with archives stored at University Archive Services. Our dedicated server for the project has a comprehensive backup schedule to University Computing Service, which gives us the added benefits of restoring files from any period in the last few months if the situation requires it. When conducting major systems work on the server we create a snapshot of the system. This necessitates downtime to stabilize the system. However, if we encounter serious problems, we can revert to a previously good state of the system very quickly.

7 Future plans

During Phase 1 of the project, we have developed an easy-to-use web interface, where no client software is required or data set updates needed by the end-user. As web technology, it is open to any computing platform with a web browser. We have comprehensive sociolinguistic metadata available as well as details about the document. This version has been tested by staff and students and proved to be fast and user-friendly.

During Phase 2 of the project, we aim to address the interlinked issues of quantity and balance, and some specifically Scottish issues. Our overall aim for the three years of the AHRC grant is to increase the corpus to at least four million words (approximately 800 texts), of which at least 20 per cent will be spoken. It is already clear that Scots survives primarily in speech, and that there should therefore be a concentration on collecting oral data. An advanced search facility will be developed so that users can choose what information to extract. We also plan an on-line concordance (see section 5) and a bulk download facility to enable downloading in plain text or XML of all documents which match a particular query. We have no immediate plans to tag the texts grammatically, although individual users may do so. An exception might be a 'light' tagging of diagnostic features of Scottish English, such as modal auxiliary verbs, present/past participle constructions and the form of past participles. In the longer term, we will consider vertical expansion to historical texts and horizontal expansion to other languages.

Planning the content of the corpus has raised many questions. We are aware of the need for a corpus to be well-balanced and representative. Most well-known corpora are created from predetermined samples to try to ensure this. The selection criteria for the BNC, for instance, are domain, time and medium, and target proportions were defined for each of these criteria, as shown below:

- **Domain:** The domain of a text indicates the kind of writing it contains. Seventy-five per cent of the written texts were to be chosen from *informative* writings: of which roughly equal quantities should be chosen from the fields of applied sciences, arts, belief and thought, commerce and finance, leisure, natural and pure science, social science and world affairs. Twenty-five per cent of the written texts were to be *imaginative*, that is, literary and creative works.
- **Medium:** The medium of a text indicates the kind of publication in which it occurs. Sixty per cent of written texts were to be books. Twenty-five per cent were to be periodicals (newspapers, magazines). Between five and ten per cent should come from other kinds of miscellaneous published material. Between five and ten per cent should come from unpublished written material such as personal letters and diaries, essays and memoranda. A small amount (less than five per cent) should come from material written to be spoken.
- **Time:** The time criterion refers to the date of publication of a text. Being a *synchronic* corpus, the BNC should contain texts from roughly the same period. The intention was that no text should date back further than 1975. This condition was relaxed for imaginative works only, a few of which date back to 1964, because of their continued popularity and consequent effect on the language.
- **Classification criteria:** a large number of other classification features were identified for the texts in the corpus. No fixed proportions were specified for these features. The criteria include such things as sample size (number of words) and extent (start and end points), topic or subject of the text, author's name, age, gender, region of origin and domicile, target age group and gender, and 'level' of writing (a subjective measure of reading difficulty). (See http://www.natcorp.ox.ac/corpus/creating.xml)

We could not follow such a model initially as we simply did not have enough information about where and how our target varieties are used, or, indeed, what they consist of. In other words, at least some of the data has to be collected before many of the questions implicit in the above categories can be answered. Is Scots used in Scottish newspapers, for example, and if so is it evenly spread throughout or restricted to certain article types such as sport or features? Is the use of Broad Scots in fiction largely restricted to dialogue or does it feature in narrative as well? To what extent, if any, are our two varieties used in informative writing? How do we define Scottish English?[8] Questions of this kind will be familiar to anyone developing a corpus for a language which is not used in all domains of life. Now that the initial data are in place, we will begin to address these questions by identifying under-represented document types and determining whether they are obtainable.

As noted in section 1, political devolution has led to increased interest in linguistic matters. One manifestation of this interest is pressure to set up an Institute for the Languages of Scotland as an umbrella organization for linguistic endeavours of all kinds. In a modern society, a corpus of the language is an essential part of such an undertaking.

Notes

1. 'Scots' is notoriously difficult to define. In this chapter it is used interchangeably with 'Broad Scots' and refers to varieties which differ substantially from English Standard English in lexis, grammar and pronunciation. The classic example is the Doric variety spoken in the rural north-east of Scotland. 'Scottish Standard English' is the educated variety, used by many people at all times and by others in writing and more formal speech. The spoken form is characterized by a Scottish accent and minor differences in lexis and grammar, such as use of *wee* 'small' and *bonnie* 'pretty', or different usage of modal verbs, such as *may* and *will*. For information on the history and development of Scots, see Murison (1977) and Smith (2000).
2. The project was funded from 2001 to 2003 by Engineering and Physical Sciences Research Council (EPSRC) Grant GR/R32772/01. From 2003–2007, it has a three-year grant from the Arts and Humanities Research Council (AHRC): B/RE/AN9984/APN17387. We are extremely grateful to both of these bodies for their support. The team currently comprises Dr John Corbett (Principal Investigator), Professor Christian Kay, Dr Jane Stuart-Smith, Jean Anderson, Dr Wendy Anderson (Research Assistant) and Dave Beavan (Computing Manager).
3. On this and related questions, see Anderson (forthcoming), Corbett *et al.* (2003), Douglas (2003).
4. The first version of the corpus went live on 30 November 2004, and is available at http://www.scottishcorpus.ac.uk/. There were 118,000 hits from 2,900 visitors on the first day, most of them coming via an article on the BBC News website. The six most popular search words were *gallus* 'bold', *muckle* 'big', *glaikit* 'stupid', *canny* 'careful', *dreich* 'dreary' and *sonsie* 'buxom'. That version contained approximately 532,000 words (385 documents). By 20 January 2005, the total had risen to around 600,000 words (425 documents). Our policy is to update whenever we have significant amounts of new data.
5. The *CSD* listing uses county names predating the 1975 local government reorganization, since most of the work for the parent *Scottish National Dictionary* was based on these divisions.
6. Most of the work on these forms was done by Dr Fiona Douglas, Research Assistant during Phase 1 of the project and now at the University of Leeds.

7. We are also grateful to the Newcastle Electronic Corpus of Tyneside English (NECTE) project team for sharing their expertise in this area with us (see Allen *et al.* in Volume 2).
8. For some answers to such questions, see Douglas (2002), and Corbett and Douglas (2003).

References

Anderson, W. (forthcoming). 'The SCOTS Corpus: a resource for language contact study'. *Studies in Eurolinguistics* 4.

Corbett, J. and F. Douglas. 2003. 'Scots in the public sphere'. *Towards our Goals in Broadcasting, the Press, the Performing Arts and the Economy: Minority Languages in Northern Ireland, the Republic of Ireland, and Scotland*, ed. by J. M. Kirk and D. P. Ó Baoill, pp. 198–210. Belfast: Queen's University.

Corbett, J., J. D. McClure and J. Stuart-Smith (eds). 2003. *The Edinburgh Companion to Scots*. Edinburgh: Edinburgh University Press.

Douglas, Fiona M. 2002. 'The role of Scots lexis in Scottish newspapers'. *Scottish Language* 21:1–12.

Douglas, Fiona M. 2003. 'The Scottish Corpus of Texts and Speech: problems of corpus design'. *Literary and Linguistic Computing* 18:23–37.

ILS Report. 2003. *An Institute for the Languages of Scotland: A Feasibility Study*, University of Edinburgh, October 2003.

Macafee, Caroline. 2000. 'The demography of Scots: the lessons of the Census campaign'. *Scottish Language* 19:1–44.

Murison, David. 1977. *The Guid Scots Tongue*. Edinburgh: James Thin/Mercat Press.

Robinson, Mairi (ed.). 1985. *The Concise Scots Dictionary*. Aberdeen: Aberdeen University Press.

Smith, Jeremy. 2000. 'Scots'. *Languages in Britain and Ireland*, ed. by G. Price, pp. 159–70. Oxford: Blackwell.

Websites

Dictionary of the Scots Language: http://www.dsl.ac.uk/

SCOTS Project: http://www.scottishcorpus.ac.uk/

Scottish Language Dictionaries: http://www.sldl.org.uk/

Institute for the Languages of Scotland: http://www.arts.ed.ac.uk/celtscot/institutelanguagesscotland/

British National Corpus: http://www.natcorp.ox.ac.uk/

For a list of Scots Web links, see also: http://www.arts.gla.ac.uk/SESLL/STELLA/links.htm#Scots

3
FRED – The Freiburg English Dialect Corpus: Applying Corpus-Linguistic Research Tools to the Analysis of Dialect Data

Lieselotte Anderwald and Susanne Wagner

1 Objectives

When, after almost two years of preliminary research, the actual compilation of FRED started in March 2000, the Freiburg team had had enough time to think about, discuss, consider possible and dismiss impossible research questions and devise a list of objectives for which the finished corpus should be suitable.[1] The research tradition of other Freiburg corpora provided two clear objectives (for F-LOB and Frown, see, for example, Mair, 2002; Mair *et al.*, 2002).

First, the corpus should permit the investigation of phenomena of non-standard morphosyntax (rather than analyses of phonetic or phonological details). Features of syntax are (almost by definition) much rarer than features of phonetics and phonology and very large quantities of text are therefore necessary (some estimates are that about 40 times the amount of text is needed for a syntactic analysis as opposed to a phonetic one). This considerably restricted the practicality of collecting our own corpus *ab initio*. Instead, we decided to try to compile a corpus from materials that were already available. We decided against collecting material with the help of questionnaires in the first phase of the project (but see Barbiers *et al.*, this volume). Questionnaires were, however, designed and distributed in the second phase of the project when, on the basis of extensive corpus analyses, interesting, transitional or rare phenomena became apparent that could not be further investigated with the help of FRED alone.

Second, we decided to collect material that would best be classified as traditional dialect data (for a diametrically opposed aim see the ICE project of Kallen and Kirk, this volume). This means that we explicitly tried to find material from speakers who grew up *before* the Second

World War, as this date seems to be the major cataclysmic event after which wide-ranging social and economic changes (with concomitant linguistic changes) came into effect. For example, highly increased mobility after the Second World War led to dialect-levelling on a hitherto unknown scale (see for example Williams and Kerswill, 1999, p. 149); mass affluence resulted, amongst other things, in television sets becoming easily available and spreading at least passive knowledge of the standard language; increased public spending made sure that education changed not only qualitatively but also quantitatively, such that children leaving school at 11 or 12 (not unusual for lower-class children only 60 or 70 years ago) is no longer possible, and so on. Only by concentrating on speakers born before the Second World War could we at least have a chance that our data would still be 'dialectal' in a regional sense, and be comparable to older dialect descriptions and dialect data (on the background of speaker selection for the *Survey of English Dialects*, see Orton, 1962, p. 14). There are a number of other arguments and preliminary considerations contributing to this decision: we had established contact with various researchers, research groups and private individuals who were either in possession of similar materials or were already working with such data, and who had kindly offered us access to them. Moreover, the only existing sources on variation in morphosyntax are based on traditional material, most importantly the *Survey of English Dialects* (Orton and Halliday, 1962–64; Orton and Dieth, 1962–71; Orton and Wakelin, 1967–68; Orton and Barry, 1969–71; Orton and Tilling, 1969–71). To guarantee comparability between these materials, it was essential that FRED should also consist of traditional dialect material without having to take factors like mobility or the influence of mass media into account.

2 FRED: make-up

Because of time constraints, but mainly for the reasons detailed above, it was considered impossible from the outset to record, digitize and transcribe all data that should make up FRED ourselves. To satisfy our research objectives, we were looking for large quantities of traditional regional speech, preferably by older local speakers with strong family affiliations in the area, that would record the use of speakers who grew up before the Second World War or, even better, before the First World War. This meant that we were looking for material preferably from the 1970s and 1980s, recording older speakers, or from the 1990s, if these recorded very old speakers. Our material had to be recorded in acceptable quality for linguistic analysis, ideally even including transcripts that were reliable on a word-by-word basis, and (most important of all) the material had to be more or less freely available to us as researchers who had not originally been part of the research design.[2] These criteria suggest a new source that has so far not (or hardly) been used for dialectological purposes, namely tape recordings and transcripts from oral history projects (but cf. Huber, 2003).

2.1 The role of oral history

As defined by the Oral History Society, 'Oral history is the recording of people's memories. It is the living history of everyone's unique life experiences' (Oral History Society at http://www.ohs.org.uk). Oral history collections sometimes originate from projects (short- or long-term) undertaken by an individual (sometimes also a group of individuals or an institution) with an interest in a specific theme or topic, often just recording life memories. Typically, these are lay persons, not professional historians, although some projects were initiated by local and academic historians, museum staff or archivists. In their 'Where you Start' section, the Society suggests a number of areas that may offer fruitful topics for an interview:

> If you haven't done any oral history interviewing before, think first about a focus or theme for your project. This could be your own family or street or block of flats, or it could be where you work, or your school. You might want to pick a topic to ask people about, for example memories of childhood, leisure, politics, religion or women's experience in wartime or memories of coming to Britain as a migrant. Whether you decide to work alone or as part of a group, having a theme will help you to decide who to interview.
>
> ('Where you Start' from http://www.ohs.org.uk/advice/)

Such a focus has certain implications concerning the content and general circumstances of an interview.[3] As the term 'oral history' and its definition above suggest, we are primarily dealing with *history*, and most projects focus on past events or customs which in the opinion of the researcher should be preserved for future generations by recording them. Interviewees are generally pensioners in their sixties or older, and only rarely do we find projects that have as many female as male speakers.[4]

The recording situation makes oral history material ideal for linguistic investigation. The interviewers were usually true insiders, coming from the area, often still speaking the dialect themselves, which tends to relax the interview situation considerably. A second advantage is that the speaker's attention was genuinely on what was being said, rather than on *how* it was being said. Fortunately, the Oral History Society ('After the interview' at http://www.ohs.org.uk/advice/) advises all potential interviewers to give a copy of the tapes to their local library or archive, and these are the places where oral history material can be found today across Great Britain.[5]

Members of the Oral History Society are advised to at least 'write a synopsis of the interview which briefly lists in order all the main themes, topics and stories discussed' ('After the interview' at http://www.ohs.org.uk/advice/), but verbatim transcripts are not explicitly mentioned.

2.2 From original recording to text in FRED: the steps and processes

Once the oral history interview has been conducted, the question of whether or not to transcribe the data is important to the interviewer. If the respective individual or group who conducted the interviews were thinking about long-term work with the material, a transcript is a very good way to allow people from outside to get an impression of the content of the interview without actually having to listen to the tapes, which is a very time-consuming business. The intentions for the future use of transcripts largely determine how the interview was transcribed, 'how' here referring particularly to the (unfortunately very common) practice of 'normalizing' the speakers' language. Since oral history projects as a rule do not involve the employment of a professional transcriber, this is the usual course of events, which is of course perfectly justified for oral history purposes. Just to give one example consisting of several actually occurring utterances, consider (1) which could end up as (2):

(1) That pot? Oh, I, I don't know, I don't remember what I made he for. I don't collect no pots now.
(2) I don't remember what I made that pot for. I don't collect pots now.

'Normalization' here has eradicated three morphosyntactic dialect features (*he* = pot; *he* here used in an oblique context; double negation *don't ... no*), not to mention all the 'superfluous data' (repetitions and so on) that are simply left out. This kind of standardized rewritten text is of course much more useful to the general public than a transcript that uses so many instances of 'eye-dialect' to represent non-standard pronunciation as well as dialect so that it is difficult to follow the line of argument.

Despite the obvious linguistic drawbacks, we were very glad to have transcripts of at least some of our material. Although these were highly deficient from a dialectological point of view, they at least solved such difficult problems for us as deciphering correctly some specialist vocabulary, unusual place names, personal names and so on, such as the names of different apple varieties used for cider-making:

(3) #The old variety of apples have died out, haven't they, or going out haven't they, from what we used to have, 'cause years ago there was dozens, wadn't there. #More so than what there were going nowadays. #You know, there were all sorts of Hang Downs and Kingston Blacks and Greasy Pippins, Toogoods Bitters all dozens, what we, the Old Dorset, dozens that we don't think of, innit, now as you might say. Within the last years I know or perhaps maybe with the, on the more improvements it seems like, with Showerings or Coats Gaymers that it is now. (FRED Som_1)

We then carefully compared existing transcripts with the original tapes and reinserted all morphological, syntactic and discourse features, taking out irrelevant phonetic or phonological features and features of pure eye-dialect (compare 4 with 4'):

(4) And the farmer wot my gran used ter ee used ter have a white high healed collar.

(4') #And the farmer what my gran used to, he used to have a white high healed collar. (FRED WIL_011)

For the rest of the material where no transcripts were available, we transcribed the original tapes *ab initio*, mostly with the help of native speakers who either worked on the project or were associated with it in related research projects. In addition, all transcripts were carefully checked by dialectologically trained research assistants.

As a result, the actual transcripts used for FRED are verbatim equivalents of the spoken versions: hesitations, repetitions, false starts of the same sentence and so on are all included.

(5) #Her her mother (trunc) w- (/trunc) was a (trunc) ne- (/trunc) niece of the -- of the -- of this farmer ... (FRED Oxf_002)

(6) #Oh well now, I tell you, when I first made my will, Mr (gap 'name') my lawyer, (unclear) oh yes (/unclear) he's still alive, (trunc) I- (/trunc) I told him I I I says, I want to leave the Salvation Army a bit of money, and I have done. (FRED Nott_016)

In addition, as stated above, and most importantly for our research purposes, all morphosyntactic dialect features have been reinserted (in bold print in the examples).

(7) #In the last orchard I **done**, I only **come** across a photograph t' other day, and I said I guess that's the last orchard been done around here for years. (FRED Som_002)

(8) #Even the seaweed here you know, we **couldn't** get **nothing** for it. (FRED Heb_030)

(9) ... there used to be a Ginnet **what** we used to call was a Ginnet, **he were** a nice eating apple, a nice sweet apple and a good apple for cider. #When **them** apples were ripe you could pick them up and could press them like that and you'd see your thumb mark in them or any apple really when **he**'s ripe, **wadn't** it, but when **he**'s not ripe **he**'s hard, isn't **he**, (unclear) you **ain't gonna**, (/unclear) well, anything at all. (FRED Som_001)

Among the features likely to have been 'corrected' in the original transcript are a zero relative in (7), double negation/negative concord in (8), a *what*-relative, demonstrative *them* and 'gendered' pronouns in (9) (see also section 4).

A variety of phonological features were also kept, either if they were already represented in the original transcripts, or if we suspected that they might interact with morphosyntax, for example contracted forms like *wanna, gonna, s'pose* and so on. It should be noted that we use the semi-phonetic form *mi* for /mi:/ used as the possessive pronoun not as 'eye-dialect' but in order to facilitate searches. (For severe criticism of gratuitous eye-dialect, see, for example, Preston, 1985, 2000). The orthographic form *me*, although widespread in other corpora, not only suggests a certain etymology for this form (at worst, a 'substitution' of the object form of the personal pronoun for the possessive function), but also complicates computer-based searches considerably, as all instances of the object case of the personal pronoun (*He saw me*) have to be manually excluded, at least for as long as the corpus remains untagged for word class.

We also represent certain paralinguistic features like laughter, long pauses, or indistinct stretches of conversation (marked as gaps, unclear passages or truncated words; see also the examples above).

(10) ... I thought he might have a (gap 'indistinct') him perhaps, but when I got to the ... (FRED Gla_002)

(11) ... and you pull it like that there (unclear) until you saw (/unclear) the bricks through, through the wires, onto these boards ... (FRED Ntt_013)

(12) #Had a month before I got demobbed to come home and eh (long pause) one of mi uh mi daughters the eldest daughter she was born while I was on the Queen Mary going over. #She were three year old when I got home. (FRED Ntt_004)

(13) #There was no, no limit, no boundaries. #And then the later years (trunc) the- (/trunc) , they got, got boundaries, you had boundaries; well otherwise half the, half the runners was out in a field a mile away perhaps, eh. (v 'laughter') (FRED Ken_001)

As examples (10) to (13) above show, all these features are indicated in the transcripts by specific tags to minimize the risk of ambiguities.[6] This opens up the possibility for analyses on a pragmatic or discourse level. In this way we have tried to remedy the linguistic shortcomings of the original oral history material as far as possible.

As mentioned above, extralinguistic variables in FRED are constrained by intention: FRED is not designed to be a representative sociolinguistic corpus, but a regionally representative corpus of dialect speech that is as broad as possible. As has already been pointed out, our oral history projects concentrated on interviewing older people. These older people are typically very local, that is, they still live in the place where they were born, without having moved outside the region for any considerable length of time. Also, typical FRED speakers usually left school about the age of 14, often much earlier, certainly not progressing to higher education. Finally, most of our speakers are male: as is well-known, women tend to use more prestigious, in many cases more standard forms of speech where these are available to them (see, for example, Chambers and Trudgill, 1998, p. 30). In other words, most of our speakers would qualify in dialectology as typical NORMs (see Chambers and Trudgill, 1998, p. 29), that is, non-mobile old rural male speakers with little education. Although this restricts the range of investigations that can be conducted with the help of FRED in sociolinguistic terms, it represents exactly the same bias as in earlier dialectological work, where we find a preponderance of NORM speakers as well, so that results from work on FRED will be comparable to earlier studies or to material from earlier investigations.

2.3 Advantages and disadvantages of orthographic transcripts

As can be seen from the examples given above, FRED is transcribed orthographically. A number of factors (besides a simple realistic evaluation of our resources) had made it clear from the beginning of the project that orthographically transcribing the dialect material would be the only viable (short-term) procedure. First, we only had been granted a restricted amount of time (and funding) to complete the compilation and transcription of the corpus, and there has to be a natural 'trade-off' between the detail of a transcription (depth) and the coverage (breadth) (see Tagliamonte, this volume). Our aim was a large corpus that would cover a number of dialect regions, and so we had to trade in phonetic detail. As mentioned before, our explicit focus was on morphosyntactic variability, not phonetic or phonological investigation. For all morphosyntactic features that we expected to investigate and that are discussed in the dialectological literature, a phonetic or phonemic transcription would not only have been unnecessary, but even counterproductive in many cases. As well as the obvious problems of legibility and numerous technical issues (how to represent phonemic transcription on a computer), one major drawback of a non-orthographic transcript concerns comparability. A non-orthographic transcript would dramatically hamper the feasibility of searching for all tokens of a certain type (for example *be*, personal pronouns and so on), as the researcher would have no clue which forms to look for without knowing which realizations actually occur in a given interview (or even across all interviews). As a result, one would have to return to the procedure that was common in corpus linguistics before the advent of computers: reading through the texts and marking all forms of interest in the process: certainly not an ideal situation.

Finally, only orthographic transcription of the data would meet the other requirements of our corpus: the finished corpus should be machine-readable, enabling easy access, a variety of searches with various tools, and, most importantly, comparability with other corpora/projects.

As has been mentioned above, research ties between the Freiburg team and similar projects had been established. Since most of these projects were working with orthographic transcripts, this lent additional support to the decision to use orthographic transcription for FRED (see especially Barbiers *et al.*, this volume). Moreover orthographic transcription would allow us to compare our data with older collections and enable us to make comparisons between different speakers, different dialects, different dialect areas and different corpora.

A further advantage of orthographic transcription is the concentration on real (morphosyntactic) dialect features, as phonetically exceptional forms do not distract the analyst's eye from the task at hand. Similar procedures were adapted for NECTE (see Allen *et al.*, Volume 2), ONZE (see Gordon *et al.*, Volume 2) and Tagliamonte's corpora (see Tagliamonte, this volume).

On the other hand, orthographic transcripts obviously prevent phonological analysis of the material when only the transcripts are made available. However, we plan to make the interviews accessible in the form of digitized audio files so that the interested researcher may go back to the original sound files to conduct such analyses. Although the poor quality of the original recordings caused a number of problems during the digitization process (see Allen *et al.*, Volume 2, for similar experiences with NECTE), the material is now available in digital format (original wav and compressed mp3). Without digitization, access to the audio material would have to be heavily restricted, and the material would only be available *in situ* at Freiburg, which is not very 'user-friendly' (but still common practice: see, for example, Tagliamonte, this volume, whose corpora are available only on site and whose audio files are not digitized; and ONZE, which is also only available on site: see Gordon *et al.*, Volume 2. For counterexamples, see Allen *et al.*, Volume 2, and Anderson *et al.*, this volume; who have made NECTE available via the Web, using an XML format).

All transcription conventions were of course documented and thus in many cases phonetic peculiarities may be traced from the transcription and the additional databases alone without having to return to the sound files. Although an alignment of sound and transcripts as in NECTE (see Allen *et al.*, Volume 2) and (planned) ONZE (see Gordon *et al.*, Volume 2) would certainly be desirable in the long run, it is not planned for the near future because of lack of time and funding.

2.4 FRED: corpus design and area coverage

2.4.1 Word counts and areal distribution

At the time of writing, the first version of FRED has been released and can be accessed by interested researchers. It consists of 370 texts, which total roughly 2.45 million words of text or about 300 hours of speech, excluding all interviewer utterances (see Table 3.1). The FRED material is broadly subdivided to cover nine major dialect areas, following Trudgill's 'modern dialects' division of Great Britain (see Trudgill, 1999, p. 65).

Table 3.1 FRED: word counts and areal distribution

Dialect area	Size (in words)	% of total
South-west (SW)	571,421	23.3
South-east (SE)	642,613	26.2
Midlands (Mid)	359,074	14.7
North (N)	434,306	17.7
Scottish Lowlands (ScL)	169,471	6.9
Scottish Highlands (ScH)	23,137	0.9
Hebrides (Heb)	151,134	6.2
Isle of Man (Man)	10,416	0.4
Wales (Wal)	88,739	3.6
Total	2,450,311	100

Each dialect area is subdivided into different counties. A detailed breakdown of counties can be found in Table 3.2 (below).

2.4.2 *Speakers*

FRED contains data from 420 different speakers (excluding interviewers): 268 (63.8 per cent) are male, and 127 (30.2 per cent) are female (gender is unknown for the rest). In all, 77.2 per cent of the textual material in FRED is produced by male speakers, and 21.4 per cent by female speakers.

The age of speakers included in FRED ranges from six years to 102 years, with a mean age of 75.2 years. A breakdown of age groups, according to the amount of text produced by them, is given in Table 3.3 (below). As can be seen, about three-quarters of the textual material in FRED is produced by speakers older than 60 years.

The oldest of FRED's speakers was born in 1877. Overall, 14 speakers (3.3 per cent) were born between 1880 and 1889, 60 speakers (14.3 per cent) were born between 1890 and 1899, 96 speakers (22.9 per cent) were born between 1900 and 1909, and 64 speakers (15.2 per cent) were born between 1910 and 1919. This means that 89 per cent of all speakers in FRED were born before 1920. A breakdown of age groups according to the amount of text produced can be found in Table 3.4 (below).

Table 3.2 FRED: distribution of words per county

	Size (in words)	**% of dialect area total**
South-west		
Devon (DEV)	85,936	15.0
Wiltshire (WIL)	174,849	30.6
Somerset (SOM)	197,705	34.6
Oxfordshire (OXF)	13,171	2.3
Cornwall (CON)	99,760	17.5
Total	571,421	100.0
South-east		
Suffolk (SFK)	318,470	49.6
Kent (KEN)	186,538	29.0
Middlesex (MDX)	30,957	4.8
London (LND)	106,648	16.6
Total	642,613	100.0
Midlands		
Leicestershire (LEI)	8,081	2.3
Nottingham (NTT)	168,663	47.0
Ironbridge (SAL)	174,128	48.5
Warwickshire (WAR)	8,202	2.3
Total	359,074	100.0
North		
Ambleside (WES)	149,721	34.5
Newcastle (NBL)	28,241	6.5
Durham (DUR)	25,855	6.0
York (YKS)	88,454	20.4
Lancashire (LAN)	142,035	32.7
Total	434,306	100.0
Scottish Lowlands		
Angus (ANS)	17,538	10.3
Banffshire (BAN)	5,216	3.1
Dumfriesshire (DFS)	9,117	5.4
East Lothian (ELN)	32,999	19.5
Fife (FIF)	3,414	2.0
Kincardineshire (KCD)	7,004	4.1
Kinrosshire (KRS)	2,218	1.3
Lanarkshire (LKS)	3,478	2.1
Mid Lothian (MLN)	28,813	17.0
Peebleshire (PEE)	14,041	8.3
Pertshire (PER)	20,181	11.9
Selkirk (SEL)	8,922	5.3
West Lothian (WLN)	16,530	9.8
Total	169,471	100.0

Table 3.2 FRED: distribution of words per county– *continued*

	Size (in words)	% of dialect area total
Scottish Highlands		
Sutherland (SUT)	10,311	44.6
Ross and Cromarty (ROC)	9,700	41.9
Inverness-shire (INV)	3,126	13.5
Total	23,137	100.0
Hebrides (Heb)	151,134	100.0
Wales		
Denbighshire (DEN)	37,282	42.0
Glamorganshire (GLA)	51,457	58.0
Total	88,739	100.0
Isle of Man (IOM)	10,416	100.0

Table 3.3 FRED: speakers' ages

Age group	Number of speakers	% of textual material in corpus produced
0–14 years	9	0.5
15–24 years	14	1.2
25–34 years	2	0.2
35–44 years	2	0.1
45–59 years	14	3.8
60+ years	233	74.8
Unknown	145	19.4

Table 3.4 FRED: speakers' birth dates

Date of birth (dob) of speaker	Number of words produced	% of all speakers
1870–79	6,297	0.3
1880–89	148,627	6.1
1890–99	479,872	19.6
1900–09	772,335	31.5
1910–19	455,261	18.6
1920–29	158,901	6.5
1930–39	31,135	1.3
1940–49	1,614	0.1
1950–59	5,181	0.2
Total	2,059,223	84.0
No information on date of birth available	393,282	16.0

2.4.3 Recordings

The material included in FRED was recorded between 1968 and 1999. A detailed breakdown of recording dates can be found in Table 3.5.

Over two-thirds of all interviews thus come from the 1970s and 1980s, guaranteeing comparability with much dialectological work conducted at that time.

Table 3.5 FRED: interview recording dates

Recording date	Number of speakers	% of all speakers
1961–69	2	0.5
1970–79	122	29.1
1980–89	163	38.9
1990–99	61	14.6
Unknown	71	16.9

3 Linguistic consequences of using oral history material

The decision to base our FRED corpus predominantly on sources of oral history projects has had a range of linguistic consequences, some of them foreseen, others not predictable at the outset. Perhaps the most clearly predictable linguistic consequences stem from the fact that oral history material necessarily involves the speaker talking about his or her life story at great length: very often, in fact, the speakers are actively encouraged to talk almost exclusively about their past. In the realm of tense and aspect, a predominance of past-time narratives implies a predominance of past-tense contexts (although not infrequently of course stretches of past-time narratives are narrated in the historical present tense as well). This is an advantage for studies concentrating on past-tense paradigms (for example, Anderwald, 2008), but a clear disadvantage for any investigation into the present tense, as the data typically yield too few examples to make a regional comparison reliable (see Anderwald, 2004). It also means that any features that are *linked* to the present-tense domain can be expected (and indeed shown) to be under-represented: for example, use of the (present) progressive versus the simple form; forms for the 'recent past' (for example the 'after'-perfect in Hiberno-English); uses, if any, of a habitual present and so on.

A second feature one would expect, considering the fact that FRED speakers tend to tell their own life stories, is a skewing in pronoun frequencies. Based on the monologic nature of many of the interviews in FRED, we might expect first person singular and first person plural contexts to be over-represented. However, a comparison with the more balanced demographic part of the British National Corpus (BNC) that records everyday spontaneous conversations reveals that this is not the case (see Table 3.6).

Table 3.6 Personal pronouns in FRED and the BNC

	FRED		BNC spoken	
Pronoun	**Occurences**	**% of total**	**Occurences**	**% of total**
I	61,458	23.4	309,797	26.8
he	29,733	11.3	75,442	6.5
she	9,418	3.6	42,879	3.7
it	41,776	15.9	254,049	22.0
we	27,240	10.4	108,698	9.4
you	54,163	20.6	268,642	23.2
they	38,608	14.7	96,672	8.4
Total	262,396		1,156,179	

Despite the impression one gets when reading through FRED transcripts, first person contexts are not over-represented in the corpus, but account for roughly one-third of all personal pronoun contexts in both FRED and the spoken part of the BNC. Although there are slight deviations in frequencies for individual third person contexts (which can easily be explained on the basis of the nature of the recording situations), the overall frequency of first versus third person contexts is surprisingly similar at 33.8 per cent versus 45.5 per cent in FRED and 36.2 per cent versus 40.6 per cent in the BNC (spoken). Based on these figures, we expect that comparative analyses of FRED and other corpora of spoken English involving the category 'person' will produce representative results.

Finally, in the realm of discourse, it has to be stressed that FRED does not contain genuinely spontaneous, everyday conversations, as for example the BNC does. In the worst case, some (but fortunately only a tiny minority of) speakers actually read from prepared notes, as witnessed by pages rustling in the background and distinctive pauses where pages are turned: obviously, these speakers prepared too well (for our purposes) for the interviews and were afraid of forgetting interesting details during the course of it! Although this worst case is mercifully rare, many interviews are nevertheless monologic: understandably, the interviewers tried to keep in the background most of the time. FRED for this reason would probably not lend itself well to the investigation of discourse strategies. However, this limitation is probably not specific to FRED, but applies to dialectological and sociolinguistic interviews alike, as the main objective is always to record the speakers' speech, rather than one's own (see Feagin, 2002).

4 First results

Early investigations of FRED were conducted at the same time as the corpus was being compiled. Naturally, these investigations had to be restricted to high-frequency phenomena, as here it seemed most feasible to accomplish much in a comparatively short time, with a continuously expanding set of data. The main advantage of FRED, geographic comparability, could not be exploited in these early studies, and the first detailed studies concentrated on individual dialect areas. Lukas Pietsch investigated the Northern Subject Rule, finding conclusive evidence that this subject–verb-concord phenomenon was introduced into Northern Ireland not from Scotland alone, but from the central English north (Pietsch, 2005); Tanja Herrmann collected and examined relative clauses (Herrmann, 2005); and one of the present authors studied the distribution of 'gendered' pronouns in the English Southwest (Wagner, 2005). Again, one of the most striking results was the fact that a phenomenon generally assumed to be predominant in a traditional dialect area has in fact a different geographic distribution.

'Gendered' pronouns are masculine pronominal forms (*he, him* and South-western *un, en* < OE *hine*) referring to inanimate referents. An example from FRED is given in (14) below; also recall example (9), reproduced here as (15) for convenience's sake.

(14) #He used to say 'Put **un** [candle] where ye can zee '**im** [candle] and I can zee '**im** [candle] as well.' (FRED Wil_024)

(15) ... there used to be a Ginnet what we used to call was a Ginnet, **he were** a nice eating apple, a nice sweet apple and a good apple for cider. #When them apples were ripe you could pick them up and could press them like that and you'd see your thumb mark in them or any apple really when **he**'s ripe, wadn't it, but when **he**'s not ripe **he**'s hard, isn't **he**, (unclear) you ain't gonna, (/unclear) well, anything at all. (FRED Som_001)

'Gendered' pronouns are a feature of the traditional dialects in the South-west, typically associated with 'Wessex' dialect, that is, the speech of rural, remote areas. Detailed analysis of the distribution of 'gendered' pronouns in the *SED* and FRED revealed one big surprise: the dialect of West Cornwall, traditionally assumed to be more standard than that of East Cornwall and the neighbouring counties (see, for example, Wakelin, 1975, p. 100), shows by far the highest percentage of 'gendered' pronouns per speaker (see Table 3.7).

Table 3.7 Frequency of 'gendered' pronouns per county and location (*SED* fieldworker notebooks)

County	No. of examples	No. of locations	Examples per location	No. of speakers	Examples per speaker
Cornwall	163	7	23.3	20	8.2
Dorset	40	5	8.0	8	5.0
Devon	126	11	11.5	26	4.8
Wiltshire	70	9	7.8	15	4.7
Somerset	88	13+1*	6.3	28	3.1
Total	487	46	10.6	97	5.0

*For unknown reasons, Montacute was not included in the Basic Material, though the questionnaire had been completed.

Based on these results, it is possible that the status of Cornwall, and particularly West Cornwall, in the world of English dialects should be re-evaluated. Earlier studies on English in Cornwall have largely focused on phonological or lexical variables, with only brief comments (Wakelin, 1975) or without commenting at all on morphosyntactic features (for example, Fischer, 1976; Bremann, 1984). It is by no means impossible that the results from more detailed morphosyntactic analyses will shed new light on the not-so-old English dialect of Cornwall.

Comparisons across the whole FRED material have not been possible for very long yet, so most truly comparative projects are currently still work in progress. These include a comparison of multiple negation (Anderwald, 2008), past-tense paradigms (Anderwald, 2005), pronoun systems (Hernández, in progress), syntactic priming (Szmrecsanyi, 2006) and complementation patterns (Kolbe, in progress). In addition, a whole range of Master's theses have been or are being completed on the basis of material from FRED. An up-to-date account can be found on the project homepage at http://www.anglistik.uni-freiburg.de/institut/lskortmann/fred.

Notes

1. The compilation of FRED was supported by the German Research Foundation (DFG grant Ko 1181-1/1-1,2,3). For the original motivation linking dialectology and typology, see, for example, Anderwald and Kortmann, 2002; Kortmann, 2002a, 2002b, 2003.
2. See also Gordon *et al.*, Volume 2, whose ONZE corpus also contains material which was collected for a non-linguistic purpose originally.
3. 'There are some points to cover in every interview: date and place of birth, what their parents' and their own main jobs were. And whatever the topic, it usually helps to get the interviewee talking if you begin with their earlier life: family background, grandparents, parents and brothers and sisters (including topics such as discipline), then onto childhood home (housework, chores, mealtimes), leisure (street games, gangs, sport, clubs, books, weekends, holidays, festivals), politics and religion, schooling (key teachers, friends, favourite subjects), early relationships, working life (first job, a typical working day, promotion, pranks and initiation, trade unions and professional organizations), and finally later family life (marriage, divorce, children, homes, money, neighbours, social life, hopes). Most people find it easier to remember their life in chronological order, and it can sometimes take you two or three sessions to record a full life story' ('Preparing questions' from http://www.oralhistory.org.uk/advice/).
4. The advantages and disadvantages of using oral history material for linguistic studies will be discussed in detail in section 3.
5. However, this procedure also raises the unfortunate problem of copyright (see also Anderson *et al.*, this volume). Especially for our older material, where many of the speakers have already passed away, it is near impossible to gain copyright clearance. Museums and archives are also often reluctant to provide copyright clearance, so that in the foreseeable future FRED will only be accessible to academic research, and cannot be published in its present form.
6. The tags in use at the moment include pauses, different types of non-verbal elements, truncations, editorial corrections, indirect speech, dubious items, uncertain transcriptions, gaps in transcription.

References

Allen, W. H., J. C. Beal, K. P. Corrigan, W. Maguire and H. L. Moisl 2007. 'A linguistic 'time-capsule': The Newcastle Electronic Corpus of Tyneside English'. *Creating and Digitizing Language Corpora: Diachronic Databases (Volume 2)*, ed. by J. C., Beal, K. P. Corrigan and H. L. Moisl, pp. 16–48. Basingstoke: Palgrave Macmillan.

Allen *et al.*: Anderson, J., D. Beavan, and C. Kay 2007. 'SCOTS: Scottish Corpus of Texts and Speech'. *Creating and Digitizing Language Corpora: Synchronic Databases (Volume 1)*, ed. by J. C. Beal, K. P. Corrigan and H. L. Moisl, pp. 17–34. Basingstoke: Palgrave Macmillan.

Anderwald, L. 2004. 'Local markedness as a heuristic tool in dialectology: the case of *amn't*'. *Dialectology Meets Typology*, ed. by B. Kortmann, pp. 47–67. Berlin/New York: Mouton de Gruyter.

Anderwald, L. 2005. 'Negative concord in British English dialects.' *Aspects of Negation*, ed. by Y. Iyeiri, pp. 113–137. Amsterdam/Philadelphia: John Benjamins.

Anderwald, L. 2008. *The Morphology of English Dialects: Verb-Formation in Non-Standard English*. Cambridge: Cambridge University Press.

Anderwald, L. and B. Kortmann. 2002. 'Typology and dialectology: a programmatic sketch'. *Present Day Dialectology, Volume I: Problems and Discussions*, ed. by J. van Marle and J. Berns, pp. 159–71. Berlin/New York: Mouton de Gruyter.

Bremann, R. 1984. *Soziolinguistische Untersuchung zum Englisch von Cornwall*. Frankfurt: Peter Lang.

Chambers, J. K. and P. Trudgill. 1998. *Dialectology*, 2nd edn. Cambridge: Cambridge University Press.

Feagin, C. 2002. 'Entering the community: fieldwork'. *The Handbook of Language Variation and Change*, ed. by J. K. Chambers, P. Trudgill and N. Schilling-Estes, pp. 20–39. Oxford/New York: Blackwell.

Fischer, A. 1976. *Dialects in the South-West of England: A Lexical Investigation*. Bern: Francke.

Gordon, E., M. Maclagan and J. Hay 2007. 'The ONZE corpus'. *Creating and Digitizing Language Corpora: Diachronic Databases (Volume 2)*, ed. by J. C. Beal, K. P. Corrigan and H. L. Moisl, pp. 82–104. Basingstoke: Palgrave Macmillan.

Hernández, N. (in progress). 'Pronouns in British English dialects: the non-standard uses of subject, object and self forms in spoken English'. PhD dissertation, Freiburg University.

Herrmann, T. 2005. 'Relative clauses in English dialects of the British Isles'. *A Comparative Grammar of British English Dialects: Agreement, Gender, Relative Clauses*, by T. Herrmann, L. Pietsch, and S. Wagner, pp. 21–123. Berlin/New York: Mouton de Gruyter.

Huber, M. 2003. 'The corpus of English in south-east Wales and its synchronic and diachronic implications.' *The Celtic Englishes III*, ed. by H.L.C. Tristram, pp. 183–200 Heidelberg: Carl Winter.

Kolbe, D. (in progress). 'Complementation patterns in English dialects'. PhD dissertation, University of Hanover.

Kortmann, B. 2002a. 'New approaches to dialectology: introduction'. *Anglistentag 2001 Wien – Proceedings*, ed. by D. Kastovsky, G. Kaltenböck and S. Reichl, pp. 3–6. Trier: Wissenschaftlicher Verlag.

Kortmann, B. 2002b. 'New prospects for the study of English dialect syntax: impetus from syntactic theory and language typology'. *Syntactic Microvariation*, ed. by S. Barbiers, L. Cornips and S. van der Kleij, pp. 185–213. Amsterdam: Meertens Insitute.

Kortmann, B. 2003. 'Comparative English dialect grammar: a typological approach'. *Fifty Years of English Studies in Spain (1952–2002). A Commemorative Volume*, ed. by I. M. Palacios, M. José López Couso, P. Fra and E. Seoane, pp. 65–83. Santiago de Compostela: University of Santiago.

Mair, C. 2002. 'Three changing patterns of verb complementation in Late Modern English: a real-time study based on matching text corpora'. *English Language and Linguistics* 6:105–31.

Mair, C., M. Hundt, G. Leech and N. Smith. 2002. 'Short-term diachronic shifts in part-of-speech frequencies: a comparison of the tagged LOB and F-LOB corpora'. *International Journal of Corpus Linguistics* 7:245–64.

Orton, H. 1962. *Survey of English Dialects – Introduction*. Leeds: Arnold.
Orton, H. and M. V. Barry (eds). 1969–71. *Survey of English Dialects. The West Midland Counties*. Leeds: Arnold.
Orton, H. and E. Dieth (eds). 1962–71. *Survey of English Dialects. The Basic Material*. Leeds: Arnold.
Orton, H. and W. J. Halliday (eds). 1962–64. *Survey of English Dialects. The Six Northern Counties and the Isle of Man*. Leeds: Arnold.
Orton, H. and P. M. Tilling (eds). 1969–71. *Survey of English Dialects. The East Midland Counties and East Anglia*. Leeds: Arnold.
Orton, H. and M. F. Wakelin (eds). 1967–68. *Survey of English Dialects. The Southern Counties*. Leeds: Arnold.
Pietsch, L. 2005. '*Some do and some doesn't*: verbal concord variation in the north of the British Isles'. *A Comparative Grammar of British English Dialects: Agreement, Gender, Relative Clauses*, by T. Herrmann, L. Pietsch and S. Wagner, pp. 125–209. Berlin/New York: Mouton de Gruyter.
Preston, D. R. 1985. 'The Li'l Abner syndrome: written representations of speech'. *American Speech* 60: 328–36.
Preston, D. R. 2000. 'Mowr and mowr bayud spellin': confessions of a sociolinguist'. *Journal of Sociolinguistics* 4: 614–21.
Szmrecsanyi, B. 2006. *Morphosyntactic Persistence in Spoken English: A Corpus Study*. Berlin/New York: Mouton de Gruyter.
Trudgill, P. 1999. *The Dialects of England*, 2nd edn. Oxford: Blackwell.
Wagner, S. 2005. 'Pronominal gender in varieties of British English'. *A Comparative Grammar of British English Dialects: Agreement, Gender, Relative Clauses*, by T. Herrmann, L. Pietsch and S. Wagner, pp. 211–367. Berlin/New York: Mouton de Gruyter.
Wakelin, M. F. 1975. *Language and History in Cornwall*. Leicester: Leicester University Press.
Williams, A. and P. Kerswill. 1999. 'Dialect levelling: change and continuity in Milton Keynes, Reading and Hull'. *Urban Voices: Accent Studies in the British Isles*, ed. by P. Foulkes and G. Docherty, pp. 141–62. London: Edward Arnold.

Websites

FRED Project home page: http://www.anglistik.uni-freiburg.de/institut/lskortmann/ FRED
Oral History Society: http://www.ohs.org.uk

4

The Syntactic Atlas of the Dutch Dialects (SAND): A Corpus of Elicited Speech and Text as an Online Dynamic Atlas

Sjef Barbiers, Leonie Cornips and Jan Pieter Kunst

1 Background information

The Syntactic Atlas of the Dutch Dialects (SAND) corpus is one of the outputs of a large-scale dialect syntax project conducted between 2000 and 2003 in The Netherlands and the Dutch-speaking parts of Belgium and France.[1] The goal of the project was twofold:

1. To create an electronic atlas serving as a tool for linguistic research. This freely accessible web-based dynamic atlas (DynaSand; http://www.meertens.nl/sand/)consists of a data corpus, a user-friendly search engine and cartographic software for the online generation of maps. It contains data from 267 dialects collected in oral and telephone interviews and in a postal survey.
2. To produce a more traditional printed atlas that visualizes syntactic variation in the dialects of Dutch. Every map in the atlas is provided with: (a) a linguistic description of specific syntactic variables, (b) a discussion of the attested geographical distribution (including a diachronic perspective when that is applicable), and (c) a bibliography. Volume I (Barbiers *et al.* appeared in June 2005. Volume II is expected to appear in 2007).

1.1 Corpus size and type of data

In all three types of interview – oral, telephone and postal – test sentences were offered to the informants (see Barbiers and Vanden Wyngaerd, 2001a and 2001b, for the written and oral questionnaires). In general, the subjects were asked to translate them and/or to establish whether the sentence occurred in their dialects (see section 2 on 'Methodology').

The postal survey was a pilot study taking stock of the extent to which dialects varied at the syntactic level and to get a first impression of the geographic distribution of key syntactic variables. The complete data set obtained from the postal survey comprises about 156,000 question–answer pairs (424 test sentences × 368 informants). The data resulting from the fieldwork form the core of the database, as we think that the methodology applied in these oral interviews yields the most reliable data (see section 2.3). The transcriptions of the fieldwork interviews include about 45,000 question–answer pairs (1,200,000 words) in 267 different dialects. These transcriptions have been partially enriched with part-of-speech (POS) tagging (see section 5). In the future we hope to provide a fully tagged corpus. The spoken data from these interviews (425 hours of speech in total) have been added to the database and lined up with the transcriptions to make them searchable.

In addition to the elicited data, the spoken part of the corpus will contain spontaneous ten-minute dialogues in the 267 dialects. Each ten-minute dialogue precedes the actual interview. One of the goals of these dialogues was to create a natural, realistic and relaxed dialect atmosphere to make sure that, during the interviews, the informants would speak their dialects in the way they normally do. The spontaneous dialogues are particularly useful for phonological and phonetic research. They are also important because the dialects involved in this project are expected to change rapidly or even disappear in the near future. Obviously, we would have preferred to record much longer dialogues, but the interviews themselves were too time-consuming to allow that.

The telephone interviews were conducted to ask some of the original questions from the fieldwork interviews again in cases where they had not produced a useful answer. In addition, a number of new questions were asked, for example to make certain paradigms complete.[2] The data from the telephone interviews roughly include 26,000 question–answer pairs (105 test sentences × 252 different locations).

Because of the striking amount of syntactic variation that is still present in Dutch dialects, the questions in the various interviews were restricted to four empirical domains: (a) the left periphery of the clause, (b) the right periphery of the clause, (c) negation and quantification, and finally (d) pronominal reference. Particularly well-represented are data on complementizer agreement (example 1; see Van Koppen, 2005); complementizer doubling (example 2); subject pronoun doubling (example 3; see de Vogelaer, 2005); relative and Wh-clauses (example 4; see Van Craenenbroeck, 2004); word order in verbal clusters (example 5, see Barbiers, 2005); verbal morphosyntax (such as the *Infinitivus pro Participio* (IPP) effect (example 6), the *Imperativus pro Infinitivo* (IPI) effect (example 7), the *Participium pro Infinitivo* (PPI) effect (example 8), DO-support (example 9), negative concord (example 10; see Neuckermans, forthcoming; Zeijlstra, 2004), the negative particle (example 11) and the form and distribution of (long and short distance) reflexives and pronouns (example 12; see Barbiers and Bennis, 2003).

(1) Complementizer agreement
   a. [...] da Lisa zo schoon is of Anna (West Flemish)
      that Lisa as beautiful is as Anna
      'that Lisa is as beautiful as Anna.'
   b. [...] da-*n* Bart en Peter sterker zijn (West Flemish)
      that.PLUR Bart and Peter stronger are
      'that Bart and Peter are stronger.'

(2) Complementizer doubling
   Ik weet niet *of dat* Jan komt (colloquial Dutch)
   I know not if that John comes
   'I don't know whether John will come.'

(3) Subject pronoun doubling
   As *ze* *zulder* voor hun werk leven [...] (Flemish)
   if they.WEAK they.STRONG for their work live
   'If they live for their work, [...]'

(4) Relative clauses (variation in form of relative pronoun depending on grammatical function and depth of embedding)
   a. de man *die* ik denk *die* het verhaal verteld heeft (East Flemish)
      the man who I think who the story told has
      'the man who I think told the story.'
   b. de man *die* ik denk *dat* ze geroepen hebben (East Flemish)
      the man who I think that they called have
      'the man who I think they called.'

(5) Word order in verbal clusters
   a. [...] dat iedereen *moet* *kunnen zwemmen* (Standard Dutch)
      that everbody must.FIN can.INF swim.INF
      'that everybody should be able to swim.'
   b. [...] dat iedereen *zwemmen kunnen moet* (Frisian)
      that everyone swim.INF can.INF must.FIN
      'that everybody should be able to swim.'
   c. [...] dat iedereen *moet* *zwemmen kunnen* (eastern Dutch)
      that everyone must.FIN swim.INF can.INF
      'that everybody should be able to swim.'

(6) *Infinitivus pro Participio* (infinitive instead of expected participle)
   a. Vertel maar niet wie zij had roepen *kend* (Groningen dialect)
      *tell just not who she had call.*INF *can.*PARTICIPLE
      'Just don't tell her who she could have called.'
   b. Vertel maar niet wie zij had *kunnen* roepen (Standard Dutch)
      *tell just not who she had can.*INF *call.*INF
      'Just don't tell her who she could have called.'

(7) *Imperativus pro Infinitivo* (imperative instead of expected infinitive)
   Hij ging naar de bakker en *koop* een broodje (Groningen dialect)
   *he went to the baker and buy.*IMP *a sandwich*
   'He went to the bakery to buy a sandwich.'

(8) *Participium pro Infinitivo* (participle instead of expected infinitive)
   a. Zou hij dat *gedaan* hebben gekund? (Frisian)
      *would he that done.*PARTICIPLE *have.*INF *can.*PARTICIPLE
      'Would he have been able to do it?'
   b. Zou hij dat hebben kunnen *doen*? (Standard Dutch)
      *would he that have.*INF *can.*INF *do.*INF
      'Would he have been able to do it?'

(9) DO-support
   Ik *doe* even de kopjes afwassen (Northern Brabantish)
   I do just the cups wash
   'I am just washing the dishes.'

(10) Negative concord
   't Wil *niemand nie* dansen (West Flemish)
   it wants no-one not dance
   'Nobody wants to dance.'

(11) Negative particle
   Pas op da ge nie *en* valt (Brussels)
   look out that you not NEG.PART *fall*
   'Don't fall!'

(12) Reflexives
   a. Jan kent *zich-zelf* goed (Standard Dutch)
      John knows REFL.PRON-*self well*
      'John knows himself well.'

b. Jan kent *zijn-eigen* goed (Central Dutch)
John knows his-own well
'John knows himself well.'

c. Jan kent *hem-zelf* goed (Frisian)
John knows him-self well
'John knows himself well.'

d. Jan kent *zijn-zelf* goed (West Flemish)
John knows his-self well
'John knows himself well.'

1.2 Main applications

The primary application for which the dynamic atlas was developed is to assist research into syntactic microvariation from various perspectives, including theoretical, typological, geolinguistic, historical and quantitative. Since the corpus contains the original spoken data, which are lined up with the transcriptions (see section 6; see Anderson *et al.*, this volume, and Allen *et al.*, Volume 2), it is an excellent tool for morphological, phonological and phonetic research too. The corpus may also serve educational purposes, that is to give students the opportunity to get hands-on experience in syntactic and other types of linguistic research. Finally, the corpus can be used for forensic purposes, for example to locate a suspect by his or her speech.

1.3 Some research questions and results

Central questions in current syntactic research are:

1. What are the limits of syntactic variation?
2. What is the locus of syntactic variation in the grammar model?
3. Is there a principled difference between macrovariation (the differences between genetically less related languages) and microvariation (the differences between closely related dialects)?

The first question should lead to a theory about syntactic variation. More specifically, it should provide a characterization of universal grammar (UG: the syntactic properties that all languages have in common) and the notion of (im)possible natural language. As for the second question, in its strongest form (see Chomsky, 1995, and related Minimalist work) the UG hypothesis states that syntactic variation does not exist. Apparent syntactic variation, such as word order variation, should then be reducible to the lexicon, namely, the parametrization of morphosyntactic features, or to phonological form, that is, different ways to spell out one and the same syntactic structure phonologically. The third question should lead, for example, to an explanation of why a sentence such as (13a) does not occur in any Dutch dialect, even though this is the common order in Standard English (13b), a genetically not very distant language.

(13) a. * Jan heeft gelezen het.
b. John has read it.
c. Jan heeft het gelezen.
John has it read

The SAND corpus is highly relevant for all of these research issues. The advantage of studying microvariation is that many variables can be kept constant, making it easier to trace the effects of small, for example, morphosyntactic, differences in one part of the grammar on other parts of the grammar, such as word order. Another advantage of studying microvariation on a large scale is that it becomes possible to make statistically valid statements about possible and impossible syntactic structures.

Many of the results of research on the basis of the SAND corpus have been reported in the papers and dissertations referred to in section 1.1. We give two examples here. In relation to the questions stated in the previous paragraph, Barbiers and Bennis (2003) explain the impossibility of certain conceivable strong reflexives (**hem-eigen* 'him-own', see (12) above) and reflexive systems from general syntactic principles such as the requirement that the two elements in a strong reflexive should agree. For word order variation in verb clusters (see the examples in (5) above), Barbiers (2005) shows that there is one word order that does not occur in verbal clusters (14a), and that there is another order that only occurs when the hierarchically highest verb is a perfective auxiliary (14b, c). He argues that these restrictions follow from general syntactic principles such as the ban on destroying original embedding relations, and the condition that reordering of verbs in a cluster requires agreement between the reordering verbs. He further claims that the other orders are the result of optional movement in the syntactic component (contra the strong Minimalist hypothesis mentioned above).

(14) a. * [...] dat iedereen gaan moet zwemmen
that everyone go.INF must.FIN swim.INF
Intended meaning: 'that everyone should go swimming.'

b. *[...] dat iedereen gaan zwemmen *moet*
*that everyone go.*INF *swim.*INF *must.*FIN
Intended meaning: 'that everyone should go swimming.'

c. [...] dat iedereen gaan zwemmen *is*
*that everyone go.*INF *swim.*INF *is.*FIN
'that everybody went swimming.'

2 Methodology of data collection

The main methodological and theoretical frameworks underpinning the compilation of the SAND corpus are generative linguistics, typology, dialectology and sociolinguistics. All possible sources have been used to prepare the questionnaires. From the comparative syntactic research common in the generative and typological frameworks much potential variation could be deduced (see Barbiers *et al.*, 2002). In addition, generative theory makes a number of specific predictions regarding the kind of variation that may be expected. The dialectological literature provides a number of syntactic variables that had to be taken into account, although they were less than we had hoped. Syntactic microvariation is a relatively neglected area in dialectological research. It has been received wisdom since the 1920s that there was hardly any syntactic variation (left) in the Dutch language area, as opposed to lexical, morphological and phonological variation (see Kloeke, 1927). Finally, sociolinguistic insights were particularly relevant for the development of an adequate and systematic data collection strategy.

2.1 Informants

In the oral and telephone interviews, the following social variables of the local dialect speakers were homogenized, as much as possible in order to be able to examine geographical variation and, hence, to exclude social variation as much as possible: (i) all subjects are native speakers of the local dialect, (ii) both the subject and their parents were born in the same community and have lived there until adulthood, (iii) the subjects did not leave their community for longer than seven years, (iv) the subjects speak their local dialect in several functional domains, (v) the subjects belong to the lower middle class, and (vi) the subjects are aged between 55 and 70 years.

2.2 Elicitation techniques

The corpus has been collected by carefully designed elicitation procedures for the written, oral and telephone surveys. The use of elicitation techniques has the advantage of systematically gathering dialect data in a large geographical area within a short time span. Moreover, it enables the researcher to standardize both the collection and the analysis of the material. One of the elicitation techniques is an acceptability judgement task reminiscent of the successful experimental methods described in Labov (1972, 1996). Rather than eliciting direct intuitions by the formula: 'can/do you say X?' or 'do you judge X a grammatical/good sentence?', informants were asked the more indirect: 'do you ever encounter this variant in the local dialect?' Hence, direct questioning is one of the conditions that promotes answers in the direction of a socially standard superordinate norm over the native dialect system (Labov, 1996, p. 100). These answers may reflect the (syntactic) variant which the informants believe has prestige or is 'correct' and, hence, the standard form rather than the form they actually use (Labov, 1972, p. 213; Cornips and Jongenburger, 2001; Cornips, 2002; Cornips and Poletto, 2005).

An example in the written questionnaire is provided in Figure 4.1. In general, the written questionnaire is offered in Standard Dutch although some questions accommodate to a specific geographical distribution of the variant by inclusion of specific local dialect features such as subject-doubling.

Moreover, an indirect relative judgement task was used to collect quantitative and qualitative data about variability in word orders in three-verb clusters. This task required the subjects to rank orders within nine types of three-verb clusters from most to least acceptable on a

---

In some dialects we encounter sentences such as:

Misschien ga'k 'et (e) (k) ik wel krijgen

Betekenis: Misschien gaik het wel krijgen

meaning: "maybe, I'll get it"

(i) Do you encounter sentences such as (1) in your local dialect?

Yes/No

Figure 4.1 Acceptability judgement task

five-point scale (representing *, ?*, ??, ?, ok), as illustrated in Figure 4.2 for the three-verb cluster containing two modals as the hierarchically highest verbs and a lexical verb as the lowest verb. In the written questionnaire, all six possible orders were presented to the subjects.

		Encounter	**Uncommon-common**
a.	Ik weet dat Jan hard *moet kunnen werken*	yes/no	1-2-3-4-5
	I know that Jan hard,must, can, work		
b.	Ik weet dat Jan hard *moet werken kunnen*	yes/no	1-2-3-4-5
c.	Ik weet dat Jan hard *kunnen moet werken*	yes/no	1-2-3-4-5
d.	Ik weet dat Jan hard *kunnen werken moet*	yes/no	1-2-3-4-5
e.	Ik weet dat Jan hard *werken kunnen moet*	yes/no	1-2-3-4-5
f.	Ik weet dat Jan hard *werken moet kunnen*	yes/no	1-2-3-4-5

Figure 4.2 Relative judgement task

Subsequently, the different degrees in acceptability judgements can be related to one another and can be interpreted in the analysis. According to Rickford (1987, p. 159), such elicited 'intuitions' are in a way similar to those which formal linguists use, but differ from them considerably in at least two respects: (i) they are elicited from a sample of community members rather than being derived from the linguist's own introspection, and (ii) heterogeneity is assumed by providing several alternatives (Cornips and Corrigan, 2005). This judgement task leaves room for native-speaker introspection in reflecting a considerable degree of individual variability (see Cornips and Poletto, 2005). This is in accordance with the more recent plea that linguists should strive towards a more systematic collection strategy for intuitions in 'spontaneous' and experimental elicitation settings, particularly given the open-ended nature of syntax and the fact that this research methodology produces data that has become increasingly subtle and, in many ways more challenging.

2.3 Task effects

The elicitation techniques were designed such that they take into account possible task effects so as to enhance their validity and reliability. *Oral elicitation* techniques differ from written in that the former enable the researcher (i) to elicit a more natural reflection of ordinary language use, and (ii) to observe and immediately respond to the reactions and answers of the subjects. However, there is a high risk that the subjects will accommodate, that is adjust from the dialect towards the standard-like varieties or more formal speech styles of the interviewer. A solution to this problem is to summon the assistance of other dialect speaker(s) from the same community with the same social characteristics, as in the SAND project (see Cornips and Poletto, 2005).

Two examples convincingly show how easily speakers switch between the (base) dialect and the standard variety in the oral interview in the southern part of the province of Limburg (see Cornips, 2006). One of the locations involved in the project was Nieuwenhagen (Landgraaf) a very small 'rural' village in the surroundings of Heerlen. In the local dialect of Nieuwenhagen proper names are obligatorily preceded by the definite determiner *et* or *der*, 'the', depending on whether the proper name refers to a female or male, respectively. The presence of the definite determiner preceding a proper name is fully ungrammatical in Standard Dutch. The recording of the first session between the Standard Dutch-speaking fieldworker and the local 'assistant interviewer' translating Standard Dutch into his dialect shows that the definite article in his translation is absent: that is, the proper names *Wim* and *Els* show up without it, as illustrated in (15). These sentences were elicited in order to investigate the order in the verbal cluster (right periphery):

(15) 1st session (dialect–standard)
Ø *Wim* dach dat ich Ø *Els* han geprobeerd e kado te geve
Wim thought that I Els have tried a present to give
'Wim thought I tried to give a present to Els.'

During the second session, however, in which the 'assistant interviewer' exclusively interviews the other dialect speaker in the local dialect, the latter utters the definite article both with the subject and object Determiner Phrase (DP) as 'required':

(16) 2nd session (dialect–dialect)
Der Wim menet dat ich *et Els* e boek probeerd ha kado te geve
the Wim thought that I the Els a book tried.pcpl had present to give
'Wim thought I had tried to give a book to Els.'

Problematic, however, remains the fact that the use of *written* and *oral elicitation* experiments induce numerous well-known task effects such as: (i) repetition effect, that is the subjects repeat exactly the sentence offered to them; (ii) sentences are rejected on the basis of lexical items, knowledge of the world and context of the sentence; (iii) subjects give judgements on the basis of interpretability rather than grammaticality; (iv) habituation effect: when a given sentence type is offered repeatedly, acceptability tends to increase; (v) order effect: the relative order in which test sentences are presented to the subject has an influence on the judgements; (vi) written forms are unduly influenced by prescriptive educational practices. These task effects have been taken into account, both in the design of our elicitation methods and in the resulting analysis.

The elicitation tasks in the oral and written phases included: (i) Indirect grammaticality judgement task combined with a scale; for example, the subjects have to indicate how uncommon (lowest value = 1) or how common (highest value = 5) the variant is in their local dialect; (ii) Translation task; (iii) Empty spots task; the subject has to fill in the relevant (function) word(s) from their dialect; (iv) Completion task; the subject has to finish the sentence; (v) Meaning questions; in this task the subject is asked to provide the meaning of a sentence (Cornips and Jongenburger, 2001).

2.4 Sociolinguistic perspective

From a sociolinguistic point of view, the corpus of elicitation data gives (i) enough frequency of syntactic data throughout the geographic grid, (ii) it provides insight into which variants are related to which syntactic variables, and hence it is able to overcome aspects of the open-ended nature of syntax, (iii) all social or external variables and also accommodation effects can be controlled for as far as practicably possible, (iv) style level can be controlled for, and finally, (v) we can examine reactions to sentence types that might occur only very rarely in spontaneous speech or written data.

2.5 Formal perspective

In addition, from the perspective of formal syntax, this corpus (i) provides insight into which syntactic variants are ungrammatical, (ii) it permits immediate comparison and analysis of the syntactic variants, (iii) we are able to elicit syntactic variables that do not always show up in interaction with other relevant syntactic variables in spontaneous speech, but that are predicted by theoretical concerns to do so, (iv) we are able to derive a scale of grammaticality concerning a given phenomenon, which would never arise by the observation of spontaneous speech or written corpora, and finally, (v) for certain phenomena, the corpus provides complete syntagms and paradigms.

3 Digitization

The fieldwork interviews were recorded with DAT recorders. Therefore, these tape recordings could be read into the computer directly without conversion. The recordings were read into the computer with the system Sadie DAW. The sample frequency was 44.1 kHz, 16 bits. This sampling rate was chosen to ensure a sound quality high enough to make phonetic research possible.

4 Transcription

Transcription was carried out in Praat (Figure 4.3), a free software tool developed by the phoneticians Paul Boersma and David Weenink (University of Amsterdam).[3] Although Praat is primarily intended as a tool for phonetic research, it can be conveniently used for transcription purposes. Praat enables the transcriber to line up the speech signal with the transcription directly, such that searching through the tran-

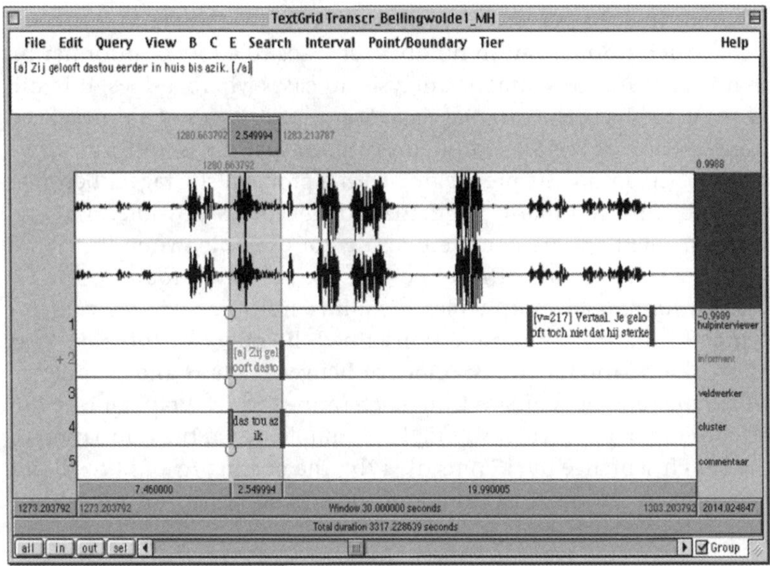

Figure 4.3 Transcription in Praat

scriptions makes it possible to find the corresponding sound fragment. Another advantage of Praat is that it allows the user to divide the transcription into different tiers, which makes it possible to separate the contributions of the speech participants.

For the SAND interviews, we used separate tiers for the speech of the first informant, the second informant and the fieldworker, the comments of the transcriber, and for clitic clusters.[4] The comment tier also contains metalinguistic information, that is, codes referring to the location of the interview, the two informants and the fieldworker. For reasons of privacy, the personal data of the informants and the fieldworker are kept in a separate database. In the future, the personal data of the informants and fieldworker will be anonymized and then added to the database such that it becomes possible to investigate sociolinguistic variables such as gender.

A detailed protocol was devised for the transcription of the spoken data (see Barbiers and Vanden Wyngaerd, 2001c). Every question (test sentence) and every answer received a special code, to make it possible to search for a particular question or answer. For reasons having to do with resource limitations, we chose to transcribe orthographically, with distinct guidelines for lexical and functional morphemes. Lexical words were transcribed according to Standard Dutch orthography and abstracting away from sound differences. For example, when the word for *know* in a dialect was *kinne* it was transcribed as Standard Dutch *kenne*. Such normalization hardly ever leads to a loss of information that is relevant for syntactic analysis. In cases where it does, it is still possible to check the original data. Some advantages of a normalized transcription of lexical morphemes are: (i) spelling is uniform across dialects, (ii) automatic pre-tagging with a probabilistic tagger becomes possible, (iii) automatic lemmatization becomes possible, and (iv) searches yield a more complete result, for example, when 'kenne' is used as a search term both 'kenne' and 'kinne' will be found.

Since functional morphemes including inflection are relevant for syntactic analysis, they were transcribed 'literally'. In this case, this means a one-to-one correspondence between sound and grapheme, where the rules of Standard Dutch determined which grapheme had to be chosen for a particular sound. For example, when the translation of the Dutch sentence in (17a) reads (17b), the missing /t/ of *wat* will not be added to the transcription, and the additional /n/ on *wie* will be transcribed as such.

(17) a. Wat denk je wie ik gezien heb? (Dutch)

b. *Wa* denk je *wien* ik gezien heb? (dialect)
what think you who I seen have
'Who do you think I saw?'

Clitic clusters got a special treatment in the transcription. The problem with clitic clusters is that their segmentation is not given a priori and can be obscured by phonological processes. To find the correct segmentation often requires a significant amount of analysis which takes into account the full system of the relevant dialect. Since such analysis would slow down the transcription process considerably, it is to be avoided. However, transcribing clitic clusters as unsegmented wholes has important disadvantages too. In particular, it will be harder to directly access the separate morphemes in a search or in an automatic tagging task. In addition, fieldworkers/transcribers working in a particular dialect area often have valuable intuitions about the proper segmentation of clitic clusters. We therefore decided that the transcriptions should contain both an unsegmented and a segmented rendering of the clitic cluster. Thus, a clitic cluster like (18a) uttered by informant 1 would be transcribed as such on the informant 1 tier, whereas on the cluster tier it would come out as in (18b).

(18) a. danzetzunder
that-they-it-they
b. dan ze 't zunder
that.PLUR they.NOM.WEAK it they.NOM.STRONG

Other cases in which the orthographic conventions of Standard Dutch had to be lifted include separable particle verbs *opeten* (literally, *up-eat*, 'eat up'), pronominal Prepositional Phrases (PPs) such as *daarmee* (literally, *there-with*, 'with that') and preposition–complementizer collocations such as *voordat* (literally, *before-that*, 'before'). In all of these cases Dutch orthography prescribes that the two morphemes be written as one word. However, we decided to split these words up since this is advantageous for automatic tagging and search, and can be easily defended on syntactic grounds.

5 Part-of-speech tagging

Part-of-speech (POS) tagging of large corpora is a tedious task that should preferably be carried out by computers. Unfortunately, automatic probabilistic taggers require a sufficiently large training set to perform well on a certain language or dialect. As we did not have enough data for each of the 267 dialects to train an automatic tagger, fully automatic tagging was not an option. However, since most of the lexical morphemes were transcribed as Standard Dutch morphemes, it proved worthwhile to use the automatic memory-based tagger developed at the University of Tilburg as a pre-tagger (see Daelemans *et al.*, 2002). The tag set we used is based on the Corpus of Spoken Dutch (so called CGN tags; see Van Eynde, 2001) which, in turn, is based on the EAGLES standard.[5] We added a number of refinements to be able to deal with dialect material (see Barbiers and Vanden Wyngaerd, 2001d, for the full tag set). In addition, we decided to build in a number of attributes that, strictly speaking, belong to the level of syntactic annotation rather than to POS tagging. These attributes mainly involve information about syntactic function, word order and hierarchy and will be useful until a full syntactic annotation has been provided. A tagging application was built that automatically translates the tags assigned by the pre-tagger (see Figure 4.4, second column: 'CGN-tags') to SAND tags. Manual tagging then consists of checking and correcting the assigned

Interval 5 uit tier 'informant' van file 1 uit Bellingwolde (C165p)

Terug naar intervallen van file Transcr_Bellingwolde1_MH.TextGr

Interval 5 uit tier 'informant' van file 1 uit Bellingwolde (C165p)

[a] Vertel maar niet wel ze roep kend ha. [/a]

	CGN-tags	SAND-woordsoort	toegekende SAND-tags
vertel	WW(pv,tgw,ev) vertellen 100.00 anders		V(inv,tt,imp,2,s,trans) [56]
maar	BW() maar 95.84 SPEC(meta) _ 0.00 N(soort,ev,basis,onz,stan) maar 0.00 N(soort,ev,basis,zijd,stan) maar 0.00 VG(neven) maar 0.00 anders	ADV	
niet	BW() niet 99.98 SPEC(meta) _ 0.00 N(soort,ev,basis,onz,stan) niet 0.00 N(soort,ev,basis,zijd,stan) niet 0.00 WW(pv,tgw,ev) nieten 0.00 anders	ADV	
wel	BW() wel 99.98 N(soort,ev,basis,onz,stan) wel 0.00 N(soort,ev,basis,zijd,stan) wel 0.00 TSW() wel 0.00 WW(pv,tgw,ev) wellen 0.00 anders	ADV	
ze	VNW(pers,pron,stan,red,3,ev,fem) ze 93.52 VNW(pers,pron,stan,red,3,mv) ze 6.12 SPEC(meta) _ 0.00 TSW(dial) ze 0.00 anders	PRON	
roep	N(soort,ev,basis,zijd,stan) roep 100.00 WW(pv,tgw,ev) roepen 0.00 anders	N	

Done

Figure 4.4 Tagging application I

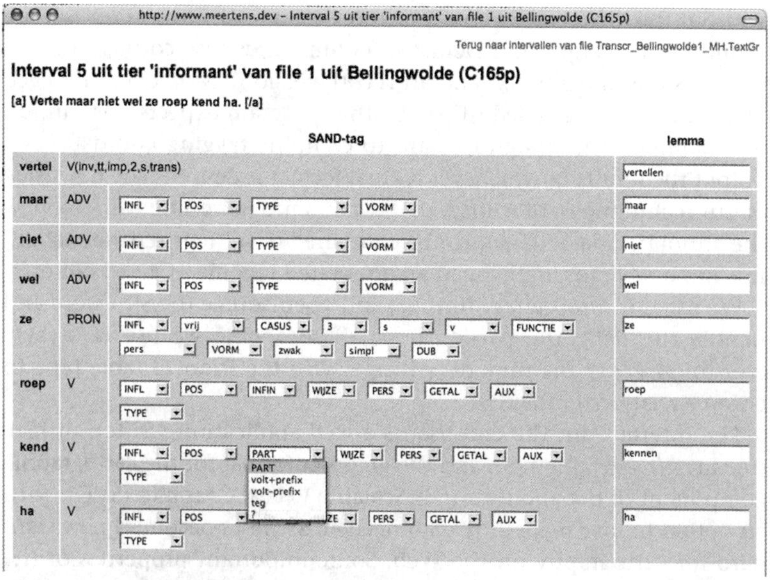

Figure 4.5 Tagging application II

tags and supplying missing attributes/values (see Figure 4.4, third column: 'SAND-woordsoort', and Figure 4.5). The tagging application also suggests tags on the basis of already assigned tags (see Figure 4.4, fourth column: 'toegekende SAND-tags'). A considerable part of the corpus (6,400 question–answer pairs) has already been provided with tags.

6 Database, search engine and cartographic tool

6.1 General principles

In contrast to most other linguistic corpora described in the present volume, the SAND corpus is a relational database at its core rather than a collection of tagged text files with a database only used for metadata (see for example Anderson *et al.*, and Tagliamonte, this volume). Our reason for using a relational database is to have more flexibility for adding annotations to linguistic data, because it is possible to keep the data and the annotations separately from each other, in different database tables, which are linked with unique keys. When the data are stored in this way, it is possible to add many different kinds of annotation to a single data set without having to use multiple copies of the linguistic data (with all the versioning problems that this entails), and without the different annotations interfering with each other (see for example van Bergen and Denison, Volume 2, whose corpus exists in two versions, a plain text and an HTML version). Moreover, if tagged text files are ever needed (if some other program expects XML input, for example) it is straightforward to combine tagging and data, and output the results in whichever textual format is desired. The downside of our technique is, of course, that it takes programming work to view the annotated data: data must be combined from their separate tables. It is impossible to simply open an annotated text file in a text editor.

We use non-proprietary formats and open-source tools to store and handle the data: the particular database engine we use is MySQL (version 4.1.9 at the time of writing), with the InnoDB table type to enforce relational integrity.

The interface for the end-user is a web application written in PHP (see http://www.php.net), and the graphics format for the cartographic component of the application is Scalable Vector Graphics (SVG), with an option to save maps as JPEG if needed. SVG has become a new standard for cartography on the Web. Some important properties of the SVG format are scalability, direct availability of the original data on which the map is based and retrievability by search engines of the objects that constitute a map.

Planned for the near future is adding the sound of the interviews to the web interface. As will be shown later in a detailed description of the table structure, the start and end times for each interval within its sound file are stored in the database. We will use QuickTime Streaming Server (see Anderson *et al.*, this volume; and Allen *et al.*, Volume 2) to host the sound files on a separate server. As we can predict start and end times, the interval links can be added to the web interface so that the particular slice of the audio file relevant to the interview can be correlated with the audio server.

The main advantages of hosting the data centrally and using a web application are: there is only one master copy of the database, so there are no problems with distributing updates to end-users if the structure of the database changes; the user needs no special software to access the data since any modern web standards-compliant browser (with SVG support for the cartographical component) will suffice.

Disadvantages are that a centrally hosted database of course also means a single point of failure (if the Meertens website is down, the SAND database is also unreachable); the user needs a net connection to access the database; we need to work within the limits of a web browser using the HTTP protocol. The trade-off for being cross-platform, and not needing anything besides a web browser and an internet connection, is of course that the amount of interactivity and 'bells and whistles' that would be possible with a dedicated desktop application is also out of reach.

The corpus is not distributed to end-users as raw data, although it would be possible to reconstruct the original form of the textual data from the database, or to output the tagged data as XML files, if that were a desired feature. It is already possible to view every interview in its entirety via the web interface. For now, the user is expected to use the web interface to search the data (see Figure 4.10). Search modes which are planned (and are already partly operational) are textual searches (with basic regular expression support), searches for part-of-speech tags, searches for lemmata, searches by the name or code of the municipality, searches by test sentence/sentence number and searches by keywords.

6.2 An artificial example

We now provide a simple 'toy' example to clarify the way our data is stored. Say our corpus consists of one five-word sentence. It would be possible to store it like this in a relational database system, in a table called 'word' (Figure 4.6).

We can uniquely address each individual word of this sentence, and it is still possible to recreate the whole sentence from its parts, with the

```
+--------+-------+-------+-----------+
| word_id | word   | offset  | sentence_id |
+--------+-------+-------+-----------+
|       1 | thanks |       1 |           1 |
|       2 | for    |       2 |           1 |
|       3 | all    |       3 |           1 |
|       4 | the    |       4 |           1 |
|       5 | fish   |       5 |           1 |
+--------+-------+-------+-----------+
```

Figure 4.6 Relational database table

hopefully self-evident SQL command (SQL = Structured Query Language, the standard way to query a relational database) shown in Figure 4.7.

```
SELECT word FROM word WHERE sentence_id=1 ORDER BY offset;

+--------+
| word   |
+--------+
| thanks |
| for    |
| all    |
| the    |
| fish   |
+--------+
```

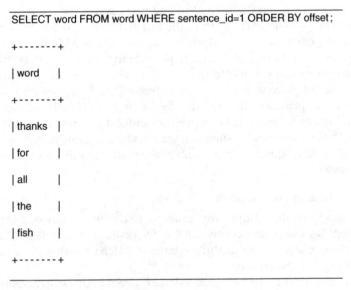

Figure 4.7 SQL query to recreate a sentence

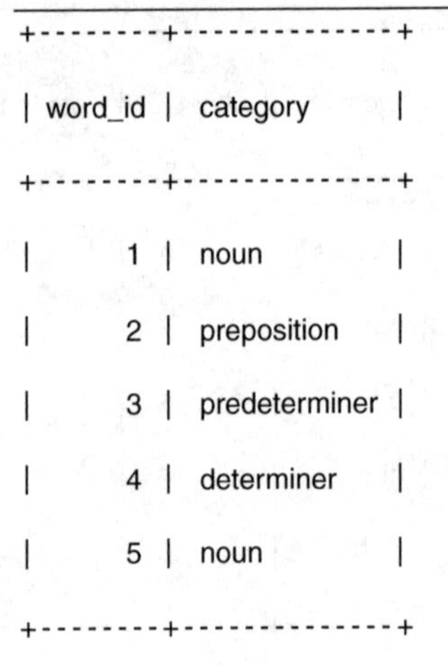

word_id	category
1	noun
2	preposition
3	predeterminer
4	determiner
5	noun

Figure 4.8 Category annotation

Suppose we want to add category annotations to these words. This is a simple matter of creating another table, called 'category', where the words are linked to categories with the word_id key (Figure 4.8).

The word_id column in the category table refers to the word_id column in the word table. Thanks to this relation, it is now possible to get all nouns from the database with the query shown in Figure 4.9.

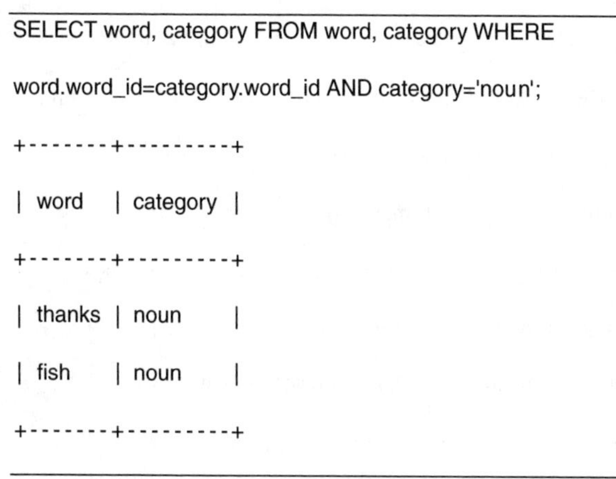

```
SELECT word, category FROM word, category WHERE
word.word_id=category.word_id AND category='noun';
+-------+---------+
| word   | category |
+-------+---------+
| thanks | noun     |
| fish   | noun     |
+-------+---------+
```

Figure 4.9 Selecting all nouns in the database

In the same vein, let us assume that we also want to add meaning annotations to the words. Because we have unique identifiers for the words (the word_id column in the word table) it is possible to do this without interfering with our category tagging. We create a table called 'meaning' where we store these annotations (where applicable) (Figure 4.10).

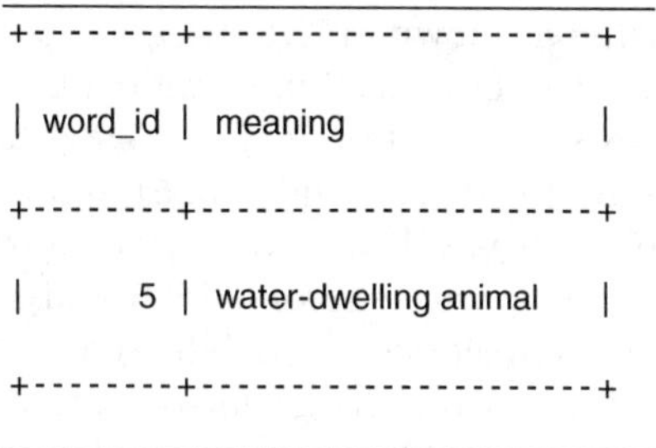

```
+--------+---------------------+
| word_id | meaning               |
+--------+---------------------+
|       5 | water-dwelling animal |
+--------+---------------------+
```

Figure 4.10 Meaning annotation

And we can now query the database for categories and meanings separately, as described above for nouns, or together if we want. The combined query is represented in Figure 4.11, for example, which gives us all nouns and, where existing, their meanings. If there is no meaning assigned we get the special value NULL which means 'no data here'.

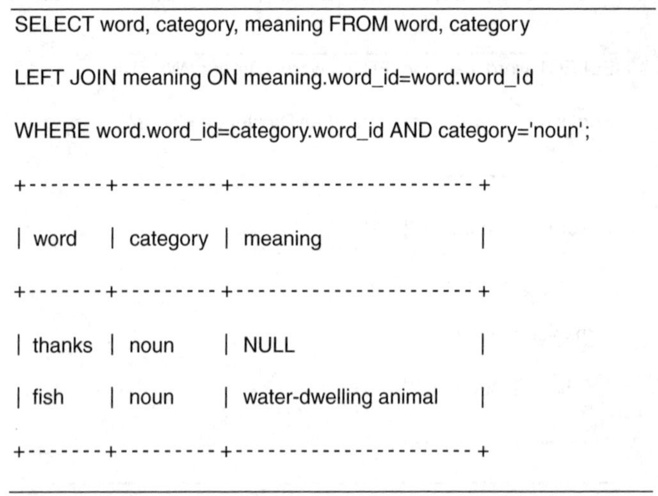

```
SELECT word, category, meaning FROM word, category

LEFT JOIN meaning ON meaning.word_id=word.word_id

WHERE word.word_id=category.word_id AND category='noun';

+-------+--------+--------------------+

| word   | category | meaning              |

+-------+--------+--------------------+

| thanks | noun     | NULL                 |

| fish   | noun     | water-dwelling animal |

+-------+--------+--------------------+
```

Figure 4.11 Combined query

6.3 A real-world example

The general principle of how the linked tables in the SAND database work is hopefully made clear by the previous 'toy' example. What follows is an example of a real tagged sentence in the database.

The raw data we had to work with are the plain text TextGrid files which the aforementioned Praat transcription program uses. An example of a snippet of such a file, from the interview of the Flemish municipality of Aalter, is shown in Figure 4.12.

This is part of the tier of the first informant (name = 'informant1') in Aalter, which consists of 438 intervals (size = 438), starts with the time counter at zero (xmin = 0) and ends 10261 seconds later (xmax = 10261.xx). The 105th interval (intervals [105]) was assigned by the transcriber to the part between second 2535 and second 2537, and consisted of the text 'k weet datij zal moete were keren' ('I know that he will have to return') which is labelled as an affirmative answer ([a=j], 'yes, this does occur') to the question which was asked by the interviewer.

```
item [1] :
class = "IntervalTier"
name = "informant1"
xmin = 0
xmax = 10261.727312500001
intervals: size = 438
intervals [1] :
xmin = 0
xmax = 333.38206557922769
text = " "
[...]
intervals [105] :
xmin = 2535.0850715889242
xmax = 2537.0411135329987
text = "[a=j] k weet datij zal moete were keren. [/a] "
[...]
```

Figure 4.12 TextGrid Praat file

We wrote PHP scripts to parse these Praat files and insert the data from the intervals into a database table called 'praat_interval' (Figure 4.13).

The [a=j] part of the transcribed text is now redundant, strictly speaking, but we did, as a matter of principle, not want to throw away any information which was entered in the transcription stage: the part between " " in the Praat file was inserted 'as is' in the database. If we did things like 'delete characters between [] in transcribed texts' this could easily lead to the deletion of real data, for example, caused by small transcription errors like [a[instead of [a].

```
+---------------
| interval_id | 3817
| tier_id     | 32
| interval_nr | 53
| xmin        | 2535.0850715889242
| xmax        | 2537.0411135329987
| tekst       | [a=j] k weet datij zal moete were keren. [/a]
| type_zin    | a
| vraag_nr    | 830
| komt_voor   | j
+------------+---
```

- interval_id: an automatically generated identifier for this particular interval;
- tier_id: the (at another point of the data inserting process) automatically generated identifier for the particular tier that the interval is a part of;
- interval_nr: ordinal number of the interval within its tier; this is different from the number in the Praat file (105) because empty intervals are an artefact of the Praat transcription and hence were not inserted in the database;
- xmin, xmax, tekst: should be self-evident;
- type_zin (sentence type) is 'a', meaning that this interval is an answer to a question by the interviewer;
- vraag_nr (question number): the answer is an answer to question number 830. This particular piece of information is not there in the interval itself and had to be derived at a later stage; this was possible because the question, which is transcribed in another tier, is labelled with its number: ' [v=830] ... [/v] '. (This would have been easier if the answer had been labelled with its question number at the transcription stage; now it took extra work to connect the answers with the question after the fact. On the other hand, the transcription would have been more work, and, by definition, more error-prone, since it is not possible to enforce constraints in Praat: transcription is free-form text entry. This is a trade-off which must be made constantly if free-form human-entered data, which always contains mistakes, is to be processed automatically at a later stage.)
- komt_voor ('does this occur') is affirmative: 'j' (for *ja*, "yes").

Figure 4.13 praat_interval table

Now we have the text of an interval as the smallest unit, but we need the individual words. The next step was splitting up the *tekst* field of the praat_interval table into its constituent words. Basically, this consisted of removing punctuation and parts between [], splitting on whitespace and converting to lower case. (Things like [a[instead of [a] caused trouble every now and then, but this could be repaired manually because we always had the original text in the *tekst* column of the praat_interval table.)

The interval under consideration has an interesting twist: one of the words is a cluster (see section 4 of this article). In the cluster tier 'datij' is interpreted as consisting of two words: *dat hij* ('that he'). See Figure 4.14 for how this looks in the Praat transcript.

For a human who is looking at the screen, it is obvious that 'dat ij' in the cluster tier belongs to 'datij' in the informant 1 tier. However, this

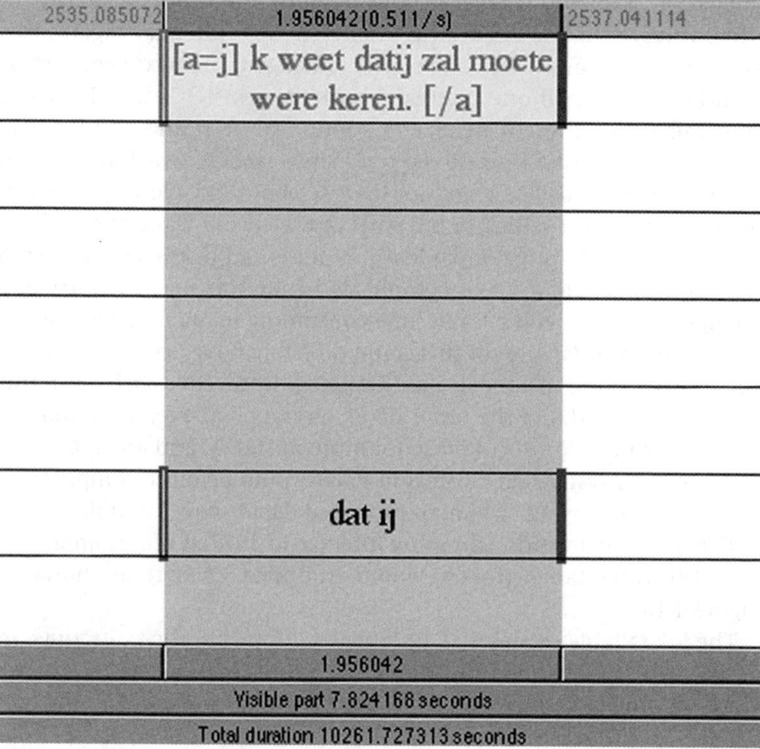

Figure 4.14 Praat transcript with cluster

is not necessarily the case for a computer program. This particular interval is a good illustration for the heuristic we used for connecting split clusters to words in the transcript, which roughly amounts to 'if you find something in the cluster tier, then find the interval in the interview which is "directly above" (that is, which has the same start and end time as the current cluster interval) and look in there for a string which is equal to the words of the cluster tier put together'. In this case, 'datij' is found without problems. But in many cases, things got rather error-prone: there could be more than one cluster in the same interval in the cluster tier, hence it was not clear (again, to a computer program) where one cluster ended and the next began; there could be more than one interval 'above' the cluster interval (that is, intervals from different tiers); sometimes, the start and end times of interview and cluster interval did not match exactly, which meant that it was difficult to decide if an interval was 'above' the cluster interval at all; and often the spelling of the parts of the cluster was different from the cluster itself, for example 'datij' represented in the cluster tier as 'dat hij'. All in all, a lot of complicated code was needed to try and recognize clusters, and a lot of time-consuming manual correcting was needed afterwards. A lot of this could probably have been prevented if the transcription protocol was designed from the start with this problem in mind. On the other hand, as argued above, more rules in the transcription protocol make for more mistakes, and an ambiguity-free notation system for clusters in Praat would be quite complicated. Automatic processing of human-produced data is never trouble-free.

The individual words, still using interval_id 3817 as our example, are stored in three tables (token, woord and praat_cluster), as shown in Figure 4.15.

The token table contains all unique word forms in the transcripts. In accordance with the relational database principle of *normalization*, we store, as much as possible, each piece of data only once, and use unique identifiers to refer to each particular piece of data in other places. Thus the form 'k' ('I', short for 'ik') is not stored directly in the woord table which contains all the individual words; instead, the form 'k' is stored only once, in the token table which contains all unique word forms, and its identifier, 278, is stored in the woord table.

Since interval_id 3817 contains a cluster, there are two possible strings of words which make up the text: one with the cluster intact, one with the cluster split up into its constituent parts. These are mutually exclusive: since a cluster and its constituent parts occupy the same place in the string, they cannot both be present at the same time. This is represented in the woord table by the combination of the cluster_id, offset and offset_no_cl ('offset without clusters') columns.

The cluster_id column only has a value if the word in the row in question is part of a cluster. The value is the word identifier of the complete cluster. In the example above, we see that word identifiers 16669 and 16670 ('dat' and 'ij', respectively) both have the value 12343 in the cluster_id column, which is the word identifier of 'datij'. This is how parts of clusters are connected to their clusters.

token_id	token
278	k
3	weet
1029	datij
206	zal
633	moete
1590	were
1591	keren
5	dat
661	ij

woord_id	interval_id	token_id	cluster_id	offset	offset_no_cl
16669	3817	5	12343	NULL	3
16670	3817	661	12343	NULL	4
12341	3817	278	NULL	1	1
12342	3817	3	NULL	2	2
12343	3817	1029	NULL	3	NULL
12344	3817	206	NULL	4	5
12345	3817	633	NULL	5	6
12346	3817	1590	NULL	6	7
12347	3817	1591	NULL	7	8

interval_id	cluster
3817	dat ij

Figure 4.15 token, woord and praat_cluster tables

Words which are not part of clusters have the special value NULL ('no data'/'not applicable') in this column.

The two columns offset and offset_no_cl contain the ordinal numbers of the word identifiers within their interval, respectively with unresolved clusters and resolved clusters. To reconstruct the text with unresolved clusters, one would select all words of this interval where offset is not NULL (or where cluster_id is NULL, which amounts to the same thing) and order by offset. To reconstruct the text with clusters resolved, select all words where offset_no_cl is not NULL and order by offset_no_cl.

The third table, praat_cluster, is redundant, strictly speaking, but it exists, like the tekst column of the praat_interval table, for performance reasons. The tekst column is used for textual searches of the data, because it would be an unacceptable performance hit to reconstruct the text from the token and woord tables every time a textual search is requested. The praat_cluster table exists so that it is possible to quickly show the resolved clusters in an interval without having to go back to the token/woord tables.

Of course, the end-user never looks directly at these tables: all queries are programmatically generated by PHP scripts via a web interface with familiar features like check boxes, drop-down menus and text input fields.

Continuing our real-world example of interval_id 3817 from Aalter, let us now consider the tagging. Word 12345 from this sentence is *moete* (Standard Dutch form is *moeten*) which means 'have to'.

A SAND tag consists of two parts: a label for the category, and a set of attributes. Written out in readable form, the tag for word 12345 is as shown in Figure 4.16.

This is stored in three database tables: sandtag_toegekend_woordsoort (SAND tag-assigned category), sandtag_toegekend_attribuut (SAND tag-assigned attribute) and sandtag_toegekend_compleet (SAND tag-assigned complete).

V(-e,eind2,inf,mod)

Main category: V = verb; with four attributes defined: *-e* (inflexion is -e); *eind2* ('end', it is the second highest verb, hierarchically, in the verb cluster); *inf* (it is a verbally used infinitive); *mod* (it is a modal auxiliary verb).

Figure 4.16 SAND tag

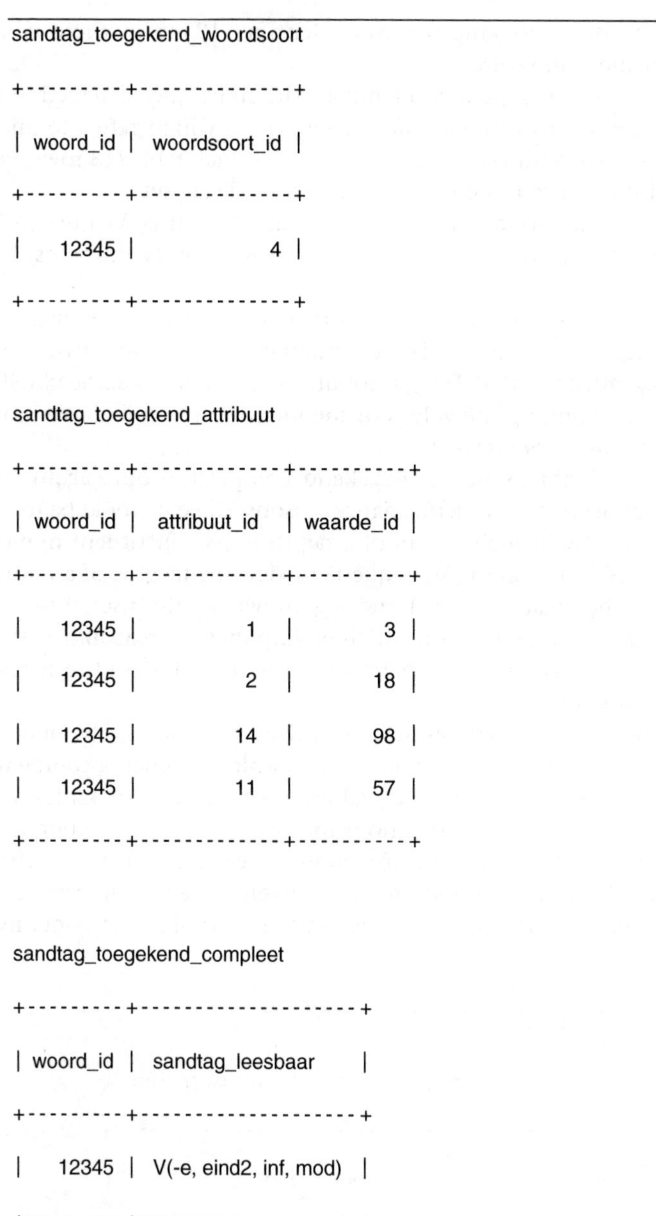

sandtag_toegekend_woordsoort

woord_id	woordsoort_id
12345	4

sandtag_toegekend_attribuut

woord_id	attribuut_id	waarde_id
12345	1	3
12345	2	18
12345	14	98
12345	11	57

sandtag_toegekend_compleet

woord_id	sandtag_leesbaar
12345	V(-e, eind2, inf, mod)

Figure 4.17 Tables for POS tagging

The result of looking up word identifier 12345 in these tables is shown above in Figure 4.17.

Category is, as should be a familiar pattern by now, assigned to word 12345 by means of a *numerical identifier* (4) which refers to another table (sand_woordsoort, SAND category): a small table (13 rows) which contains all word categories used in the SAND tag set.

Category identifier 4 is shown in Figure 4.18. It is 'V-infin' (infinitival verb), the short form of which, for readability purposes, is just 'V'.

The attributes are stored like attribute–value pairs, as usual with numerical identifiers. These numbers refer to two tables: sandtag_attribuut (SAND tag attribute) and sandtag_waarde (SAND tag value). Looking up the values of the identifiers found above in these tables results in Figure 4.19.

The third table, sandtag_toegekend_compleet, is once again redundant but necessary for performance reasons, since it would be too slow to recreate the readable form of a tag from its constituent numerical identifiers every time a user requests to view the tagging of an interval.

It will be clear now that the tag shown to the user, V(-e,eind2, inf,mod), is actually a form which is simplified for readability: the tag is stored as attribute–value pairs, but only the values of the attribute–value pairs are shown.

There are, besides sandtag_woordsoort, sandtag_attribuut and sandtag_waarde, which contain, in no particular order, a complete list of categories, attributes and values, two associative tables which contain the possible combinations thereof: sandag_x_attribuut_woordsoort contains the possible attributes for each category, whether an attribute is optional or required for a given category, and the order of the attributes; sandtag_x_waarde_attribuut_woordsoort contains the

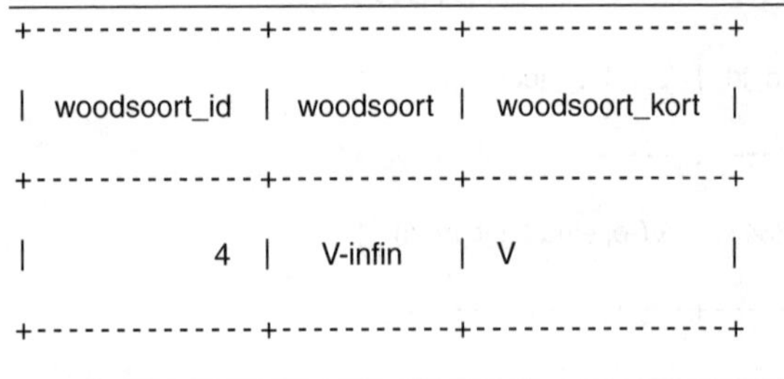

woodsoort_id	woodsoort	woodsoort_kort
4	V-infin	V

Figure 4.18 Table for word categories

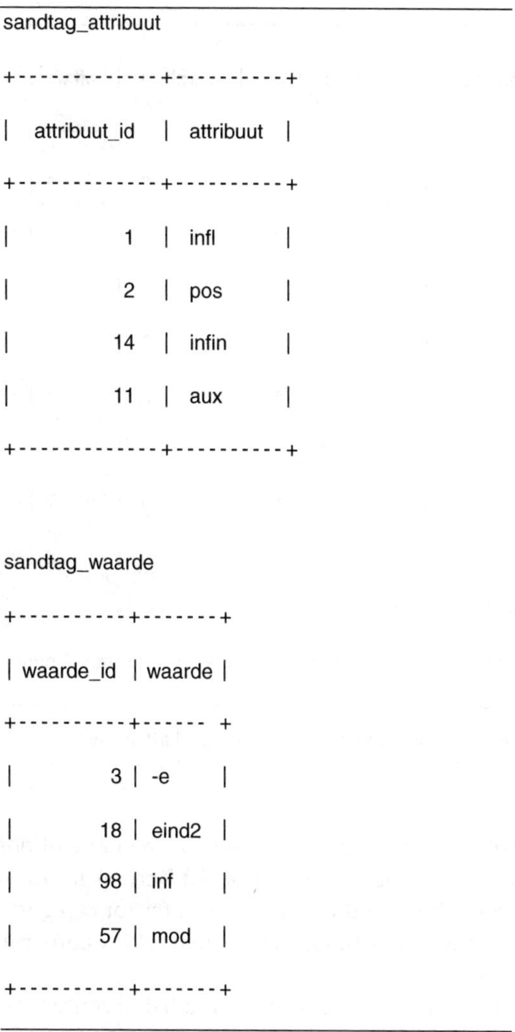

sandtag_attribuut

attribuut_id	attribuut
1	infl
2	pos
14	infin
11	aux

sandtag_waarde

waarde_id	waarde
3	-e
18	eind2
98	inf
57	mod

Figure 4.19 Tables for POS attributes

possible values for each attribute within a given category. As an example of how these tables are structured, the list of possible attributes for category 4 (V-infin) is shown in Figure 4.20.

It should not come as a surprise that the table does not contain actual attribute names, but attribute identifiers which refer to the

woordsoort_id	attribuut_id	verplicht	offset
4	1	0	1
4	2	1	2
4	14	1	3
4	10	0	4
4	4	0	5
4	5	0	6
4	11	0	7
4	12	0	8

(verplicht means 'required': an attribute with verplicht = 0 optional).

Figure 4.20 Associative table for categories and attributes

sandtag_attribuut table. The same goes for the table of possible values for each attribute, which we will not list here; it looks quite similar, just longer (54 values total in eight attributes for category 4) and with different numerical identifiers. These five tables constitute the complete SAND tag set.

The output of a search (Figure 4.21) is a list of sentences and a list of municipality codes of the places in which the searched variable occurs (Figure 4.22, first column). There is an option to show the dialogue context and a tagged version of the sentence.

The list of municipality codes resulting from a query can be used as the input for a map that shows the geographical distribution of the syntactic variable (Figure 4.23). This can be done automatically or manually. In the latter case, the user can specify many properties of the map, such as symbol colour, size and shape, areal division, legend and so on. It is also possible to combine various syntactic variables in

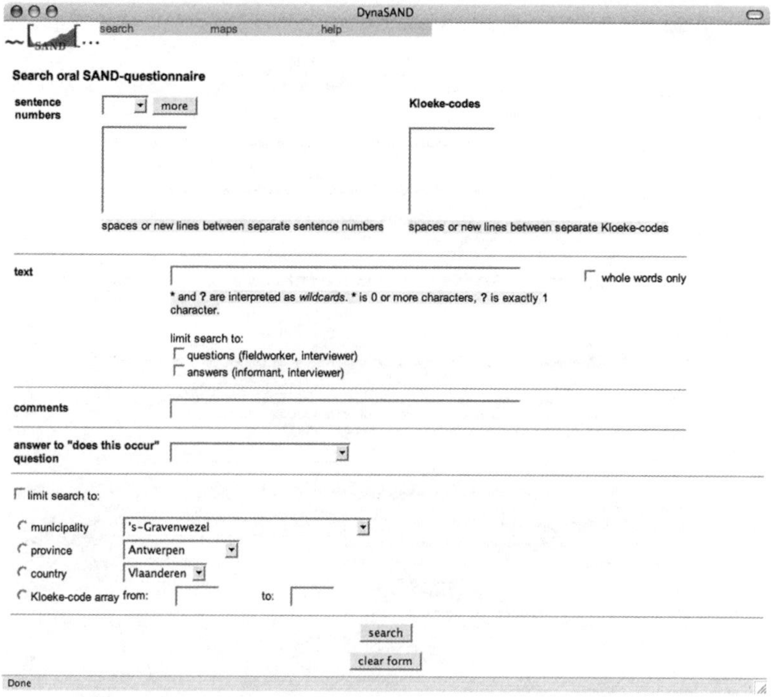

Figure 4.21 Search screen SAND database

one map to see if the geographical distribution of certain variables coincides.

As was mentioned above, the maps are dynamic which makes it possible to directly access the data behind the maps by clicking on a certain location. The search results and maps can be stored in an online archive. Researchers who want to store their search results and maps will be asked to provide a map description in a standard format, such that the archive will function as an ever-growing map collection.

7 Future prospects

The cooperation between formal linguists, sociolinguists and database/search-engine developers results in a joint approach to selecting

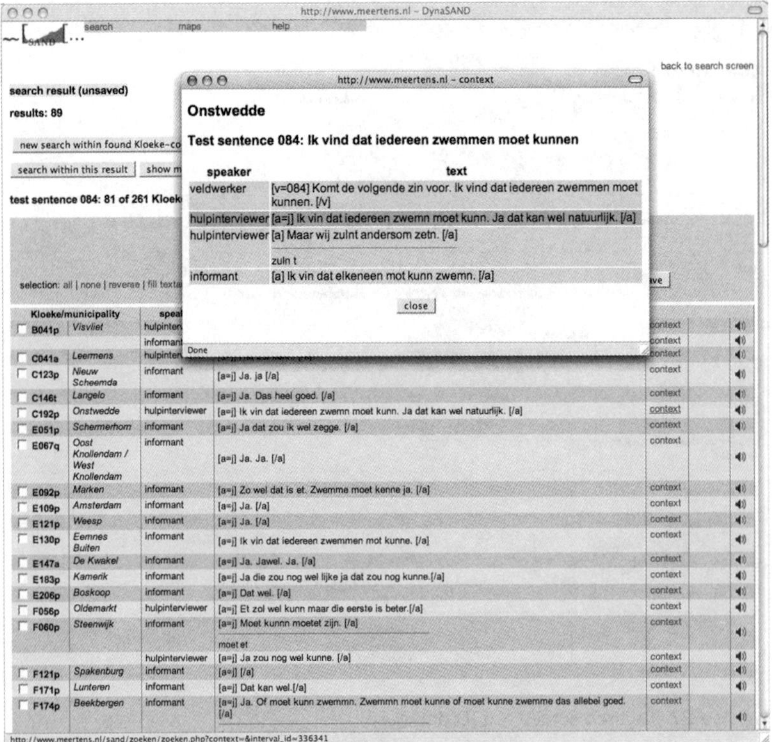

Figure 4.22 SAND database: search results

the empirical domains, collecting the data and developing technical ways to make the data accessible and searchable, as described in this chapter. We believe that this opens interesting avenues for further research. The approach that has been taken in this SAND project, incorporating as it does a range of generative, methodological and technical criteria, appears to be a fruitful method for comparing 'empirical' syntactic microvariation.

There is a second sense in which we want SAND to be dynamic. In our current European Dialect Syntax initiative (Edisyn: http://www.meertens.knaw.nl/projecten/edisyn/), we try to support the creation of projects across Europe that are methodologically and technically com-

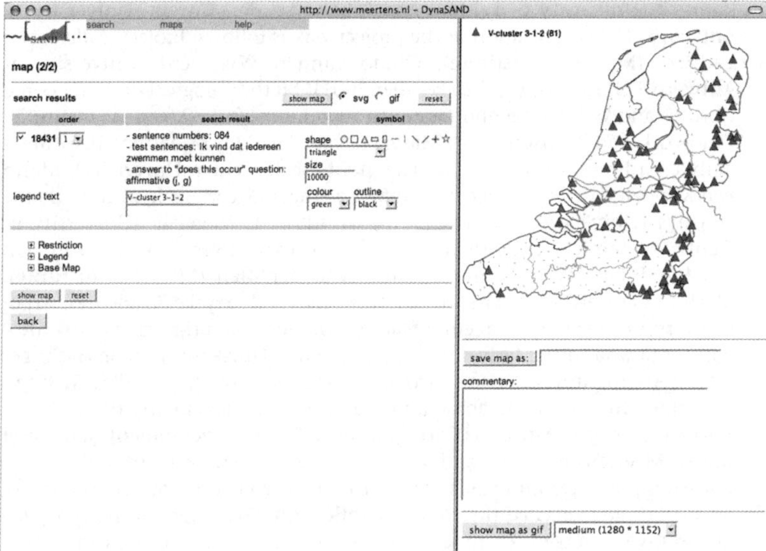

Figure 4.23 SAND database: cartographic tool

parable to SAND. The databases resulting from such projects should become part of an on-line network of databases that are searchable with a single common seach engine and analysable with identical cartographic and satistical software. This will eventually provide the linguistics community with a research tool that greatly enhances the empirical basis of dialectological typological and formal linguistic research.

Notes

1. The project was funded by the Flemish–Dutch Committee for Dutch Language and Culture (VNC) (a cooperation between the Fund for Scientific Research, Flanders (FWO) and the Netherlands Organization for Scientific Research (NWO)), the Meertens Institute, Amsterdam and the Royal Netherlands Academy of Arts and Sciences (KNAW). The project was launched and supervised by Hans Bennis (Meertens Institute), Hans den Besten (University of Amsterdam), Magda Devos (University of Gent), Johan

Rooryck (University of Leiden) and Johan van der Auwera (University of Antwerp). The organization of the project was as follows. Project leaders: Sjef Barbiers (Meertens Institute), Guido vanden Wyngaerd (University of Antwerp/KUBrussels, until December 2001). Methodological design: Leonie Cornips and Willy Jongenburger (until September 2001) (Meertens Institute). Fieldwork and Transcription: Margreet van der Ham (Meertens Institute – daily coordination), Jeroen van Craenenbroeck (Leiden University), Marjo van Koppen (Leiden University), Irene Haslinger (Meertens Institute), Hedde Zeijlstra (University of Amsterdam), Gunther De Vogelaer (University of Gent), Annemie Neuckermans (University of Antwerp), Vicky Van den Heede (University of Gent), Susanne van der Kleij (Meertens Institute), Mathilde Jansen (Meertens Institute), Henk Wolf (Fryske Akademy), Arjan Hut (Fryske Akademy). Tagging: Margreet van der Ham (Meertens Institute – daily coordination), Marjo van Koppen (Leiden University), Irene Haslinger (Meertens Institute), Vivien Waszink (Meertens Institute), Alies Maclean (Meertens Institute). Database and search engine development: Jan Pieter Kunst (Meertens Institute). Cartographic software development: Jan Pieter Kunst (Meertens Institute) and Ilse van Gemert (Meertens Institute).

2. For example, after an evaluation of the data from the oral interviews we decided that we needed the complete inflectional paradigm of the verb *gaan* 'go' in inversion contexts to test a certain generalization. Since the oral interviews did not include all the members of this paradigm we tested those in the telephone interviews.
3. See http://www.fon.hum.uva.nl/praat/
4. See below and section 6 for a discussion of clitic clusters.
5. See the EAGLES home page: http://www.ilc.cnr.it/EAGLES96/home.html

References

Allen, W. H., J. C. Beal, K. P. Corrigan, W. Maguire and H. L. Moisl, 2007. 'A linguistic 'time-capsule': The Newcastle Electronic Corpus of Tyneside English'. *Creating and Digitizing Language Corpora: Diachronic Databases (Volume 2)*, ed. by J. C. Beal, K. P. Corrigan and H. Moisl, pp. 16–48. Basingstoke: Palgrave Macmillan.

Barbiers, S. 2005. 'Word order variation in three-verb clusters and the division of labour between generative linguistics and sociolinguistics'. *Syntax and Variation: Reconciling the Biological and the Social (Current Issues in Linguistic Theory, 265)*, ed. by L. Cornips and K. P. Corrigan, pp. 233–64. Amsterdam/Philadelphia: John Benjamins.

Barbiers, S. and H. Bennis. 2003. 'Reflexives in dialects of Dutch'. *Germania et alia. A Linguistic Webschrift for Hans den Besten*, ed. by J. Koster and H. van Riemsdijk. Groningen: Electronic publication, University of Groningen. http://odur.let.rug.nl/~koster/DenBesten/contents.htm

Barbiers, S., H. Bennis, M. Devos, G. de Vogelaer and M. van der Ham: 2005. *Syntactic Atlas of the Dutch Dialects*. Volume 1. Amsterdam: Amsterdam University Press.

Barbiers, S., L. Cornips and S. van der Kleij (eds), 2002. *Syntactic Microvariation.* Electronic publication of the Meertens Instituut. http://www.meertens.knaw.nl/projecten/sand/synmic/

Barbiers, S. and G. vanden Wyngaerd. 2001a. *Schriftelijke vragenlijst* [written questionnaire]. Amsterdam: Meertens Institute.

Barbiers, S. and G. vanden Wyngaerd. 2001b. *Mondelinge vragenlijst* [oral questionnaire]. Amsterdam: Meertens Institute.

Barbiers, S. and G. vanden Wyngaerd. 2001c. *Transcriptieprotocol* [transcription protocol]. Amsterdam: Meertens Institute.

Barbiers, S. and G. vanden Wyngaerd. 2001d. *Woordsoortetikettering voor het project Een Syntactische Atlas van de Nederlandse Dialecten* [POS tagging and tag set]. Amsterdam: Meertens Institute.

Chomsky, N. 1995. *The Minimalist Program*. Cambridge, Mass.: The MIT Press.

Cornips, L. 2002. 'Variation between the infinitival complementizers *om/voor* in spontaneous speech data compared to elicitation data'. *Syntactic Microvariation*, ed. by S. Barbiers, L. Cornips and S. van der Kleij, pp. 75–96. Electronic publication of the Meertens Instituut. http://www.meertens.knaw.nl/projecten/sand/synmic/

Cornips, L. 2006. 'Intermediate syntactic variants in a dialect – standard speech repertoire and relative acceptability'. *Gradience in Grammar. Generative Perspectives*, ed. by G. Fanselow, C. Féry, M. Schlesewsky and R. Vogel, pp. 85–105. Oxford: Oxford University Press.

Cornips, L. and K. P. Corrigan. 2005. 'Convergence and divergence in grammar'. *The Convergence and Divergence of Dialects in Contemporary Societies*, ed. by P. Auer, F. Hinskens and P. Kerswill, pp. 96–134. Cambridge: Cambridge University Press.

Cornips, L. and W. Jongenburger. 2001. 'Elicitation techniques in a Dutch syntactic dialect atlas project'. *Linguistics in The Netherlands*, vol. 18, ed. by H. Broekhuis and T. van der Wouden, pp. 53–64. Amsterdam/Philadelphia: John Benjamins.

Cornips, L. and C. Poletto. 2005. 'On standardising syntactic elicitation techniques'. *Lingua* 115(7):939–57.

Daelemans, W., J. Zavrel, A. van den Bosch and K. van der Sloot. 2002. *MBT: Memory Based Tagger, version 1.0, Reference Guide*. ILK Technical Report 02/09/2002. ILK pub: ILK-0209.

de Vogelaer, G. 2005. 'Subjectmarkering in de Nederlandse en Friese dialecten' [Subject marking in the Dutch and Frisian Dialects]. PhD Dissertation, University of Ghent.

Kloeke, G. G. 1927. *De Hollandse expansie in de zestiende en zeventiende eeuw en haar weerspiegeling in de hedendaagsche Nederlandsche dialecten, proeve eener historisch-dialect-geographische synthese* [The Hollandic expansion in the 16th and 17th century and its reflection in the contemporary Dutch dialects]. Noord- en Zuid-Nederlandse dialectbibliotheek 2, Nijhoff: 's-Gravenhage.

Labov, W. 1972. *Sociolinguistic Patterns*. Philadelphia: University of Pennsylvania Press.

Labov, W. 1996. 'When intuitions fail'. *Papers from the 32nd Regional Meeting of the Chicago Linguistics Society*, 32:76–106.

Neuckermans, A. (forthcoming). Negatie in de Vlaamse dialecten. [Negation in the, Flemish dialects]. PhD Dissertation, University of Ghent.

Rickford, J. R. 1987. 'The haves and have nots: sociolinguistic surveys and the assessment of speaker competence'. *Language in Society* 16(2):149–77.
van Bergen, Linda and David Denison. 2007. 'A Corpus of Late Eighteenth-Century Prose'. *Creating and Digitizing Language Corpora: Diachronic Databases (Volume 2)*, ed. by Joan C. Beal, Karen P. Corrigan and Hermann L. Moisl, pp. 228–46. Basingstoke: Palgrave Macmillan.
van Craenenbroeck, J. 2004. 'Ellipsis in Dutch dialects'. PhD dissertation, Leiden University. LOT Dissertations 96.
van Eynde, F. 2001. *Part of speech tagging en lemmatisering*. Technical report, Centrum voor Computerlinguistiek, K.U.Leuven. http://lands.let.kun.nl/cgn/publicat.htm
van Koppen, M. 2005. 'One probe, two goals: agreement phenomena in Dutch dialects'. PhD dissertation, Leiden University.
Zeijlstra, H. 2004. 'Sentential negation and negative concord'. PhD dissertation, University of Amsterdam. LOT Dissertations 101.

Websites

DynaSAND: http://www.meertens.knaw.nl/sand/
CGN (Corpus of Spoken Dutch): http://lands.let.kun.nl/cgn/home.htm
EAGLES (Expert Advisory Group on Language Engineering Standards): http://www.ilc.cnr.it/EAGLES96/home.html
Edisyn: http://www.meertens.knaw.nl/projecten/edisyn/
Praat (P. Boersma and D. Weenink): http://www.fon.hum.uva.nl/praat/

5
Coding and Analysing Multilingual Data: The LIDES Project[1]

Penelope Gardner-Chloros, Melissa Moyer and Mark Sebba

1 Introduction

Over the last few decades, the study of bilingual and plurilingual talk has been an important focus for linguists. Data have been collected through projects, large and small, in many countries and involving many different languages and dialects. This has been in the form of monographs describing particular linguistic situations where code-switching (CS) is prevalent (Bentahila, 1983; Agnihotri, 1987; Gibbons, 1987; Heath, 1989; Nortier, 1990; Gardner-Chloros, 1991; Myers-Scotton, 1993a; Sebba, 1993; Treffers-Daller, 1994; Haust, 1995; Backus, 1996; Halmari, 1997; Zentella, 1997; McCormick, 2002; Nivens, 2002). Two books have been devoted to the grammatical aspects of CS (Myers-Scotton, 1993b; Muysken, 2000), as well as a further volume by Myers-Scotton (2002) developing her grammatical theory in the broader context of language contact. Chapters or sections have been devoted to CS in the principal volumes on bilingualism and language contact which include Romaine's *Bilingualism* (1994), Coulmas's *Handbook of Sociolinguistics* (1997), Hamers and Blanc's *Bilinguality and Bilingualism* (2000), Li Wei (2000), Thomason (2001), Clyne (2003). A number of edited collections and special issues of journals have been devoted to different aspects of CS (Heller, 1988; Eastman, 1992; Milroy and Muysken, 1995; Auer, 1998; Jacobson, 1998; and Dolitsky, 2000). CS is regularly the subject of papers in the two main journals on bilingualism, the *International Journal of Bilingualism* and *Bilingualism, Language and Cognition*.

It has become a source of frustration for many who work in this area that there is no basic standard for transcribing data of this kind, nor any central resource to enable researchers to share their data with each other. Meanwhile, as pointed out by MacWhinney (this volume), researchers in some fields have begun to take advantage of new technological developments to enable data to be shared. Researchers in language acquisition have both standard ways of transcribing and coding data, and international databases to which they can contribute and on which they can draw for comparative data.

The purpose of the LIPPS initiative, and of the people behind it, is to provide support and propose a system for transcribing and coding bilingual data that takes into account research questions specifically related to multilingual communities and individuals. Researchers in the field may benefit from the LIPPS initiative in two ways:

1. By following the step-by-step guidelines to carry out the transcription and coding which make it possible to use already existing computer-based analytical tools. For the beginner, we hope to provide answers to many of the basic questions relating to transcription of bilingual data. Where we cannot provide answers, it may at least help researchers to consider what they are doing and how their decisions affect the ways in which their data may be useful to other researchers. We hope that the LIPPS recommendations will be adopted widely as 'best practice'.
2. The existence of a set of basic standards for transcribing and coding bilingual data should encourage research on language interaction from an interdisciplinary perspective. Thus, a special effort is made to cater for the needs of researchers working in very different disciplines within the field. The proposals made here are equally intended to help those who are interested in quantitative and qualitative research. Useful guidelines are provided so that solutions may be found for problems that may arise in the processes of transcription and coding. In addition, some user-friendly computational tools are discussed which provide support in exploring and analysing language interaction data. LIPPS is an ongoing project and new recommendations are being developed to improve and refine the present proposals. In this chapter we have mentioned various initiatives that did not appear in earlier versions.

We have adopted the term 'language interaction' rather than the more commonly used terms 'code-switching' and 'language contact' in order to include all manifestations of language contact, whether or not the varieties under study are held to belong to two discrete systems.

2 The goals of LIDES

The majority of language interaction studies involve the collection of new sets of data by individual researchers; so it seems likely that the endless collection of more data for analysis will no longer constitute the most productive application of research efforts. In spite of the high level of interest, no coordinated system has yet been developed for researchers to make use of one another's data. On the contrary, the data are only available, if at all, in widely disparate forms, and coding and transcription practices vary significantly. Access to the original data (usually audio recordings) may be necessary in order to verify the significance of the written transcripts, but it is even rarer for anyone except the original researcher to gain access to this material.

The acronym LIDES stands for Language Interaction Data Exchange System and it is based on the child language data exchange system (CHILDES) enterprise established by Brian MacWhinney (see MacWhinney, this Volume). It consists of a set of standards and computational tools for analysing language acquisition data and a collection of data sets contributed by diverse researchers (MacWhinney and Snow, 1990; MacWhinney, 1995), and shows the advantages of being able to access a database in research fields where data on spoken, spontaneous language are essential. The LIDES project is conceived as a network of researchers who, in addition to carrying out their own research on language interaction data, are committed to the overall goal of producing a database and developing coding schemes and guidelines. Each researcher works independently on their own data set, but a common set of overall goals is kept in mind.

The reasons why it is desirable to achieve a coordinated approach go beyond the advantages of simple data-sharing. What researchers typically want to know about patterns of language interaction is to what extent these patterns are dictated by the particular language combination and/or the context and circumstances which are relevant in their study, and to what extent they are universal or at least common to similar language sets or similar combinations of sociolinguistic circumstances. For example, one major strand of research on code-switching focuses on grammatical constraints that stipulate where a switch can occur within the sentence. Time after time, constraints proposed on the basis of one data set (and often put forward as potentially universal) have been disproved when new data sets have emerged (for a survey, see Muysken, 2000). Furthermore it is not possible, without making comparisons of the kind we propose, to establish the relative role of linguistic features as such and sociolinguistic, psycholinguistic and/or contextual factors in the language interaction patterns that are observed. Both of these are fundamental problems with approaches based on a single data set.

In this section, we discuss the rationale for basing LIDES on the CHILDES system and the codes for the human analysis of transcripts (CHAT) coding protocol. Section 3 is devoted to the basic steps for preparing language interaction data for analysis. Special attention is dedicated to the steps involved in the preparation and organization of the data and to the minimal requirements for transcription and tagging. Section 4 runs through the essential elements of a CHAT data file. Section 5 takes the reader through the transcription process step by step. In section 6 we mention some ways of coding data for specific research interests. Section 7 describes some of the programs that automate data analysis. Finally, section 8 contains practical information about contact addresses and obtaining the LIDES programs and data sets.

2.1 Why use CHILDES?

CHILDES has been successfully used for fifteen years and is equipped with an institutional support base,[2] specific detailed guidelines for transcribing and coding data (the CHILDES coding manual) within an existing format (CHAT) and a set of software, the computerized language analysis (CLAN) programs, which researchers can use to carry out a large range of automated analyses of the data in the database. The programs for analysis of bilingual data can be obtained by contacting Brian MacWhinney. A number of people associated with the LIPPS Group had already used CHILDES for encoding their multilingual data.

There were also some arguments *against* using the existing CHILDES system for our purposes. CHILDES was not designed for adult, multilingual, speech data. It was set up to provide a database of conversations involving mainly monolingual adult–child interactions. Therefore, the CHAT format was not initially the most appropriate one for the type of data researchers in this area were collecting, and the CLAN programs were not designed to answer the type of questions that researchers working in the field of multilingualism would want to ask. However, the CHAT coding scheme and the CLAN tools in CHILDES were adopted precisely because they are open to further elaborations and additions. Existing tools can be accommodated to language interaction purposes and new coding schemes and tools can be developed. In fact, some adaptations, necessary to cope with multilingual data, can already be found in CHILDES and others have been developed by the LIPPS Group. Even greater possibilities are offered by the development of a framework based on XML for CHILDES and TalkBank (see MacWhinney, this volume). The CHILDES database contains data from many different languages, and the way transcription problems have been solved for these different languages can be of help when transcribing language interaction data.

More important in this respect are the bilingual data already available. A separate chapter of the CHILDES manual (MacWhinney, 1995) is devoted to data available on bilingual acquisition, which is becoming an important field of research. This chapter presents data sets collected by De Houwer, Deuchar, Guthrie, Hayashi, Serra, Snow and Velasco among others. In the CHILDES system different types of information are coded on a series of 'dependent tiers' linked to the 'main tier' which carries the transcription. A separate dependent tier is proposed to code information on the language of the utterance on the main tier (see below), the language of the preceding speaker and the dominant language of the speaker (see De Houwer, 1990; MacWhinney, 1995, p. 63, for a good example of this type of system). There is also a separate subsection on code-switching in the CHILDES manual (MacWhinney, 1995, subsection 9.4) in which some useful coding options are proposed.

Another point in favour of the CHILDES system is the formal way in which the system is set up. One development that was incorporated in 2003 is an interface between CHAT and XML formats. XML is a markup metalanguage of the World Wide Web with powerful tools for analysing data on the Web. It is a standard way of marking up texts (both spoken and written), which is independent of any word processor or computer system. Because XML is designed to be read by a computer rather than a human, 'readability is less of a concern than computational tractability' (Edwards, 1995, p. 21), with the result that researchers tend to interact with XML via an interface which hides the complex coding. One of the present tasks of the LIPPS Group is to offer a universal set of codes for language interaction data in XML. The new system will also offer user-friendly interfaces which will allow researchers to encode numerous different scripts and have a choice of how to present the transcribed and encoded data in print and on the computer screen. A program for converting CHAT files to XML can be downloaded from the CHILDES web page. This prospect matches the view of MacWhinney (1995, p. 437):

'As our work in database development proceeds, we want to think in terms of a more general database of all the varieties of spoken human language.'

Another recent innovation to CHILDES that has also been incorporated by LIDES is the adoption of the Unicode encoding system. CLAN programs presently recognize this new system. Unicode is important for research on multilingual data because it allows language interaction researchers to use their computer keyboard to represent a character from any language including Arabic, Chinese or the International Phonetic Alphabet (IPA) that have different script types. A further advantage to using Unicode is that it permits researchers working in the field of discourse and conversation analysis (CA) to use the CA-CLAN programs developed to analyse utterances, turns and overlaps as well as other conversation phenomena used in the transcription conventions put forth by Atkinson and Heritage (1984).

A far-reaching expansion that has also been developed in recent years is the linking of original digitized audio and digitized audio–video recordings to transcribed files. Linking can also be done at the same time as one carries out the transcription. New avenues for spoken language analysis and possibilities for checking and revising transcriptions can easily be carried out. More detailed information on linking is provided with the CHILDES programs. A computer program called Praat, with which it is possible to analyse, synthesize and manipulate speech, has been developed by Paul Boersma and David Weenik. This program is especially useful for splicing short audio files into a single large file. The CHILDES project is currently developing further CLAN support for this program.

2.2 Why use CHAT?

The existing CHAT transcribing and coding conventions are very flexible, making it possible for the researcher to reflect many kinds of phenomena that occur in natural speech data. We give some examples of existing CHAT transcription and coding options below. Furthermore, you can add any type of code you want, as long as you use it consistently and define it properly, which is what you would have to do anyway, be it in a more traditional format or the CHAT format.

You can see from examples (1) and (2) that transcribing in CHAT is not that different from the traditional way of transcribing, and that the basic transcribing and coding conventions are not that difficult:

(1) A 'traditional' transcription (Moyer, 1992)

The participants in this conversation are Yvonne and Natalie, both housewives. The languages used are Spanish and English. English is given in plain typeface, Spanish in italic typeface.

YVO: Excuse me could we have two coffees and some scones please?
NAT: Yvonne *para mí no vayas a pedir* scones *de esos*
Yvonne for me not go to ask scones of these
que ahora me estoy tratando de controlar un poquito antes de Pascua
that now me are trying to control a little-bit before of Christmas
'Yvonne, don't order these scones for me because now I am trying not to put on weight before Christmas.'
YVO: *si* Christmas *ya está* round the corner *mujer*
yes Christmas already is round the corner woman
'Mind you, Christmas is already round the corner.'

In this traditional transcription we can see:

- There is a short introduction giving details of speakers and languages used.
- Each speaker's turn is put in a separate paragraph following an indication of who is speaking.
- Normal and italic fonts are used to indicate the language of each word/phrase.
- The literal gloss for each word is placed on the line beneath.
- There is a free translation of the conversation provided.

In the following example the same data are given in CHAT format:

(2) A CHAT transcription (Moyer, 1992)

@Begin
@Participants: YVO housewife1, NAT housewife2
@Languages: English (1), Spanish (2)
*YVO: excuse@1 me@1 could@1 we@1 have@1 two@1 coffees@1 and@1 some@1 scones@1 please@1?
*NAT: Yvonne@1 para@2 mí@2 no@ vayas@2 a@2 pedir@2 scones@1

	de@2 esos@2 que@2 ahora@2 me@2 estoy@2 tratando@2 de@2 controlar@2 un@2 poquito@2 antes@2 de@2 Pascua@2.
%glo:	Yvonne for me not go to ask scones of these that now me are trying of control a little-bit before of Christmas.
%tra:	Yvonne, don't order these scones for me because now I am trying not to put on weight before Christmas.
*YVO:	si@2 Christmas@1 ya@2 está@2 round@1 the@1 corner@1mujer@2.
%glo:	if Christmas already is round the corner woman
%tra:	mind you, Christmas is already round the corner
@End	

Transcription (2) uses the coding system recommended by LIDES and, as you can see, the data look somewhat different. However, the same information is present:

- There is a set of 'headers' giving details of speakers and languages used (@Participants, @Languages).
- Each utterance is put on a separate line (the 'main tier') following an indication of who is speaking.
- Language tags (@1 and @2) are used to indicate the language of each word/phrase.
- There is a separate line or 'dependent tier' following the main tier for the literal gloss, the %glo tier.
- There is a dependent tier for a free translation of each utterance, the %tra tier.

From the above examples, it is clear that the CHAT transcription is actually very similar to the traditional one. Some extra work is inevitable, for example, tagging each word with a language code, though word processors or 'editors' are currently being developed to help do this task automatically.[3] However, once you have done this work, the benefits are substantial. To name a few, you can add as many dependent tiers as you need. You can create additional headers which provide information such as the socio-economic status or age of the participants, the name of the transcriber and the date of the recording. You can create additional dependent tiers on which you can provide a gloss (%glo), a translation (%tra), or code grammatical, pragmatic or other information. You can devise codes to label problematic words which do not clearly belong to one language or another, such as <in> when dealing with English, Dutch and a range of Germanic languages. Once your transcription is complete, you can print it, selecting just those tiers you want to appear on the page, from among all those you have included in your transcription.

An enormous benefit, obvious to every researcher who has done frequency counts using pen and paper on a relatively large set of data, is the fact that you can use the CLAN programs to search your data for patterns or provide certain statistics. This is because all LIDES transcriptions can use Unicode characters and a common set of transcription and coding guidelines. The latter also makes it easier to exchange and compare data with other researchers, inside or outside the LIDES database.

Finally, although the LIDES system recommends the use of a transcription system based on CHAT to transcribe data, existing data in different formats will not be excluded from LIDES. Such data can still be used productively by other language interaction researchers if included in the database. One of our aims is to develop adequate tools to convert these data sets into the transcription format utilized by the CLAN automatic analysis programs.

3 The basics of transcription

Transcription is not pre-theoretical, but is a form of interpretation of the data, as discussed by Ochs (1979). For any set of spoken data, there is no single 'correct' method of transcription, but a variety of theory-dependent options. The problems, both theoretical and practical, which are inherent in the transcription of monolingual discourse, are multiplied when two or more language varieties are present. Where plurilingual data are involved, most researchers want a transcription system which provides a way of differentiating between the languages (or language varieties) found in the data. One solution may be to use the conventional writing system of the languages concerned, if there is one. If the researcher chooses a 'language-neutral' alphabet such as IPA, they will need some method of indicating which stretches of transcription are in which language. There will still be problems. For some utterances it will not be easy to assign them to either language: for example, fillers like *<er>* and *<um>* and word fragments of various sorts which are not necessarily language-specific. What to do in these cases involves theoretical decisions being made by the individual researcher. It is not simply a matter of choosing a method. Assigning a word, by means of some transcription convention, to either L1 or L2, may have consequences later for the outcome of the investigation. The researcher must have a principled basis on which to make these decisions, and may have to take into account aspects of syntax, phonology and pragmatics. Where more than two languages or related varieties are involved, things are even more complicated.

If researchers are to be able to establish large usable machine-readable corpora of code language interaction data, then a *standard format* is needed for transcribing and coding the data that fulfils at least the following requirements:

- It should allow information contained in transcriptions (for example, language labels) to be stored in a format which is not word processor-dependent. This involves using a system-independent format such as Unicode along with a standard markup language such as XML. This enables data transcribed by one researcher to be compared easily with data from another, as well as promoting a more universal software to carry out rapid searches and analyses of data.
- It should encourage researchers to include in their transcriptions, for their own benefit as well as for that of other researchers, information which is relevant to the analysis of language interaction data. This is desirable as a way of helping researchers new to the transcription of language interaction data to include features which will be useful for their own analysis at the time, and to others who may want to use their data later for another purpose.
- It should be flexible enough to accommodate the present and (as far as is predictable) future needs of researchers in terms of what requires to be represented in a transcription. Researchers should feel in control of the transcription process rather than being forced into a straitjacket. These guidelines have no value if researchers do not find them suitable for their own needs.

CHAT allows researchers to include all the information needed for the analysis of their data. Since language interaction data differ according to the language pairs involved, researchers also may ask very different questions regarding their data and thus will want to codify different types of information in order to carry out an analysis. CHAT has the advantage of being adaptable to individual research needs. We give some examples below of language interaction data transcribed and coded in CHAT, including some of the proposed LIDES adaptations.

In the following example a tier (%add) has been inserted to indicate the addressee. From this it is possible to see that the speaker changes the language according to the person they speak to:[4]

(3) Catalan/Castilian (Torras, 1998)

@Begin	
@Participants:	OWN owner stall_owner, CU1 customer_one customer, CU2 customer_two customer
@Languages:	Catalan (1), Castilian (2), unintelligible (0)
*OWN:	digui'm@1.
%tra:	can I help?
*CU2:	esa@2 xxx@0 de@2 la@2 paletilla@2 de@2 aquella@2 la@2 màs@2 chiquita@2 que@2 tengas@2.
%tra:	that xxx of the shoulder over there the smallest you have.
*OWN:	ahora@2 mismo@2 te@2 lo@2 miro@2.
%tra:	I'll have a look for you right now.
%add:	CU2
*OWN:	qué@2 me@2 da@2 señora@2?
%tra:	what are you giving me madam?
%add:	CU1
*OWN:	dos@1 centes@1 setanta@1 dos@1.
%tra:	two hundred and seventy two.
%add:	CU1
*OWN:	molt@1 bé@1 gràcies@1 xxx@0 reina@1.
%tra:	very good thanks xxx love.
%add:	CU1
@End	

Key to symbols

xxx	unintelligible speech

A more complicated example is the following. In this example, codes for *speech acts* are added on the speech act coding line (%spa:) to show how a positive answer was given in the same language as the question was (B answers her mother's question twice, first in English, second in Cantonese, both times using the same language as her mother used), whereas a negative answer is given in another language than that in which the question was put (when A asks C in English whether he wants some spring rolls, the answer is 'I don't want' in Cantonese):

(4) Cantonese/English (Milroy and Li Wei, 1995, p. 149), adapted to CHAT conventions.

@Begin
@Participants: MOT mother, DAU daughter, SON son
@Languages: Cantonese (1), English (2), undetermined (0)
@Age of B: 9
@Age of C: 11

*MOT: who@2 want@2 some@2?
%add: DAU, SON
*MOT: <crispy@2 a@1> [>].
%spa: $i:yq
*DAU: <yes@2> [<].
%spa: $i:aa
*MOT: yiu@1 me@1?
%spa: $i:yq
%glo: want some?
*DAU: hai@1 a@1.
%spa: $i:aa
%glo: yes.
% %add: SON
%spa: $i:yq $i:cl
*SON: ngaw@1 m@1 yiu@1.
%spa: $i:an
%glo: I don't want.
*MOT: m@1 yiu@1 a@1?
%spa: $i:yq
%glo: Don't want?
*MOT: crispy@2 la@1
*SON: mm@0
%gpx: shaking head
%spa: $i:an
@End

Key to symbols

<...> scope of phenomenon

[>]	overlap follows
[<]	overlap precedes
%glo:	gloss; LIDES recommendation
%spa:	speech act coding tier
%act:	activity
%gpx:	gestural and proxemic activity coding tier

Speech act codes (MacWhinney, 1995, pp. 101–3)

$i:	illocutionary force code follows
yq	yes/no question
aa	answer in the affirmative to yes/no question
an	answer in the negative to yes/no question
cl	call attention to hearer by name or by substitute exclamations.

Other interesting features in this example are the way overlaps are transcribed (using <>, [<], [>]), and how various non-linguistic activities are rendered in CHAT (%act:, %gpx:).

4 The essentials of a CHAT data file

Once the researcher has completed transcribing and encoding the data, their data set will contain three or four files: the CHAT *data file*, a *readme* file, the *depfile* and possibly a *depadd file*.

4.1 The CHAT data file

A CHAT data file typically consists of three components: *file headers*, *main tiers* and *dependent tiers*. For all of these components the following general requirements obtain (MacWhinney, 1995, p. 8):

a. Every character in the file must be in the basic Unicode character set.
b. Every line must end with a carriage return (= enter).

Other requirements obtain only for a specific component, and will be given where the component in question is discussed.

4.1.1 File headers

File headers are lines of text which provide information about the file and they appear at the beginning of any transcript. They all begin with the sign @ followed by the name of the header. Some headers require nothing more; these are the 'bare' headers (for example, @Begin). Other headers must be followed by information regarding the participants, the situation and so on. This information is called the entry. Headers that require an entry are followed by a colon and a tab after which the entry is given. For example:

(5) @Participants: SHO shopkeeper, RES researcher, SEA seamstress

Besides the distinction between bare headers and headers requiring an entry, CHAT makes a distinction between *obligatory* and *optional* file headers. Obligatory file headers (MacWhinney, 1995, pp. 13–14) are required for the CLAN automatic analysis programs to work. These are the following:

@Begin	The first line of any transcription file. This is a bare header.
@Participants:	This header states who the participants of the conversation are. It requires an entry which may consist of two or three parts: a speaker ID (obligatory) which is composed of one up to three characters (letters in capitals and/or numbers), for example MAR or S09; the speakers' names (optional); and the speakers' role (obligatory), for example Interviewer. A role which is not included in the depfile must be added in the depadd file (see glossary and section 4.3). The latter two parts may consist of multiple elements, but they must be connected with an underscore, for example, Penelope_Gardner_Chloros or sister_in_law
@End	The last line of any transcription file. @End is a bare header.

There are two types of optional headers: *constant* and *changeable*. Constant headers contain useful information that does not change throughout the file.[5] They must be placed at the beginning of the file before any of the actual spoken utterances. Because of the interaction of different languages in LIDES files, the following two file headers are recommended to be used consistently:

@Languages:	This header indicates what the main language or languages of the transcription files are.

@Language of XXX: This header can be used to indicate the primary language(s) of a given participant, if there is any.[6]

Changeable headers contain information that can change within the file, for example, showing how the conversation can be divided into several stages each associated with a different activity. These headers appear, then, at the point within the file where the information changes. Besides these headers, new headers may be created to fulfil specific needs as long as they are added to the depadd file located in the same directory as your data files.

4.1.2 The main tier

The actual utterances are transcribed on what is known as the *main* (speaker) *tier*. This is the line that reproduces in written form what each one of the participants says. Requirements for the main speaker tiers are as follows (MacWhinney, 1995, pp. 8–9):

- Main lines indicate what was actually said and they begin with an asterisk (*). Each main line should contain one and only one utterance[7] (but can extend over several computer lines).
- After the asterisk * on the main line comes a code (the speaker ID: see the Participant header) for the participant who was the speaker of the utterance being coded. After the speaker ID comes a colon and then a tab, for example, *MAR:	I'm tired.
- Continuations of main tiers over several computer lines begin with a tab.
- Utterances must end with an utterance terminator, that is full stop (.), exclamation mark (!), or question mark (?).

4.1.3 Dependent tiers

Dependent tiers are lines typed below the main tier containing codes, comments and descriptions of interest to the researcher. It is important to have all this information on separate lines because the use of complex codes on the main tier would make it unreadable. Though all dependent tiers are optional, we recommend having at least a *gloss* tier (%glo) and a tier in which a *free translation* of the utterance is given (%tra). Requirements for dependent tiers are the following (MacWhinney, 1995, pp. 8–9):

- Dependent tiers typically include codes and/or commentary on what is said and begin with the symbol %.

- After the % symbol comes a three-letter code in lower-case letters for the type of dependent tier, a colon, and then a tab; for example, %glo: I am tired.
- Continuations of dependent tiers over several computer lines begin with a tab.

Dependent tiers do not require ending punctuation. The researcher's interests determine the number and nature of dependent tiers in a transcript. In the examples above, we saw the following dependent tiers:

%add: specifies the addressee(s) of the utterance.
%glo: gives a word-by-word or even morpheme-by-morpheme gloss of the utterance.
%spa: this tier is for coding speech acts. Any sort of speech act can be used to describe the utterance on the main tier. A proposal for codes to be used on this line can be found in MacWhinney (1995, ch. 13).
%tra: tier where a free translation (in English or some other widely known language) of the utterance is given. We propose to use %tra instead of the %eng tier in the CHILDES manual, %tra being more language neutral.

Other useful tiers include:

%gpx: gestural and proxemic activity coding line, for example %gpx: shaking head
%mor: coding of morphological information for the words on the main tier. Codes used on the %mor tier can be found in MacWhinney (1995, ch. 14).

In order to make it possible to exchange all the data coming from different researchers using different computer systems (Macintosh, PC, UNIX and so on) and printers, we strongly recommend that data be transcribed in Unicode format, by using a true Unicode editor. In the CHILDES manual (1995), you can find the description of a Unicode editor specially created for the transcription (and coding) of CHAT files: the so-called CED editor. This allows the user to link a full digitized audio recording of the interaction directly to the script. Furthermore, the CED editor supports the display of non-ASCII roman-based characters such as á, ñ or ç, as well as non-Roman characters from Cyrillic, Japanese, Chinese and other languages. In all cases, CED displays these fonts correctly, but the underlying file is saved in Unicode characters. The CED editor is included in the CLAN package, which can be downloaded from the internet site (see web address in the final section).

4.2 The readme file

All data sets should be accompanied by a readme document (00readme.doc), which is aimed at providing general information about them. Information which is specific about a particular file in this set should not be included here but in the header of the specific file. Below is a checklist of information that the readme file should specify:

- Acknowledgements
- Researcher (name, institution, history of the project and so on)
- Characteristics of the community to which informants belong
- Informants (age, sex, class)
- Sampling techniques
- Number of hours recorded
- Number of hours transcribed
- Special transcription and coding practices
- Interaction type
- Working definitions used to identify given language interaction phenomena
- Warnings about limitations on the use of the data (that is, what has been transcribed and coded and what has not)
- List of files
- Instruments used for data collection
- Changes made in the 00depadd file

This list is not meant to be exhaustive. Contributors may add whatever they consider useful for future users. It may be helpful to comment on a particular aspect of a language or variety so that readers unfamiliar with it have a better understanding of the data. For example, a researcher dealing with Swahili data may want to provide an outline of the null prefix system of this language because they think this is relevant to the study of their corpus.

4.3 Depfile and depadd files

These are files which list the codes used in the data file and are needed by the CLAN programs for them to be able to check your transcription and carry out analyses. Depfile.cut is a standard file that is delivered with the CLAN programs. The 00depadd file is a file you make yourself. For more information on the contents of the CHILDES depfile, and their meaning, see MacWhinney (1995, pp. 162–4).

For analysing language interaction data, it is possible to extend the CHAT depfile by creating an additional file, a depadd file called '00depadd.cut', which you should place into the same directory as the files being checked. All new codes must be included in this corpus-specific LIDES depadd file: new header codes, new dependent tiers and the possible strings that may occur on those tiers. The LIDES depadd file (changed only if necessary) should also remain with the data files as a form of documentation of the particular divergence from the standard CHAT depfile and the standard LIDES depadd file. In the readme file, you should describe any changes you made in the standard LIDES depadd file.

5 A step-by-step outline of the minimal transcription process

This section gives a step-by-step outline of the basic information a data file should contain in order to enable researchers to carry out the analysis of switches between languages. You can find the details of various steps in the sections referred to at these steps. There are eight steps (data from Moyer, 1992):

- Step 1. Do a written transcription.

Y: Excuse me, could we have two coffees and some scones, please?
N: Yvonne, Para mí no vayas a pedir scones de esos que ahora me estoy tratando de controlar un poquito antes de Pascua.
Y: Si Christmas ya está round the corner, mujer. Yo ya no hago dieta hasta por lo menos enero, febrero y eso con suerte.

- Step 2. Use Obligatory File Format.

@Begin
@Participants: YVO housewife1, NAT housewife2

*YVO: Excuse me, could we have two coffees and some scones, please?
*NAT: Yvonne, para mí no vayas a pedir scones de esos que ahora me estoy tratando de controlar un poquito antes de Pascua.

*YVO: Si Christmas ya está round the corner, mujer.
*YVO: Yo ya no hago dieta hasta por lo menos enero, febrero y eso con suerte
@End

- Step 3. Run the CHECK programs.
In order to check the overall structure, the CHILDES system provides special CHECK programs which run twice over the files. In the first pass, CHECK searches for errors by comparing the files to the prescribed format. If errors are found (for example, no @Begin and @End markers at the beginning and end of files) the offending line is printed, followed by a description of the problem. On the second pass it checks if the used symbols and codes are declared in either 'depfile.cut', or in '00depadd.cut'.
Run the CHECK programs now to check if the basic format is correct.

- Step 4. Add the language tags.

@Begin
@Participants: YVO housewife1, NAT housewife2
@Languages: English (1), Spanish (2)

*YVO: Excuse@1 me@1 could@1 we@1 have@1 two@1 coffees@1 and @1 some@1 scones@1 please@1?
*NAT: Yvonne@1 para@2 mí@2 no@2 vayas@2 a@2 pedir@2 scones@1 de@2 esos@2 que@2 ahora@2 me@2 estoy@2 tratando@2 de@2 controlar@2 un@2 poquito@2 antes@2 de@2 Pascua@2.
*YVO: Si@2 Christmas@1 y@2 está@2 round@1 the@1 corner@1 mujer@2.
*YVO: Yo@2 ya@2 no@2 hago@2 dieta@2 hasta@2 por@2 lo@2 menos@2 enero@2 febrero@2 y@2 eso@2 con@2 suerte@2.
@End

- Step 5. Insert the %glo and the %tra dependent tiers.

@Begin
@Participants: YVO housewife1, NAT housewife2
@Languages: English (1), Spanish (2)

*YVO: excuse@1 me@1 could@1 we@1 have@1 two@1 coffees@1 and@1 some@1 scones@1 please@1?
*NAT: Yvonne@1 para@2 mí@2 no@2 vayas@2 a@2 pedir@2 scones@1 de@2 esos@2 que@2 ahora@2 me@2 estoy@2 tratando@2 de@2 controlar@2 un@2 poquito@2 antes@2 de@2 Pascua@2.
%glo: Yvonne for me not go to ask scones of these that now me are trying of control a little-bit before of Christmas
%tra: Yvonne, don't order these scones for me because now I am trying not to put on weight before Christmas
*YVO: si@2 Christmas@1 ya@2 está@2 round@1 the@1 corner@1 mujer@2.
%glo: if Christmas already is round the corner woman
%tra: mind you, Christmas is already round the corner
*YVO: yo@2 ya@2 no@2 hago@2 dieta@2 hasta@2 por@2 lo@2 menos@2 enero@2 o@2 febrero@2 y@2 eso@2 con@2 suerte@2.
%glo: I already not make diet until for the less January or February and that with luck
%tra: I am not going on a diet until at least January or February and even then with a bit of luck
@End

- Step 6. Run the CHECK programs again.
  Once the transcription and tagging are completed, the next stage is to check again the overall structure of the files, and the symbols and codes used in the main and dependent tiers as declared in the CHILDES depfile and the LIDES depadd file.

- Step 7. Make changes in the depadd file.
  Eventually, it may be necessary to add symbols to the LIDES depadd file for your own special data set of files. In this case the depadd file must be changed using an ASCII editor and then you can run the CHECK programs once again.

- Step 8. Create a readme document to accompany the transcription file.

6 Using CHAT for language interaction data

The transcription and coding requirements of language interaction data differ according to whether the language pairs under study are genetically related, typologically similar, or whether the mixed pairs are isolating, agglutinative, inflective or incorporative languages. This section presents some suggestions as to how to deal with specific transcription issues faced by researchers studying language interaction.

6.1 Expanding the language tags

The language tag can be expanded by using more numbers. One could, for example, use the language tag not only to signal the languages used, but also to assign a tag to mixed words. One could also use the language tag to code single word calques, borrowings and so on. Aside from expanding the language tag for language interaction types and/or mixed words, one can also expand the language tag to a two- (or more) digit system, where, for example, the first digit denotes the language of the word and the second digit word class, or vice versa.

6.2 Coding at morpheme level

For some research in language interaction data it is necessary to look not only at words, but also at smaller morpheme units. There are two ways in CHAT to dissect words into morphemes. The first is to code morphemes on the main tier. Alternatively, one can use the %mor tier for more extensive morphological coding. For more information on coding on the %mor tier we refer the reader to MacWhinney (1995).

6.3 Coding turns

Turns are not basic units in CHAT, and without adaptations (like separately coding for turns) the CLAN programs cannot make analyses pertaining to turns. There are, however, various options for representing turns in a transcription file, for example by representing turns as a main tier.

7 Automated data analysis

The CLAN tools provide many possibilities for automatic analysis, although they are not a substitute for the researcher's efforts in analysing and interpreting the data. They are especially helpful when large amounts of language data have to be processed. In the following sections we present a few of the most obvious applications of the CLAN tools to multilingual data. There is extensive information on this in the CHILDES manual. Three of the most useful analytical tools are FREQ, COMBO and FLO.

7.1 FREQ: frequency counts

The FREQ program makes frequency counts, which are useful for many different purposes. FREQ has properties which make this tool effective in handling multilingual files for other types of counts as well, but we will start with straightforward word counts.

7.2 COMBO: pattern matching

COMBO is a CLAN tool which provides the user with ways of composing complex search strings. The strings or patterns defined are used to find matches of letters, words or groups of words in the data files specified. With the COMBO tool the language tags on the main tier can be used, for example, for capturing switches within utterances.

7.3 FLO: output for other programs

There are sometimes advantages in looking at the data in their 'pure' form, particularly when a large amount of information and coding is added through the dependent tiers. By applying the FLO tool all coding and other information on the dependent tiers is left out. This output file can be made the input file for the statistical package SPSS.

A comparison of the Gibraltar oral corpus with the Gibraltar written corpus (Moyer, 2000) illustrates how FREQ and COMBO, two of the most useful CLAN programs, yield quantified information of the major differences between oral and written code-switching styles.[8] Prior classification and codification of the data following the LIDES recommendations according to major structural and conversational units (that is, word, phrasal constituents, utterances and turns) by language are needed for running the CLAN programs.

The FREQ program can tell us about: (a) the language that dominates in each corpus, (b) the number and type of syntactic constituent in each language, (c) the number of utterances by speaker (and language), (d) the number of turns by speaker (and language). Table 5.1 (on page 113) shows the output of a FREQ program showing in percentages the language of switched phrases in the oral and the written corpora.

The COMBO program allows for more complex searches such as the combination of language switches within an utterance or turn of a given speaker. Table 5.2 on page 113 illustrates the results in percentages for the combination of language and turn in oral and written code-switching styles.

Corpus-based studies and quantitative information about code-switching patterns provide important empirical support for formal and interpretative claims. Furthermore, the LIDES project offers data sets from a variety of language pairs as well as the necessary tools for carrying out the analysis.

Table 5.1 Switched phrasal categories by language in oral and written texts (in percentages)

Switched phrasal categories	Texts		Percentage of total
	Oral texts	Written texts	
Sentence			36.0
English	32.0	8.7	16.0
Spanish	21.0	19.0	20.0
Noun phrase			35.0
English	18.0	11.0	13.0
Spanish	9.9	27.0	22.0
Verb phrase			4.0
English	–	2.4	1.7
Spanish	–	3.4	2.4
Adjective phrase			6.1
English	7.7	0.5	2.7
Spanish	–	4.8	3.4
Prepositional phrase			16.0
English	10.0	6.8	7.7
Spanish	2.2	11.0	8.4
Adverbial phrase			3.0
English	–	1.0	0.7
Spanish	–	3.4	2.4
Total	100%	100%	100%
(Absolute number)	(91)	(206)	(297)

Source: Moyer (2000).

Table 5.2 Turns by language in oral and written texts (in percentages of turns)

Language of turns	Oral texts	Written texts	Percentage of total
English	21.0	13.0	18.0
English–Spanish	8.3	56.0	23.0
Spanish	40.0	4.8	29.0
Spanish–English	15.0	22.0	17.0
Equal number*	0.5	3.6	1.5
Unknown	15.0	0.4	10.0
Total	100%	100%	100%
(Absolute number)	(531)	(250)	(781)

* 'Equal number' refers to turns that have the same number of words in both English and Spanish.

Source: Moyer (2000).

8 Practical information

8.1 Data sets currently available in the LIDES database

At the moment, the LIDES database contains sample corpora with the following language combinations: Dutch/Turkish, Dutch/French, Alsatian German/French, Catalan/Spanish, Catalan/Spanish/English, English/Spanish, English/German, English/Punjabi, English/Greek Cypriot Dialect, English/Jamaican Creole.

These corpora vary widely in their size and their degree of development. For more up-to-date and detailed information, please consult the LIPPS website indicated below.

8.2 Research contacts

Researchers interested in participating in the LIPPS Group and the LIDES database are advised to contact the Steering Committee. A list of email addresses is provided below:

Penelope Gardner-Chloros: p.gardner-chloros@bbk.ac.uk
Roeland van Hout: roeland.vanhout@kub.nl
Melissa G. Moyer: melissa.moyer@uab.es
Mark Sebba: m.sebba@lancaster.ac.uk

More information can be found on the LIPPS home page on the World Wide Web. The URL for the LIPPS homepage is: http://www.ling.lancs.ac.uk/staff/mark/lipps/lipps.htm

8.3 How to obtain the CLAN programs

You can download the CLAN tools together with a CHAT depfile from the CHILDES internet pages: http://childes.psy.cmu.edu

Glossary of terms

(This glossary is adapted from the LIDES Coding Manual, *International Journal of Bilingualism* (2000) 4(2):131–270.)

Alternation. A psycholinguistic concept introduced by Muysken (1995) to characterize code-switching within a sentence or between sentences. It involves the use of stretches of language from different systems which do not necessarily make up a syntactic constituent. Alternation contrasts with *insertion* and *congruent lexicalization.* In *insertion*, the grammar of a single language predominates incorporating a word or larger syntactic constituent from another language. In *congruent lexicalization*, the syntax of the two languages in the sentence is the same, thus allowing the lexical items from either language to be used.

Borrowing. In language interaction research, lexical borrowing typically refers to the linguistic forms being taken over by one language or language variety from another. A crucial methodological issue is the distinction between borrowing and code-switching. Difficulties involved in this distinction include estimating, and deciding the relevance of, the degree of morphological, phonological and syntactic integration of the borrowed item.

Changeable headers. A CHAT data file may contain information which changes within the file (for example, a change in the activity being carried out by the participants). Changeable headers may be placed within the body of the transcription file and they are preceded by the symbol @ (for example, @Activities: PAT tries to get CHI to put on her coat). Changeable headers should be distinguished from constant and obligatory file headers which are preceded by the same symbol @. Obligatory file headers are essential if a researcher wants to use the CLAN automatic analysis programs (see section 4.1.1).

CHAT. The transcription system created by MacWhinney (1995 [1991]) for the CHILDES project. This transcription scheme has been adapted and elaborated further by LIDES to deal more precisely with the theoretical and practical problems raised by language interaction data.

CLAN programs. The analytical tools developed by MacWhinney (1995 [1991]) for the CHILDES project, which can be used by researchers to carry out automated analyses of their data files.

Code-switching. This is a general term which refers to the alternate use of two or more languages or language varieties by bilinguals for communicative purposes. Code-switching embraces various types of bilingual behaviour such as switching within and between utterances, turns and sentences. A theoretically neutral and less confusing term adopted for code-switching is *language interaction*.

COMBO program. The main use of this CLAN program is to search transcription files for specific expressions, words or strings. The COMBO search command is constructed with a set of Boolean operators (i.e. AND, OR, NOT) which are used to define the parameters of the search string which may be some aspect of the coding (that is, language tags) or words or utterances from the text data file. Searches may be carried out on main or dependent tiers. An example of a COMBO search command to find all lexical items which cannot be assigned to a given language and which are coded on the main tier as @0 is: combo +s *\ @0^*^* gibraltar.doc OJO

Constant headers. A CHAT data file may contain non-obligatory constant headers at the beginning of the file in order to specify information relevant to the conversation text transcribed. Such information may include gender or age of participants, level of education, social economic status, information about coders and transcribers, languages spoken by each of the participants. As with the case of obligatory and changeable headers, constant headers are preceded by the symbol @ such as: @Gender of participants: CHI female, PAT male.

Depadd file. The file where a researcher using CHAT incorporates the list of their newly created symbols or coding schemes used in their transcription. Adding symbols to the depadd file is easy and it gives flexibility to the researcher to develop their own system of coding. The depadd file, like the depfile, is used by the CHECK program to verify the syntax and structure of data files.

Dependent tier. The CHAT transcription scheme makes use of dependent tiers to include information or additional coding (that is syntactic, morphological, speech acts, general comments and so on) which refer to the preceding main tier. It is possible to have any number of dependent tiers at the same time which make reference to a single main tier. All dependent tiers should be preceded by the symbol % followed by a three-letter code among those already defined in the depfile or a newly created code which should be added to the depadd file. An example of a dependent tier code for a gloss of the main tier utterance is %glo.

File headers. One of the main components of a CHAT transcript are the file headers. These are lines of text preceded by the symbol @ (for example, @ Participants). Headers can be obligatory (such as @Begin, or @End) or optional (such as @Participants, or @Coder). Different types of headers can be inserted in different places in a CHAT transcription.

Gloss. A morpheme-by-morpheme translation of one or more utterances on the main tier. This gloss is strongly recommended for researchers contributing their data to the database and it should be incorporated on a specific dependent tier (%glo).

Main tier. This is the line in a CHAT transcription which includes a person's speech transcribed in written form. It is preceded by an asterisk and the speaker's initials or other three-letter code (for example, *PAM:). Each turn of the conversation may be divided into several entries or the speech may be transcribed in a single entry.

Metacharacter. May also be referred to as a metasymbol. A metacharacter is a symbol used in coding a transcription in CHAT (for example, %, *). Metasymbols or characters are used for various types of coding in the headers, the main tier and dependent tiers. Any non-letter character is a metacharacter.

Readme file. Provides important background information about the files belonging to a data set. This information is crucial for other researchers working with this data. The original researcher may include any comment which is important for understanding the particular data set or the particular way it has been transcribed and coded. The readme file is a separate document or file which is included with all data contributed to the LIDES database.

SGML. This acronym stands for Standard Generalized Markup Language. It is a metalanguage which is used as a standard way of marking up a text (both spoken and written), and is independent of any word processor or computer system.

XML (Extensible Markup Language). This language is a flexible text format derived from SGML (see above). XML is a metalanguage written in SGML which allows a user to design customized markup languages. XML now provides the framework for the CHILDES and TalkBank databases (see MacWhinney, this volume). See http://www.w3.org/XML/ for more information.

Notes

1. LIDES = Language Interaction Data Exchange System. LIPPS = Language Interaction in Plurilingual and Plurilectal Speakers. A fuller description of these proposals can be found as a Special Issue of the *International Journal of Bilingualism*, 4(2), June 2000. However, this obviously does not include the developments to the system which have been made since then. The authors of that volume were the LIPPS Group and included (in alphabetical order) Ruthanna Barnett, Eva Codó, Eva Eppler, Montse Forcadell, Penelope Gardner-Chloros, Roeland van Hout, Melissa Moyer, Maria Carme Torras, Maria Teresa Turell, Mark Sebba, Marianne Starren, Sietse Wensing. The authors of the present chapter would like to acknowledge the contribution of the original authors and the permission of the Editor of *IJB*, Li Wei, to base this chapter on the Special Issue.
2. The CHILDES system is maintained by Brian MacWhinney at Carnegie Mellon University, Pittsburgh, USA and the University of Antwerp, Belgium; email: macw@cmu.edu; internet: http://childes.psy.cmu.edu or http://atila-www.uia.ac.be/childes/index.html
3. For example, you can use a macro to build up a lexicon of words to be coded by language.
4. This example contains a number of non-ASCII characters (ñ, é, à). It is good practice to replace these with sets of Unicode symbols, making clear the mapping between these and the orthographic characters they represent.
5. Some headers may be considered either constant or changeable: for example, date, location, situations and so on.
6. There are different views as to whether it is possible, always or even sometimes, to decide which is the primary language, and if so how this should be done. The reader is referred to discussions surrounding the 'Matrix Language' as defined by Myers-Scotton (see for example, Gardner-Chloros and Edwards, 2004; pp. 117–20).
7. The notion of utterance may vary from one researcher to another depending on specific research interests. LIDES purposely does not provide a single definition of utterance. Some criteria for distinguishing an utterance can be a single word, an intonation unit, a long pause and so on. Because of the possibility of sound linking to the transcripts the issue of where to put boundaries on an utterance may become somewhat less arbitrary, but we do not expect it will solve the segmentation problem completely.
8. The Gibraltar oral corpus is made up of 16 recordings from eight different contexts in Gibraltar. A total of 6,765 words have been transcribed. The written corpus is made up of 16 written constructions of oral speech used by two speakers. The size of this corpus is 5,049 words.

References

Agnihotri, R. 1987. *Crisis of Identity: The Sikhs in England*. New Delhi: Bahri.

Atkinson, J. M. and J. Heritage. 1984. *Structures of Social Action: Studies in Conversation Analysis*. Cambridge and New York: Cambridge University Press.

Auer, P. 1998. *Bilingual Conversation*. Amsterdam/Philadelphia: John Benjamins.

Backus, A. 1996. *Two in One. Bilingual speech of Turkish Immigrants in the Netherlands*. Tilburg: Tilburg University Press.

Bentahila, A. 1983. *Language Attitudes among Arabic-French Bilinguals in Morocco*. Clevedon: Multilingual Matters.

Clyne, M. 2003. *Dynamics of Language Contact*. Cambridge: Cambridge University Press.

Coulmas, F. (ed.). 1997. *The Handbook of Sociolinguistics*. Oxford: Blackwell.

De Houwer, A. 1990. *The Acquisition of Two Languages from Birth: A Case Study*. Cambridge: Cambridge University Press.

Dolitsky, M. (ed.). 2000. Special Issue on Code-switching. *Journal of Pragmatics* 32.

Eastman, C. M. (ed.). 1992. *Codeswitching*. Clevedon: Multilingual Matters.

Edwards, J. 1995. 'Principles and alternative systems in the transcription, coding and mark-up of spoken discourse'. *Spoken English on Computer* ed. by G. Leech, G. A. Myers and J. A. Thomas, pp. 19–34. London: Longman.

Gardner-Chloros, P. 1991. *Language Selection and Switching in Strasbourg*. Oxford: Clarendon Press.

Gardner-Chloros, P. and M. Edwards. 2004. 'Assumptions behind grammatical approaches to code-switching: when the blueprint is a red herring'. *Transactions of the Philological Society* 102(1):103–29.

Gibbons, J. 1987. *Code-Mixing and Code-Choice: A Hong Kong Case Study*. Clevedon: Multilingual Matters.

Halmari, H. 1997. *Government and Code-switching: Explaining American Finnish*. Amsterdam/Philadelphia: John Benjamins.

Hamers, J. and M. H. A. Blanc. 2000. *Bilinguality and Bilingualism*, 2nd edn. Cambridge: Cambridge University Press.

Haust, D. 1995. *Code-switching in Gambia: eine Soziolinguistische Untersuchung von Mandinka, Wolof und Englisch in Kontakt.* [*A sociolinguistic investigation of Mandinka, Wolof and English in contact.*] Cologne: Köppe Verlag.

Heath, J. 1989. *From Code-Switching to Borrowing: Foreign and Diglossic Mixing in Moroccan Arabic*. London/New York: Kegan Paul International.

Heller, M. 1988. *Code-Switching: Anthropological and Sociolinguistic Perspectives*. Berlin: Mouton de Gruyter.

Jacobson, R. (ed.). 1998. *Codeswitching Worldwide*. Berlin/New York: Mouton de Gruyter.

Li Wei (ed.). 2000. *The Bilingualism Reader*. London: Routledge.

McCormick, K. 2002. *Language in Cape Town's District Six*. Oxford: Oxford University Press.

MacWhinney, B. 1995 [1991]. *The CHILDES Project: Tools for Analyzing Talk*, 2nd edn. Hillsdale, NJ: Erlbaum.

MacWhinney, B. and C. Snow. 1990. 'The Child Language Data Exchange System: an update.' *Journal of Child Language* 17:457–72.

Milroy, L. and Li Wei. 1995. 'A social network approach to code-switching: the example of a bilingual community in Britain'. *One Speaker, Two Languages: Cross-Disciplinary Perspectives on Code-Switching*, ed. by L. Milroy and P. Muysken, pp. 136–57. Cambridge: Cambridge University Press.

Milroy, L and P. Muysken (eds). 1995. *One Speaker, Two Languages: Cross-Disciplinary Perspectives on Code-Switching*. Cambridge: Cambridge University Press.

Moyer, M. G. 1992. 'Analysis of codeswitching in Gibraltar'. Unpublished PhD dissertation, Universitat Autònoma de Barcelona.

Moyer, M. G. 2000. 'Gibraltar oral and written corpus 1987–1990'. Unpublished.

Muysken, P. 1995. 'Code-switching and grammatical theory'. *One Speaker, Two Languages: Cross-Disciplinary Perspectives on Code-Switching*, ed. by L. Milroy and P. Muysken, pp. 177–98. Cambridge: Cambridge University Press.

Muysken, P. 2000. *Bilingual Speech: A Typology of Code-Mixing.* Cambridge: Cambridge University Press.

Myers-Scotton, C. 1993a. *Social Motivations for Code-Switching: Evidence from Africa.* Oxford: Clarendon Press.

Myers-Scotton, C. 1993b. *Duelling Languages.* Oxford: Clarendon Press.

Myers-Scotton, C. 2002. *Contact Linguistics: Bilingual Encounters and Grammatical Outcomes.* Oxford: Clarendon Press.

Nivens, R. J. 2002. *Borrowing versus Code-Switching in West Tarangan (Indonesia).* Dallas, Tex.: SIL International.

Nortier, J. 1990. *Dutch–Moroccan Arabic Code Switching.* Dordrecht: Foris Publications.

Ochs, E. 1979. 'Transcription as theory'. *Developmental Pragmatics*, ed. by E. Ochs and B. B. Schieffelin, pp. 43–72. New York: Academic Press.

Romaine, S. 1994. *Bilingualism.* 2nd edn. Oxford: Basil Blackwell.

Sebba, M. 1993. *London Jamaican.* Harlow, Essex: Longman.

Thomason, S. G. 2001. *Language Contact: An Introduction.* Edinburgh: Edinburgh University Press.

Torras, M. C. 1998. 'Code negotiation and code alternation in service encounters in Catalonia'. Unpublished MA dissertation, Lancaster University.

Treffers-Daller, J. 1994. *Mixing Two Languages: French–Dutch Contact in a Comparative Perspective.* Berlin: Mouton de Gruyter.

Zentella, A. C. 1997. *Growing Up Bilingual: Puerto Rican Children in New York.* Oxford: Blackwell.

6

ICE-Ireland: Local Variations on Global Standards

Jeffrey Kallen and John Kirk

1 ICE and ICE-Ireland: background and methodology

The proposal to compile an International Corpus of English (ICE) was first published in a brief note by Greenbaum (1988). In a later discussion of the ICE project, Greenbaum (1996b, p. 3) explained that:

> its principal aim is to provide the resources for comparative studies of the English used in countries where it is either a majority first language (for example, Canada and Australia) or an official additional language (for example, India and Nigeria). In both language situations, English serves as a means of communication between those who live in these countries. The resources that ICE is providing for comparative studies are computer corpora, collections of samples of written and spoken English from each of the countries that are participating in the project.

Nelson (1996a, p. 28) further elaborates the ICE concept in describing the social characteristics of the contributors to ICE corpora:

> The authors and speakers of the texts are aged 18 or over, and have been educated through the medium of English to at least the end of secondary schooling. We use these two criteria because they are quantifiable. We do not attempt an evaluation of the language in a text as a criterion for inclusion or exclusion. Age and education can be accurately measured, and they can be applied in the same way in every country. The project, then, is not based on any prior notion of what 'educated' or 'standard' English is.

As we discuss below, there are many features of the ICE project in Ireland (ICE-Ireland) that reflect the specific historical and political forces which have shaped the Irish sociolinguistic landscape. In order to appreciate these particularities, though, we start with an examination of the salient features of ICE as an investigation of English as a world language. First, although it is true that all the countries in Greenbaum's national categories contain within them elements of dialect variation, urban vernacular speech, non-native or learner English, linguistic change in progress and a host of other sources of linguistic variation, ICE is not designed as a study of variation, but as a study of 'standard' national Englishes. Taken to extremes, it could appear that this focus on the standard language would make international comparisons redundant: if 'Standard' English is truly standardized, then all national standards should be linguistically identical and comparisons would be unrevealing. Yet built into Greenbaum's aim of 'comparative studies' is the recognition that national standard Englishes do differ in important ways: in other words, that there is diversity within English even when the English which is being studied is ostensibly that which suppresses variation. Second, we recognize that Nelson's succinct definition of the contributors to the ICE corpus also anticipates the inclusion of linguistic diversity within ICE. Second-level education, especially in those English-speaking countries where it is widely available, is not necessarily a linguistically unifying experience, that is, one which determines a focused linguistic norm for all participants. Thus it may be that considerable variety will be found among speakers and writers who meet the simple educational criterion used in ICE. Third, we point out that Nelson's reference to 'texts' indicates the essential unit of the ICE corpus: the corpus text, consisting of approximately 2,000 words of speech or writing, taken from a specified context as defined in ICE protocols (see Nelson, 1996a, pp. 28–33; Nelson *et al.*, 2002, pp. 309–31). Each ICE corpus includes 300 texts of spoken language and 200 texts of written language, yielding a total of 1 million words, orthographically transcribed and marked up using a standard ICE markup system (see Greenbaum, 1996a, for various discussions of ICE annotation. The ICE markup system is available from the ICE website).

In theory, then, the ICE project lays down simple rules which determine each national corpus based on a combination of textual and language-user definitions. This system is general enough to be applicable across a wide range of English-speaking countries, yet specific enough to ensure comparability of text type and social considerations among the different corpora. In practice, however, we have found that many decisions had to be made in implementing the ICE-Ireland corpus that could not have been determined by general ICE guidelines, but which, instead, required elaborations or modifications to the ICE procedures in order to retain the goal that ICE-Ireland should be a credible representation of Standard English usage in Ireland. We turn to a discussion of these areas first, in order to understand the methodology of ICE-Ireland in relation to other ICE protocols.

1.1 ICE-Ireland: problems of definition

An initial question for ICE-Ireland, which has faced the compilers of several other ICE corpora as well, is the simple matter of defining national boundaries. In the Caribbean, for example, where an ICE Jamaica project now exists, an early paper by Mair (n.d.) explored the possibility of establishing a pan-Caribbean ICE corpus, pointing out (p. 2) that 'a first survey of the available linguistic literature would tempt one to assume the existence of an educated Caribbean standard at least as an initial working hypothesis'. At the same time, it was recognized (p. 4) that if, for example,

> educated English in Jamaica, Trinidad and Tobago and Guyana were in fact developing different norms, then lumping these varieties together in a corpus of Caribbean English would be a waste of time because the results from an analysis of such a corpus would not represent any of the three actually emerging standards but create an artificial one that is irrelevant both in prescriptive and descriptive terms.

Conversely, while ICE East Africa does in fact include data from Kenya and Tanzania, the ICE guidelines have been modified to include 'parallel written corpora' for each country, yielding 800,000 words of text in total rather than the ICE figure of 400,000. The justification for this modification is the recognition by the compilers that 'the linguistic situation in Kenya and Tanzania differs to such an extent that we considered it to be necessary to represent both varieties of written English fully' (ICE East Africa website) (see also Sebba and Dray, this volume).

In the case of Ireland, we were faced with a problem that we have elsewhere called 'the national context issue' (see Kirk *et al.*, 2004a). This issue pertains to Ireland's status as a single English-speaking zone when considered in a geographical and historical perspective, balanced with its political division into two legal jurisdictions, Northern Ireland (within the United Kingdom) and the Republic of Ireland. The political division is less than 100 years old (not a long time in linguistic or dialectological history), yet, given the role of government, educational systems and other public institutions in shaping the use of language within many of the ICE text categories, a plausible argument could be made in favour of having a separate ICE corpus from each political jurisdiction in Ireland.

We argue, however, that determining the question of 'national English' in Ireland on a purely political or legal basis would ignore some crucial linguistic facts. In so far as the standard language reflects anything of the dialectal history of English (a point which we discuss below), the political division in Ireland would not serve linguistic analysis well. There are many features of traditional Irish English dialects which easily transcend political borders, and the Ulster dialect border as it has been documented both for English and for the Irish language corresponds not to the political border but to much older patterns of settlement and social interaction (see, especially, O'Rahilly, 1932; Ó Cuív, 1951; Adams, 1958; Wagner, 1958; Henry, 1958; Barry, 1981c; and Kallen, 2000). Moreover, the division of ICE within Ireland into two separate corpora would, by ICE rules, specifically exclude cross-border conversation and other kinds of language use, just as the British corpus (ICE-GB), for example, includes no interactions with speakers of Irish or Indian English. This exclusion would create a totally unrealistic picture of daily linguistic interaction in Ireland, and would subordinate our desire to reflect the reality of Standard English usage in Ireland to an external political consideration. In building ICE-Ireland, we could, of course, have adopted what appears to have been the approach in ICE-GB. Here, despite the existence of three large English-speaking areas (England, Scotland and Wales), each with a certain level of independent political recognition but all united geographically in Britain and politically within the United Kingdom, ICE-GB has in large measure reflected English usage, as opposed to that of Scotland or Wales. The emphasis on usage in the south of England, especially the London area, is particularly strong in the spoken texts. We could have based our picture of ICE-Ireland in Belfast or Dublin, for example, and included texts from other parts of Ireland in a random fashion. Instead of either separating Ireland into two ICE corpora or giving predominance to one specific area of Ireland, however, we chose to divide the ICE-Ireland corpus into two equal halves, one from Northern Ireland, which we designate as ICE (NI), the other from the Republic of Ireland, or ICE (ROI).

This division is not meant to be exclusive. A conversation recorded in Dublin will belong to ICE (ROI), but if a speaker from Northern Ireland happens to participate in this conversation, the speech is simply treated as part of the ICE (ROI) corpus in the normal way. Such cross-border texts do not constitute a very large portion of ICE-Ireland, but they are common enough to show that speakers from either side of the political border may be exposed to norms from the other jurisdiction, and that convergence or divergence between speakers exposed to different linguistic norms may be a feature of everyday English usage in Ireland. We thus understand the systematic division of ICE-Ireland into ICE (NI) and ICE (ROI) subcorpora, together with the opportunities for interaction between two potentially diverse sets of norms which this division presents, to constitute distinctive features of the corpus.

Consideration of the speakers and writers who contribute to ICE corpora gives rise to a second problem for ICE-Ireland, which we refer to as the 'speaker demographic issue' (Kirk *et al.*, 2004a). In deciding to divide ICE-Ireland into two equal subcorpora, we have distorted the population distribution between the two jurisdictions: the Republic of Ireland has a population of approximately 3.8 million people, as opposed to the 1.6 million residents of Northern Ireland. ICE, however, has never attempted to balance corpus sizes with populations. An ICE corpus of 1 million words is used for very large English-speaking areas such as India, the United States, Great Britain and South Africa, as well as for smaller populations such as those of Fiji, Jamaica, Singapore and Ireland. This standard size for ICE corpora is in keeping with the methodological standardization in ICE which we have already mentioned. Hence we take it that ICE corpora do not represent populations so much as they represent usage and text types in the domains specified by ICE protocols. It follows from this understanding that ICE-Ireland should represent equal quantities of texts across its two (partially overlapping) jurisdictions, rather than attempt a representation of population balances.

In looking at contributors to the ICE corpus, we have also had to consider the problem of how to define Irish users of Standard English, and how to account for migration within our population of speakers and writers. Here, too, our problem is not unique to Ireland, even though our eventual solution may be. Bauer (1991) and Holmes (1996) have discussed the question of how to determine who counts as a speaker of New Zealand English for ICE purposes. Both point out that a definition on linguistic grounds is unsuitable: as Holmes (1996, p. 164) puts it, 'selecting people who "sounded like" New Zealanders ... would have self-evidently pre-judged an issue which the corpus data was intended to illuminate'. Yet, as Bauer (1991) notes, New Zealanders include many citizens and residents who have not grown up in New Zealand, and who may have only a transient link either to English in New Zealand or to the country itself. Excluding such speakers seems an obvious choice but, as Bauer (1991, p. 3) also observes, if the definition of a native speaker of New Zealand English is pushed to an extreme criterion, for example, 'that every speaker recorded has not only grown up in New Zealand but has two parents who also grew up in New Zealand', then 'we will discover that we have very few potential informants in some sections of the population'. When factors of migration, residence and education are taken into account, the working definition for ICE in New Zealand has been that 'a speaker of New Zealand English is defined as someone who has lived in New Zealand since before the age of 10' (Holmes, 1996, p. 165).

Our solution to the problem of defining speakers of Irish English has been complicated by our division of ICE-Ireland into two subcorpora, and by patterns of Irish migration, both internally and externally. As a basic criterion, we put considerable emphasis on the location of an individual's primary and second-level education. To the best of our knowledge, anyone whose education up to the completion of second-level qualifications lies wholly outside either Irish jurisdiction is not included in ICE-Ireland. We have not, however, excluded speakers or writers who have spent a part of these years in other jurisdictions, although such people constitute only a small fraction of the ICE-Ireland total. Neither have we excluded individuals whose adult life has included periods in employment or higher education outside of Ireland. In some text categories, including academic and broadcasting contexts, it may be quite common for individuals to have spent time acquiring higher degrees or employment experience in other English-speaking countries before returning to Ireland: excluding such individuals could make the corpus unrepresentative of actual patterns of usage as they are encountered within these specific discourse genres. Our approach to internal migration has been equally flexible. If ICE (NI) and ICE (ROI) were defined on the basis that the language-users contributing to each had been raised and lived exclusively within one political jurisdiction, we would by definition have excluded all speakers whose life histories had crossed this political border at one time or another, thus creating an illusion that Standard English usage in Ireland consists of the language of only 'pure' Northern Ireland or

Republic of Ireland speakers. Just as we have allowed texts occasionally to contain speakers from both jurisdictions, and as we have included language-users with significant adult experience outside of Ireland, we also allow ICE-Ireland to include cross-border migrants. For the ICE-Ireland corpus-user, these considerations are dealt with in large part by the use of header files which contain the relevant demographic information, where available, for each contributor to the corpus.

Following the arguments above, then, the division of ICE-Ireland into ICE (NI) and ICE (ROI) reflects a primary division on the basis of the site from which the text originates. For most recorded conversations, broadcasts, classroom usage and similar categories, the definition of the site is self-evident. Most of the published material in ICE (NI) or ICE (ROI) has been written and published in its appropriate jurisdiction, by an author or authors from this jurisdiction. These definitions, however, cannot be taken too rigidly. Many Irish writers, whether writing literature, science or in the humanities, publish their work abroad, and it would again be an unrealistic restriction to exclude all such material from ICE-Ireland. Here the decision as to which subcorpus includes the material depends on the provenance of the author. The division according to this definition of the origin of material, however, is cross-cut both by mixed authorship, in which a given text may include speakers or writers from both jurisdictions, and by the effects of population mobility. Together these factors determine that ICE-Ireland texts may be (a) exclusively from speakers or writers native to Northern Ireland, (b) exclusively from speakers or writers native to the Republic of Ireland, and (c) mixed in type, including texts in which the speakers or writers come from different sides of the political border, as well as texts from language-users who have migrated within Ireland during their lifetimes. By far the majority of texts come from categories (a) and (b), yet to include only texts of this kind would be to create an artificial separation within ICE-Ireland that does not reflect linguistic reality so much as it constitutes an artefact of the linguist's method. Our hypothesis is that the mixed texts of type (c) have greater potential to demonstrate linguistic convergence and divergence between competing 'northern' and 'southern' norms than would be expected in the texts of type (a) and (b): these mixed types are therefore not simply expedient, but are important in their own right.

In the foregoing discussion, then, we can see that the compilation of ICE-Ireland has had to face problems of national definition and the definition of who constitutes an ICE speaker in much the same way as other ICE projects have done. Our solution, however, reflects some unique aspects of language and political history in Ireland, as well as our interest in using a synchronic, corpus-based analysis to shed light on elements of the historical development of Irish Standard English.

2 Contexts and texts for ICE-Ireland

ICE-Ireland was initiated in the context of early discussions held at the 1989 meeting of the International Conference on English Language Research on Computerized Corpora of Modern and Medieval English (ICAME). At that time, preliminary consideration was given to the construction of ICE corpora for England, Scotland, Wales and Ireland. As the ICE-GB project developed into a single corpus (see Nelson *et al.*, 2002), an independent ICE-Ireland corpus was initiated in 1990 by John Kirk at Queen's University Belfast, who was soon joined in the project by Jeffrey Kallen from Trinity College Dublin. With the help of Goodith White in University College Cork, the project assumed a wide geographical base, from which the first phase of data collection began in the early 1990s. The development of ICE-Ireland continued at a slow pace until 1999, when a grant from the Royal Irish Academy and British Council Social Sciences Committee made it possible to put much of the conversational material from ICE (ROI) into machine-readable form. Major funding to enable the construction of ICE-Ireland subsequently became available in 2001, with a grant (B/RG/AN1033/APN12375) from the Arts and Humanities Research Board in the UK to fund a two-year research project on the 'Sociolinguistics of Standardization of English in Ireland', for which ICE-Ireland was to be the database. This funding initiated a second phase of collection for ICE-Ireland, in which it became possible to complete the corpus according to ICE guidelines, making a maximum effort to restrict newly incorporated materials to those from the years 1990 to 1994, which is the basic time period for ICE. Retrospective collection for printed materials, television and radio broadcasting and some other text types was relatively straightforward; in some categories, however, a small number of new recordings had to be made in 2002 and 2003. Though the time span from the earliest to the latest ICE-Ireland recordings is just over ten years, we do not think this gap introduces a large amount of diachronic variation into the corpus. Some of the new recordings include politicians and broadcasters who also feature in recordings from the first phase of data collection, and adherence to the original ICE text categories (thus excluding new modes such as email and text messaging) means that newer ICE-Ireland texts are in many ways similar to those of the older period. Though a few lexical innovations (particularly related to text messaging and other electronic communication) may be found within the newer texts, we have so far not seen evidence of any structural innovations within the time span of ICE-Ireland collection. Since header files indicate the date of each text, albeit sometimes approximately, it remains open for the user to explore further the question of diachronic variation within ICE-Ireland.

The general principles that govern the selection and exclusion of texts from ICE corpora are publicly available (for example, Greenbaum, 1996a; ICE-GB, 1998; ICE website; Nelson *et al.*, 2002), so there is no need to review these in detail here. The categories of ICE texts are designed to include contexts of language usage which could be found in any English-speaking country (face-to-face conversation, news broadcasts, academic writing, journalism and so on), and Ireland generally proved to be no exception to this principle. Application of the ICE text category rules to Ireland was not, however, entirely unproblematical. For 'Legal presentations' and 'Legal cross-examinations', it emerged that legal restrictions in the Republic of Ireland would have prohibited the use of recordings of courtroom proceedings. The use of legal transcripts would not have been suitable for ICE, since legal transcription could not be expected to preserve many of the features of spontaneous speech that a linguistic transcript would necessarily include. Official recordings of sworn public testimony at legislative committee enquiries, were, however, available and have been used in the corpus: they are 'legal' in a broad sense, but not identical to courtroom proceedings. The category of 'Parliamentary debates' is also in some ways problematical, since Northern Ireland does not have an autonomous parliament. Recordings from the Northern Ireland Forum on Peace and Reconciliation date from the appropriate time period and have in many ways the overall feel of parliamentary debate, yet it is possible that close analysis would reveal some differences between Forum debates and those in autonomous legislative chambers. It also turned out that while efforts could be made to ensure gender balance in many categories of speech and writing, balance could prove elusive in other areas: it proved extremely difficult to find males who were willing to participate in 'Telephone conversation' recordings or to contribute personal letters as ICE texts.

To give a sense of what is involved in the ICE-Ireland corpus, Table 6.1 gives the distribution of text types and approximate word counts for the texts of ICE-Ireland in its two components.[1] Titles of text categories in the table reflect usage within the ICE-Ireland project

Table 6.1 Text categories and word counts, ICE-Ireland (August 2004)

	Word count		
Text category	**NI**	**ROI**	**Total**
Face-to-face conversation	90,847	98,257	18,9104
Telephone conversation	10,089	10,323	20,412
Classroom lessons	21,072	21,217	42,289
Broadcast discussions	21,139	20,180	41,319
Broadcast interviews	10,222	10,253	20,475
Parliamentary debates	10,140	10,831	20,971
Legal cross-examinations	10,059	9,869	19,928
Business transactions	10,284	10,427	20,711
Spontaneous commentaries	21,578	20,446	42,024
Unscripted speeches	29,928	30,764	60,692
Demonstrations	10,471	10,779	21,250
Legal presentations	10,282	10,147	20,429
Broadcast news	20,245	20,215	40,460
Broadcast talks	19,813	20,329	40,142
Scripted speeches (not broadcast)	10,487	9,665	20,152
Total spoken texts	306,656	313,702	620,358
Student untimed essays	10,788	10,143	20,931
Student examination essays	10,743	10,323	21,066
Social letters	16,362	15,535	31,897
Business letters	16,675	13,723	30,398
Learned publications in Humanities	10,903	11,301	22,204
Learned publications in Social Sciences	10,946	10,447	21,393
Learned publications in Natural Sciences	10,025	10,822	20,847
Learned publications in Technology	11,757	10,223	21,980
Popular publications in Humanities	10,410	10,406	20,816
Popular publications in Social Sciences	11,238	10,890	22,128
Popular publications in Natural Sciences	10,571	10,133	20,704
Popular publications in Technology	10,576	10,371	20,947
Press news reports	21,131	21,851	42,982
Administrative/regulatory prose	10,877	10,347	21,224
Skills and hobbies	11,812	10,991	22,803
Creative writing	24,169	20,553	44,722
Total written texts	219,323	208,169	427,492
Total texts	525,979	521,871	1,047,850

and sometimes differ in small but self-explanatory ways from the original ICE labels.

ICE transcriptions are orthographic. They do not include phonological information, although conventional orthography allows for some features of spoken language to be represented (see also Tagliamonte, this volume). Negative contractions, for example, are orthographically transcribed, while non-negatives are transcribed with a space before the attached auxiliary in order to facilitate searching for auxiliary verbs, as in <she 's>, <I 'll>, and so on. More purely phonological points of variation such as the choice between velar and alveolar nasal consonants in *-ing* endings for verbs and nouns are completely left out of the ICE transcription conventions. Likewise, intonation or other features of prosody are not included in ICE transcriptions. ICE has a specially designed markup system for indicating pauses, conversational overlaps, non-corpus material such as foreign language use and other non-lexical features of interaction: Nelson (1996b), Nelson *et al.* (2002, pp. 9–13) and the ICE website describe in detail the methodology for transcription and annotation of ICE corpora. ICE transcripts are meant to be machine-readable in a general sense, but ICE-GB, as the pioneer corpus in the project, has also been closely linked to specially designed software known as ICECUP (see especially ICE-GB; and Nelson *et al.*, 2002, pp. 69–231). Use of ICECUP relies on a specific system of parsing and tagging, discussed in a variety of papers in Greenbaum (1996a). ICE-Ireland has been transcribed and annotated in keeping with the general principles of the ICE project, selecting, however, options which provide relatively less detail in the markup system, and not linking the corpus to ICECUP. ICE-Ireland transcriptions are formatted as text files, allowing flexibility in the selection of standard concordancing packages to carry out whatever analysis a user of the corpus wishes to do. The data analysis which follows is based on concordances created with the Conc 1.76 concordance package from the Summer Institute of Linguistics in Dallas, Texas; the same material could be searched with equal validity by other well-known packages.

Each ICE-Ireland text thus consists of header information concerning the context of use from which the text originates, as well as information (insofar as it is available) on each speaker or writer contributing to the text, followed by a transcript based on ICE conventions. A standard questionnaire was used to elicit speaker (or writer) profile information, covering topics such as the speaker's age, sex, provenance, current residence, level of formal education, native language, other languages spoken, religious background and occupational category. Strict assurances have been made to guarantee the anonymity of all private texts, whether spoken or written. Relevant encodings in the transcriptions include those for speaker identification (<$_>), utterance initiation (<#>), pause (<,> or <,,>), conversational overlap (using square bracket notation), partial utterance of a word (<.> ... </.>), unintelligible speech (for example <unclear> ... </unclear>), and so on. The ICE-Ireland markup system closely follows the general ICE conventions as discussed by Nelson (1996b); these conventions are motivated in part by ordinary orthographic principles and in part by the need to facilitate electronic concordancing. Example (1) shows a segment of a classroom discussion using the ICE-Ireland transcription; although the <X> indicates that Speaker C is actually ex-corpus, the speech is transcribed in order to make sense of the following utterances.

(1) <$C> <X> <#> The the people that stayed behind in uh in the town <,> like the old ladies and also the uhm <,> uh the the vagabonds and the <unclear> 2 sylls </unclear> <#> What <,> you know <,> what would they eat <,> how would they live </X>

<$B> <#> Oh there 's <,> I mean <,> if you think about it this was a really productive agricultural area and the produce is still there except it 's unclean <#> I mean there 's <,> there was still animals around <,> there was all sorts of crops

<$C> <X> <#> Just abandoned </X>

<$B> <#> Yeah <#> Just abandoned because they couldn't actually continue to <.> ex </.> <,> to uhm <,> to export that sort of stuff <,> because if you export grain from the area it 's going to contaminate the rest of the country <#> It 's going to contaminate anywhere that you export it to basically <,> so they have to stop all <,> stop all movement of of produce out of the area <#> So if you looked at it in a <,> in a whole <,> in a real sense <,> it was a really productive area and anyone who didn't have anything <,> they just went there <#> There was loads of food but <,> it <.> wa </.> it 's going to make them sick you know but <,> they didn't see it that way

3 ICE-Ireland: empirical investigations

3.1 Irish Standard English and dialectal research

A linguistic corpus is not merely an inert accumulation of linguistic material: its structure, method of presentation and content will help certain kinds of linguistic investigation, but will not be of special benefit to others. In order to understand the nature of ICE-Ireland, we give here a sample of the value of the ICE-Ireland corpus for testing certain hypotheses in the sociolinguistics of Irish 'Standard' English. The study of language standardization in Ireland has received very little attention, whether in the empirical sense that forms the basis of our investigations or in the sense of analysing the process of standardization, by which efforts are made to suppress variation, codify norms and exert pressure on language users to adhere to these norms (on the process of standardization, see especially Milroy and Milroy, 1999, and Bex and Watts, 1999). Most earlier treatments of Irish English have instead focused on dialectological aspects of the language, wherein a major controversy concerns the degree to which Irish English demonstrates the effects of language transfer from Irish into English (diachronically or synchronically) versus the degree to which the distinctive features of Irish English are retentions of aspects of the language formerly common in Britain but now obsolete or obsolescent there. We can see the roots of this 'transfer vs retention' debate in the earliest modern works on Irish English (for example, Hume, 1858, 1877–78), continuing through the pioneering works of Hayden and Hartog (1909), Joyce (1910), Hogan (1927), Henry (1957, 1958), and Bliss (1979, 1984), as well as in more recent works such as those of Ní Ghallchóir (1981), Harris (1983, 1993), Filppula (1986, 1997, 1999, 2001), Lass (1990), Ó Baoill (1997), Corrigan (2000a, 2000b), Hickey (1997) and others (see also Kallen, 1999, for a review). Barry (1980, 1981b) and Adams (1981) took up the question of 'standard' pronunciation in Ulster, while Adams (1964), Barry and Tilling (1986), Braidwood (1964), Gregg (1972), Macafee (1996) and Mallory (1999), among others, have developed research on Ulster Scots and Ulster English in relation to Scots and the English of the North of England. More recently, attention has also shifted towards an examination of possible Irish influence on English in the cities of northern England (see Centre for Linguistic Research, 2004). Especially since the paradigm shift in the study of urban vernaculars which was signalled by the work of Milroy (1987) in Belfast, and arising in part from other work associated with this enterprise (for example, Milroy and Milroy, 1985), the study of English in Ireland has now come to embrace a range of newer topics. These include network studies of variation in relation to linguistic change (Collins, 1997); sociolinguistic variation and ethno-religious categories (McCafferty, 1999b, 2001); the possible rise of Irish English regiolects (Hickey, 2001); the relations between vernacular speech and linguistic theory in syntax (Henry, 1995) and phonology (Kallen, 2005); social perspectives on phonology in Dublin

English (Hickey, 1999); the links between Irish English (or Scots) and English in North America (Montgomery, 1989, 2000, 2001; Montgomery and Robinson, 1996; Clarke, 1997); and the use of historical corpora of Irish English (see Hickey, Volume 2).

As we point out in Kallen and Kirk (2001), however, in addressing the process of standardization of English in Ireland and the structural aspects of what might be termed the 'standard' variety of English, we find that empirical approaches have been almost entirely lacking (though see, especially, some general comments by Filppula, 1999, pp. 20–1; 2004, p. 73). Greenbaum (1996b, p. 10) anticipated that 'for descriptive linguistics, ICE offers the first systematic collections for many national varieties of English'. This claim would not be entirely true for ICE-Ireland: dialectal usage has been studied with various degrees of systematicity over the years and, in addition to published works on the topic, the large body of material collected by the Tape-Recorded Survey of Hiberno-English (see Barry, 1981a; Tilling, 1985) is a valuable resource whose full potential for the systematic study of dialect in Ireland has yet to be realized (see also Kirk, 1991, 1992). More recently, Irish corpus projects from specific domains of contemporary English usage have also been developed (for example, Farr and O'Keeffe, 2002). Nevertheless, we consider ICE-Ireland to be a unique empirical source for the understanding of Standard English in Ireland due to its construction as the combination of ICE (NI) and ICE (ROI) subcorpora, its breadth of coverage across a variety of spoken and written genres with (near-) universal applicability in the English-speaking world, and the attempts which have been made, through the use of header information and systematic selection of texts, to build a level of social diversity (as measured primarily by geography, age and sex) into the corpus. ICE-Ireland is also, of course, unique in its inherent comparability with ICE corpora developed elsewhere.

In the remainder of this chapter, we will be concerned to demonstrate some particularly salient linguistic features of the ICE-Ireland corpus and, by extension, features of what we take to be 'Standard' English in Ireland. As we have explained elsewhere (for example, Kallen and Kirk, 2001), our definition of what is standard in the 'Standard' English of the ICE project is not determined by linguistic content, but by the use of a standard methodology that allows for international comparisons across text types and speaker variables. We have already noted here that, apart from some well-defined reflections of morphosyntactic processes such as cliticization, phonology is not reflected in ICE corpora; the implication is that phonology is not a part of the standard language. Indeed, independent support for this position comes, for example, from Trudgill's (1984, p. 32) definition of Standard English as 'that set of grammatical and lexical forms which is typically used in speech and writing by educated native speakers'. Trudgill's (1999, p. 118) exclusion of phonology could hardly be more clear: 'There is one thing about Standard English on which most linguists, or at least most British linguists, do appear to be agreed, and that is that Standard English has nothing to do with pronunciation'. In what follows, then, we adhere to an attempt to develop an empirical definition of 'Standard' English which is based on syntax and lexicon and which is very much in keeping with Trudgill's concept of Standard English as a social dialect (see, for example, Trudgill, 1999). Because a corpus-based empirical approach to standard language always carries with it questions over the representativeness of the corpus and the validity of methods used in corpus analysis, we also devote attention here to some of the methodological problems that arise in the interpretation of ICE-Ireland. (On methodological questions for ICE-Ireland see also Kirk *et al.*, 2004a, 2004b; on work in phonology and pragmatics which arises from the ICE-Ireland project, see Kirk *et al.*, 2005).

3.2 Hypotheses in interpreting ICE-Ireland

Considering the small amount of previous research on 'Standard' English in Ireland, any discussion of what is contained in ICE-Ireland is necessarily selective. Given the existing research traditions in Irish English, it would be tempting to start with an examination of the transfer versus retention debate that is so familiar in Irish English dialect study. Our focus on standard language, however, cautions us not to assume the existence of variation within the corpus. The political subdivision within ICE-Ireland also compels us to evaluate all questions of dialectal influence in the light of possible cross-border differences. Since, as we have commented above, the notion of 'Standard' English implies the suppression of variation, what we call the *default hypothesis* with regard to the standard language is that ICE (NI) and ICE (ROI) should be virtually identical in their significant structural aspects. By extension, ICE-Ireland should also be virtually identical to other varieties of Standard English. Yet if a relationship exists between the standard language and traditional dialect patterns, this relationship would necessarily skew the ICE-Ireland corpus to reflect the different linguistic histories of Northern Ireland (which lies entirely within the Ulster dialect zone and historically includes Ulster dialects of Irish, English and Scots) and the Republic of Ireland (which includes some areas of Ulster as well as the much larger provincial areas of Connacht, Munster and Leinster in the west, south and east respectively – each of which has its own regional and local dialectal features). What we thus term the *dialect–historical hypothesis* suggests instead that there will be divisions within Irish Standard English, and that these will reflect differences in the traditional dialects of English and Irish. (For an examination of Irish and English dialect boundaries in relation to the political border, see the overview of atlas and dialect survey data in Kallen, 2000; for a detailed local study, see Zwickl, 2002). To the extent that data confirm the dialect–historical hypothesis, we would expect to see this confirmation most clearly in the relatively informal ICE text types (Face-to-face conversation, Telephone conversation, Personal letters and so on), and to find less confirmation in formal genres such as Legal presentations and Academic writing.

We have not, however, automatically assumed that the ICE-Ireland subcorpora show dialectal and historical influences. We also allow for the possibility that the processes of dialect-levelling and standardization have insulated the standard language from the variation which is observable at other levels, and that, contrary to our default hypothesis, the effect of standardization has been either (a) to create one national Standard English that is differentiated externally from other national standards but that is essentially a single unified standard throughout Ireland (support for what we term the *single-island hypothesis*), or (b) to create two different standard Englishes in Ireland, reflecting the political division between Northern Ireland and the Republic of Ireland and anticipating that the standard English of Northern Ireland will be more closely aligned to that of Great Britain on the basis of the political unity of the United Kingdom (support for a *political hypothesis*). These four hypotheses, which arise from our earlier consideration in Kallen and Kirk (2001) and which we also discuss in Kirk *et al*., (2003, 2004b), will not be evaluated in detail here, but they do form a necessary part of the background in making use of the ICE-Ireland corpus.

3.3 Dialect lexicon and standard in ICE-Ireland

Since ICE makes no systematic attempt to capture phonological detail, we are reliant on elements of lexicon and syntax in looking at ICE-Ireland and dialectal history. Rather than search the entire ICE-Ireland corpus for points of connection between dialect and standard, we concentrate our efforts here on text categories which we consider to be most likely to illuminate these relationships. Turning to the question of dialect lexicon, we are fortunate in having a growing supply of reference works against which to check ICE data, thus supplementing, for example, the major glossaries and dictionaries of Joyce (1910), Traynor (1953), and Bliss (1972) with more recent works such as those of Todd (1989, 1990), Macafee (1996, henceforth *CUD*), Moylan (1996), Ó Muirithe (1996), Fenton (2000), Wall (2001), Sammon (2002), Share (2003) and Dolan (2004). Combined with standard references such as the *Oxford English Dictionary* (*OED*), Wright (1898–1905, henceforth *EDD*), and Upton *et al.* (1994), these word lists facilitate the comparative process, albeit without offering the benefit of a machine-readable word bank of dialect lexicon to match the word lists generated by ICE (see, further, Montgomery, 1993; Görlach, 1995; and Kirk, 1999).

Searching in the categories of Face-to-face conversation, Broadcast discussions and Social letters, we do indeed find a certain amount of material which may legitimately be considered dialectal. The list which follows gives the frequency of occurrence for each term in the texts searched, and a brief discussion of the relevant meanings as they are encountered in ICE-Ireland; other attested meanings are not discussed. This list includes raw numbers for the frequency of occurrence of particular lexical items; bear in mind that the sample sizes for ICE (NI) and ICE (ROI) are roughly equal.

ARRAH – [**ROI** Face-to-face conversation × 1] Sentence- or clause-initial interjection: see, for example, Ó Muirithe (1996). Cf. also YERRAH [**ROI** Face-to-face conversation × 3], in similar function.

AULD, AUL, OUL, OULD – [**NI** Face-to-face conversation × 22; **ROI** Face-to-face conversation × 11] Dialectal pronunciation of 'old', with a pragmatic force including endearment, diminution, and other functions which differentiate it from standard English *old*. Note phrasal uses in Share (2003).

AYE – [**NI** Face-to-face conversation × 354; **ROI** Face-to-face conversation × 15; **ROI** Broadcast discussion × 1; **ROI** Social letters × 1] Affirmative particle, 'yes'. Scots dialectal marker of habituality (see Fenton, 2000) not found.

CANNAE – [**NI** Face-to-face conversation × 1] Scots *cannot.*

CRAIC, CRACK – [**NI** Social letters × 11; **NI** Face-to-face conversation × 11; **ROI** Social letters × 5; **ROI** Face-to-face conversation × 18] 'Fun, lively conversation, chat, news'. Best considered a word of dual etymology (see Kallen, 1996, pp. 112–14), *craic* in Irish covers roughly the same meaning as *crack* in dialectal English in Scotland and the North of England (*EDD*). It is equally plausible for the Irish word to have entered English in Ireland as it is for the English word to have been borrowed into Irish.

DIVIL – [**NI** Face-to-face conversation × 1; **ROI** Face-to-face conversation × 1] Dialectal pronunciation of *devil*, sometimes used as a general negator (see Odlin, 1995) but used with a pragmatic function that distinguishes it from standard English *devil*.

FISSLE – [**NI** Face-to-face conversation × 1] 'Make an attempt at something' (*EDD*).

GIRN – [**NI** Social letters × 1] 'Whimper, cry peevishly' (*CUD*).

HAMES – [**ROI** Face-to-face conversation × 1] 'A mess', usually in phrase *make a hames of* something. Taken literally, a *hames* is part of a horse's collar (*OED*); the phrase *make a horse's collar* of something is also used with the same reference.

HOOR – [**ROI** Broadcast discussion × 2] From dialectal pronunciation of *whore*, often used metaphorically; occurs in ICE in the phrase *cute hoor* 'crafty individual, especially in politics' (cf. Share, 2003).

KEECH – [**NI** Social letters × 1] 'Excrement, defecate' (Todd, 1990). Form is <keeking> in ICE-Ireland.

OCH – [**NI** Face-to-face conversation × 67; **ROI** Social letters × 2; **ROI** Face-to-face conversation × 3] Interjection, usually found sentence-initially.

POLLIES – [**NI** Face-to-face conversation × 1] 'Hornless sheep' (EDD: *poll-sheep* in same meaning).

QUARE – [**NI** Face-to-face conversation ×× 1; **ROI** Face-to-face conversation × 2] Used as an intensifier [ICE (NI) 'it saves a quare bit of travelling'] and as a dialectal pronunciation of *queer* in the sense 'odd, strange, remarkable' [ICE (ROI) 'isn't she some quare dolly', 'well he has a quare motorbike now']. We would not rule out overlap between the two meanings.

SHITE – [**NI** Face-to-face conversation × 15; **ROI** Social letters × 1; **ROI** Face-to-face conversation × 1] 'Shit', dialectal form shared with Scotland and North of England (*EDD*).

WEAN – [**NI** Face-to-face conversation × 2] Scots 'child'.

WEE – [**NI** Broadcast discussion × 2; **NI** Social letters × 6; **NI** Face-to-face conversation × 116; **ROI** Face-to-face conversation × 10; **ROI** Social letters × 5] 'Little, small', also more general diminutive connotation and discourse function.

YE – [**NI** Social letters × 3; **ROI** Social letters × 2; **ROI** Face-to-face conversation × 2] Plural of *you*.

YOKE – [**ROI** Face-to-face conversation × 7] 'A thing in general'.

YOUS – [**NI** Face-to-face conversation × 36; **ROI** Broadcast discussion × 1; **ROI** Face-to-face conversation × 9] Plural of *you*.

It is difficult at this point in the development of ICE-Ireland to evaluate results of this kind definitively. Though all dialectal items which we have identified in the least formal ICE-Ireland text files have been indicated here, it is expected that other dialect words will come up on a sporadic basis in other text files. These lexical headwords, though, give only a partial view of the use of dialect lexicon. A deeper understanding (which we have not attempted here) would also require lexical investigations into differences of meaning and usage that are invisible to standard concordancing or lexical searching, but which are nevertheless essential in order to understand the lexical choices made by speakers and writers in the ICE corpora. Examples of this type include restrictions on the use of *never* (discussed below), the use of *whenever* with punctual versus durative reference, and the use of positive *anymore* 'from now on', 'nowadays' reported on by Eitner (1991 [1951]) and Labov 1991 [1973]) and discussed in the Irish context (for example, *We can do our homework on this [desk] anymore, can't we?* and *Wool is so expensive anymore*) by Kallen (1997, pp. 152–3).

Despite the tentative state of our knowledge, we can make some general observations on the use of dialect lexicon in ICE-Ireland. It is striking, for example, that although the number of individual dialect words in the texts considered here is relatively small, a few words, notably *aye* and *wee* in ICE (NI), are used with considerable frequency. There is also a clear pattern for the words in question to have interactive and emotive functions, rather than to be used with purely denotative function: *arrah, aye, och* and *yerrah,* for example, are all interjections, while words such as *auld, craic, quare, shite* and *wee* 'little' carry with them a variety of discourse functions and connotations of emotion and interaction that go beyond pure lexical reference. Though the limitation on the amount of data which we have analysed thus far calls for caution in interpreting results, it would appear that most of the dialect words in ICE-Ireland are used on both sides of the political border. Quantitative differences, however, run counter to the apparent unity of dialectal usage in Ireland. Words from ICE (NI) such as *aye, cannae, keech, och, wain* and *wee* are relatively less common or are non-occurring in ICE (ROI), and it is plausible to attribute this difference to the influence of Ulster dialect (including Scots) in Northern Ireland (bearing in mind, as well, that some Ulster speakers and writers are naturally found in the ICE (ROI) corpus). Though *arrah, hames, hoor* and *yoke* are included as elements of Ulster English in the *CUD* and by Todd (1990), their occurrence only in the ICE (ROI) subcorpus suggests that these words are more exclusively vernacular or dialectal in Northern Ireland. A similar observation holds for *shite,* which is certainly extremely common in vernacular use in the Republic of Ireland (cf. Share, 2003, p. 290), but within ICE-Ireland is far more frequent in the ICE (NI) subcorpus than in ICE (ROI). Differences of this kind may arise by chance effects of the ICE sample, or they may reflect real asymmetries in the division between standard and vernacular usage for speakers in the two subcorpora. We are less inclined to attribute the cross-border discrepancy in the frequency of plural *yous* to the effects of sampling: our general experience of the use of the second person pronoun in the two jurisdictions leads us to suggest that the frequency distribution in ICE-Ireland represents a real distinction in the degree to which *yous* has been incorporated into the standard language across the two jurisdictions.

In sum, then, we suggest that the number of dialect words which could serve to differentiate ICE-Ireland from other ICE corpora is relatively small, but that both the high frequency of some lexical items and the general occurrence of others in the contexts of standard language make ICE-Ireland distinctive. The cumulative effect of quantitative differences of occurrence for dialect markers should not be ignored. We note, for example, that while *wee* 'little' is found in this sample of ICE (NI) and ICE (ROI) as well as in the comparable texts of ICE-GB, it only occurs once in ICE-GB and 15 times in ICE (ROI), as opposed to 124 occurrences in ICE (NI). Similarly in this ICE subset, *aye* does not occur at all in ICE-GB, while it occurs 17 times in ICE (ROI) and 354 times in ICE (NI). Thus we can say that ICE-Ireland does differ from ICE-GB in the use of dialectal lexicon; moreover, our evidence is that differences exist within ICE-Ireland that reflect different dialectal histories across the island much more clearly than they suggest a role for the political border as a conditioning factor in linguistic variation.

3.4 Dialect and syntax in ICE-Ireland: the case of *after*

Aspects of dialectal syntax in Irish English pose considerable complexities, and would not be well-suited to the brief treatment which we can only give them here. Following our sampling method, though, and in order to illustrate the potential for ICE-Ireland to shed light on the relations between 'Standard' as defined in ICE and other varieties of Irish

English, we consider here the well-known construction in Irish English with BE plus *after* used as a realization of perfect aspect. This construction is perhaps the single most debated one in Irish English: see, for example, Hume (1877–78), Hayden and Hartog (1909), van Hamel (1912), Younge (1923–24), Henry (1957), Harris (1984), Kallen (1989, 1990, 1991), Filppula (1999, 2004), Fiess (2000), Hickey (2000), and McCafferty (1999a, 2001, 2004). The factors which govern the use of the *after* perfect are complex, including socially significant speaker variables, intended illocutionary force, discourse features, verb transitivity and dynamism, and a host of other possible variables, most of which are still subjects of varying degrees of academic controversy. Though the *after* perfect is found in vernacular speech throughout Ireland, Harris (1993) suggests that semantic constraints on its usage may be different in different parts of Ireland. ICE-Ireland, then, potentially allows us to test for two questions: the degree to which the *after* perfect is found in the standard language as defined by ICE, and the degree to which patterns of usage in ICE (NI) and ICE (ROI) are congruent.

Selecting the category of Face-to-face conversation as one which allows for the kind of spontaneous speech in an informal context that might enhance the availability of *after* as a perfect form, we find that the *after* perfect is rare but not absent from ICE-Ireland. The ICE (NI) text files in this category contain 64 tokens of the word *after*, but only one of these is a token of the English perfect. This example does not use the canonical BE *after* Verb-*ing* structure, but a common nominal alternative:

(2) I'm not that long after my dinner.

The same text files in ICE (ROI), however, yield a higher frequency of use for *after* perfects. Out of 74 tokens of the word *after* in this category, four are uses of the perfect:

(3) And he's after coming back from England, you know.
(4) They thought he was after going into a coma with diabetes.
(5) The wife and children are after going out there the other day.
(6) A new fella is after taking over uhm one of the pubs at home.

It would be misleading to make an *a priori* judgement as to the robustness of the *after* construction in Irish 'Standard' English. On the one hand, it is true that the perfect with *have* greatly outweighs the *after* perfect in ICE-Ireland: within the ICE (NI) Face-to-face conversation files alone, there are some 44 tokens of perfective auxiliary *have* with the main verb form *been*. Counting other main verbs and other tenses of HAVE would multiply the number of 'standard' perfects in the corpus greatly. On the other hand, Harris (1984, pp. 316–17) also shows a relatively low level of usage for the *after* perfect within interviews that arise from the Tape-Recorded Survey of Hiberno-English. Analysing approximately 15 hours of recorded speech from nine Belfast speakers and 15 speakers from rural areas in south-west Ulster, Harris notes only three examples of the *after* perfect from the urban speakers (as opposed to 50 uses of the 'standard' perfect with *have*), and no examples of *after* perfects from the rural sample, in contrast to the occurrence of 48 uses of the 'standard' perfect within this group. Filppula (1999, p. 101) further describes the occurrence of *after* perfects in his corpus of recorded interviews as being 'generally low', noting that 25 tokens of *after* perfects in a sample of 158,000 words show the construction to be virtually absent in material from Clare and Kerry (accounting for only three tokens in 74,000 words), although a higher level of usage can be found in Dublin, with twelve tokens in 42,000 words. As demonstrated in Kallen (1991), it is not difficult to hear the *after* perfect being used in Dublin, but it is less frequent in public use between strangers and among middle-class speakers than it is among working-class speakers, and it may be favoured in certain discourse frameworks (including chastisement or 'giving out') that are not likely to occur in ICE transcripts or, for that matter, the texts analysed by Harris (1984) and Filppula (1999). In other words, while it is true that the *after* perfect is rare in ICE-Ireland compared to the 'standard' perfect with *have*, and while its occurrence in ICE-Ireland is lower than the frequency cited by Filppula (1999), there is no intrinsic expected frequency of occurrence for this form: usage depends on a host of linguistic and non-linguistic factors. Thus we would not view the five examples of the *after* perfect in the ICE-Ireland Face-to-face conversations as a 'low' or 'high' figure: it is simply the figure which reflects the outcome of various conditioning factors, some of which are already identified in previous research and others of which are still matters of controversy.

Overall, then, the examples of the *after* perfect point in the same direction as the results of our lexical searches. Given that the *after* perfect does not occur in ICE-GB, and that we do not expect to find this construction in any other ICE corpus, these examples show that dialectal and vernacular differences in national Englishes are reflected in Standard English as defined by ICE. As Milroy (1984), Harris (1985), and Wall (1990) point out, differences of this kind may be responsible for the breakdown of communication across language varieties, whether in speech or in writing, and we expect them to be salient for language users. Any electronic parsing system used in corpus linguistics must also be able to account for these cross-varietal differences. At the same time, however, it is plausible to suggest that the standardization process, whether considered as the pragmatic conditioning of language choice in specific contexts of use or as the focusing of linguistic norms towards the elimination of diversity in the grammar itself, has muted the use of the *after* construction relative to what might be observable in a variation-oriented study.

3.5 ICE-Ireland and the Irish language

The Irish language provides a further means by which ICE-Ireland may be distinguished from other ICE corpora, and by which the subcomponents of the Ireland corpus may be seen as divergent. A distinctive linguistic history in Ulster, in which English was transplanted on a large scale during the seventeenth century (well before it became a widespread language of popular use in most of the rest of Ireland), as well as the development of different governmental policies towards Irish since the foundation of the Irish Free State in 1921–22, have given the Irish language very different roles to play within Northern Ireland and the Republic of Ireland. The use of Irish shows up in ICE-Ireland in three ways: (1) code-switching, where English speakers switch into Irish for varying lengths of time, (2) the use of official terminology and names of corporate institutions in Irish, and (3) the use of isolated lexical items of Irish, variously classifiable as single-word code switches, loanwords, or historical transfer into the lexicon of Irish English (see Kallen, 1996, for further discussion). Many place names and widely used personal names are also of Irish origin and may be spelled or in other ways considered as Irish, but these words are so ubiquitous in ICE-Ireland that it seems prudent simply to treat these as if they were words of English.

ICE conventions are not well-suited to the kind of multilingualism we find in ICE-Ireland. Since large numbers of Irish words need to be integrated into the ICE-Ireland database in order to accommodate corporate, personal and place names, it seems unrealistic to treat any official terminology derived from Irish as lying outside the ICE-Ireland corpus. By extension, it becomes difficult to draw a line between these uses and single-word code switches or borrowings. These uses, too, have been included in ICE-Ireland. Only extended stretches of conversation or writing in Irish would seem to qualify for exclusion from ICE on the basis of being non-English material. Yet here the ICE designation for such excluded material, the notation <foreign>, is inadequate. It is of course historically inaccurate, since Irish is the language which long predates the coming of English to Ireland – just as it would be wrong to designate Hindi as 'foreign' in India or Chinese as 'foreign' in Hong Kong. Moreover, this designation would put Irish on an equal footing with French or Spanish (which also arise in ICE-Ireland), though it is quite clear that the influence of Irish in Irish English is of a different order from that of French and Spanish. Therefore our modification of ICE methodology has been to designate phrase- or clause-length uses of Irish with the notation 'Irish' and to transcribe this material in standard Irish orthography. No translation into English is provided. The material is thus kept available in the corpus to anyone wishing to make use of it, though it is specially designated as being independent from the use of English.

To illustrate the occurrence of Irish-language material, consider three examples of code-switching below. Example (7) is taken from a radio discussion; the speaker here uses an Irish proverb in order to illustrate a point concerning the care of individuals for members of the community, subsequently repeating the sense of the proverb in English. In (8), the writer engages in a brief bit of code-switching, adding a phrase in Irish which is not strictly grammatical but which we interpret in this context to mean 'and [from] me too', while in (9) the speaker indicates to her co-conversationalists that she is unable to see the inside of a house. Though such examples are not common in ICE-Ireland, and arise, on the basis of our analyses thus far, only in ICE (ROI), they further contribute to the sense of national difference in the ICE-Ireland corpus.

(7) <$C> <#> Yeah there is obviously like it gets back to probably you know <Irish> ar scáth a céile a mhaireann na daoine </Irish> <,> in everybody 's shadow everybody else lives basically and if 'twas over 'twould be very sad for Ireland.

(8) <#> Love from all here – <Irish> agus mise fós. </Irish>

(9) <$C> <#> You <{> <[> can't see </[>
<$A> <#> <Irish> <[> Níl mé </[> </{> in ann é a fheiceáil a chailíní </Irish>

Beyond such examples of code-switching, we consider as well the use of official terminology in Irish within ICE-Ireland (cf. Share 2001).

A lexical search of the text categories of Administrative prose, Learned natural science, Parliamentary debates, Broadcast news, Legal presentations and Face-to-face conversation (categories which include both the informal and more formal domains), reveals that, as expected, Irish terminology is much more commonly used in ICE (ROI) than in ICE (NI) (see Table 6.2 below). This difference reflects the different governmental, administrative and economic environments of the two subcorpora and gives ample opportunity to support the hypothesis that governments do affect the standard language at some level. The occurrence of terminology arising from official activity in the Republic of Ireland within ICE (NI), however, shows that the two language zones are by no means isolated from each other but, instead, share features that are not found in other ICE corpora.

Other Irish vocabulary items occur sporadically within this sample: these include *fáinne*, literally Irish 'ring', but in this context a specific type of lapel ring worn in association with the speaking of Irish; *Féile*,

Table 6.2 Sample of Irish-language titles and designations in ICE-Ireland

(a) Found in ICE (NI) and ICE (ROI)

Name	Reference
Aer Lingus	Irish national (state-supported) airlines
Radio Telefís Éireann	RTÉ – Irish public service broadcasting organization
Gardaí	Refers to *Garda Siochána* (plural of *Garda*)
Taoiseach	Head of Irish legislative body (*Dáil Éireann*), prime minister

(b) Found only in ICE (ROI)

Name	Reference
An Bord Pleanála	The Irish planning appeals board
Ceann Comhairle	Presiding officer of the *Dáil*
Cultúrlann na hÉireann	Irish cultural centre
Dáil	*Dáil Éireann* – the main Irish legislative body
Fianna Fáil	Irish political party
Garda Siochána	Irish national police force
Oireachtas	National parliament of Ireland (combined houses)
Seanad	The Senate (upper house) of the *Oireachtas*
Tánaiste	Deputy head of Irish legislative body (*Dáil Éireann*)
Taoisigh	Plural of *Taoiseach*
TD	Member of *Dáil*, from Irish *Teachta Dála*

literally a festival, but used in ICE (ROI) to refer to a specific annual music festival; *fleadh*, a traditional music festival; *Gaeltacht*, a designated area where Irish is retained as a community language; *poitín*, 'illicit distilled spirits'; and *scór* 'tally'. *Fleadh* occurs in ICE (NI) and ICE (ROI); all other words in this group are found in ICE (ROI) only.

3.6 Syntactic variation: auxiliaries and negation in ICE-Ireland

A syntactic feature of ICE-Ireland such as the *after* perfect is familiar from the study of Irish English dialectology and the substratum debate, as cited above. In the remainder of this section, however, we turn to some areas that have received considerably less attention in Irish English study, but which form part of the general study of variability in English. These aspects of variation help to show the potential for ICE-Ireland in evaluating the role of the political border in conditioning linguistic boundaries and in relating Irish usage to standard English internationally. Continuing with our method of sampling from within specific text categories, we concentrate here on elements of three distinctive topics in syntax: the auxiliary system, sentence negation, and the use of subordinate clauses (see Kallen and Kirk, 2001; Kirk *et al.*, 2003; and Kirk, 1997, on these topics respectively).

In looking at the operation of auxiliaries in ICE-Ireland, our first concern is with variation and change in the use of *have* with noun phrases. Table 6.3 shows the distribution of three main types of realization: *have* with a simple noun phrase (NP) (as in *I have this notion*); *have* plus *got* with a possessed noun phrase (*I have got this notion*); and a form in which *have* is followed by a noun phrase and a verbal participle (VP) form (*We have this topic covered*). This latter construction

Table 6.3 HAVE + NP in affirmative declarative sentences (ICE sample)

	Distribution of tokens			
	ICE (NI)	**ICE (ROI)**	**ICE-Ireland**	**ICE-GB**
S HAVE NP	517	564	1081	992
S HAVE got NP	7	6	**13**	**38**
S HAVE Object VP	15	25	**40**	**21**
Total	539	605	1144	992

Forms
I *have* this notion, and so on (S HAVE NP)
I *have got* this notion, and so on (S HAVE got NP)
We *have* this topic *covered*, and so on (S HAVE Object VP)

includes (but is not limited to) the structure which Filppula (1999, p. 107) terms the 'Medial Object Perfect'. It might be argued that such forms should not be treated as part of a set with simple noun phrase possession, but the close surface-level similarity of these three uses of *have* leads us to include them all in a single analysis. A fourth possibility, as in *We have got this topic covered,* strikes us as grammatically acceptable in some Englishes, but this form (perhaps significantly) does not arise in any of the ICE data we have considered. The data of Tables 6.3–6.5 come from text files for Social letters, Skills and hobbies, Face-to-face conversation, Classroom discussion and Broadcast discussion in the two subcorpora of ICE-Ireland and, for comparative purposes, in ICE-GB. For ease of comparison, these tables collapse data from different tense forms of realization types into single categories, so that, for example, *I have this notion* and *I had this notion* are treated as instances of what we denote as S HAVE NP. Every effort has been made here to exclude tokens of HAVE, DO and GOT in which HAVE is used with a noun phrase that is a complement to the verb rather than its object (for example, *have lunch, have the measles,* and so on), DO is used emphatically, or in which GOT is used dynamically (for example, *We had got it into the bag*). Salient differences of distribution are marked in bold to facilitate the discussion which follows.

Tables 6.4 and 6.5 consider the distribution of HAVE with noun phrases in interrogatives and negative declaratives. Visser (1969–73, pp. 1558–9) claims that it is not until 'well into the nineteenth century' that *do* and *have* were used together in questions and negatives, and the

Table 6.4 HAVE + NP in affirmative interrogatives (ICE sample)

	Distribution of tokens			
	ICE (NI)	**ICE (ROI)**	**ICE-Ireland**	**ICE-GB**
DO S have NP	**12**	**25**	37	33
HAVE S NP	7	**15**	22	**3**
HAVE S got NP	8	5	**13**	**29**
HAVE S Object VP	3	–	3	0
Total	30	45	75	65

Forms
Do you *have* any money? and so on (DO S have NP)
Have you any money? and so on (HAVE S NP)
Have you *got* any money? and so on (HAVE S got NP)
Had she her Christmas shopping *done*? and so on (HAVE S Object VP)

Table 6.5 HAVE + NP in negative declaratives (ICE sample)

	Distribution of tokens			
	ICE (NI)	ICE (ROI)	ICE-Ireland	ICE-GB
S DO NEG have NP	**42**	**27**	69	73
S HAVE NEG NP	40	33	**73**	**52**
S HAVE NEG got NP	3	13	**16**	**48**
Total	85	73	158	176

Forms
They *did* not *have* a clue, They *didn't have* a clue, and so on (S DO NEG have NP)
They *had* not a clue, They *hadn't* a clue, and so on (S HAVE NEG NP)
They *have* not *got* a clue, They *haven't got* a clue, and so on (S HAVE NEG got NP)

evidence which he produces (Visser 1969–73, pp. 1561–7) shows British examples only from 1816 onwards and American examples beginning from 1871, leaving Visser (1969–73, p. 1559) ultimately to conclude that 'it cannot be ascertained whether the usage appeared earlier in American English than in British English'. In considering Tables 6.4 and 6.5, we take the preference for HAVE and simple NP as evidence of historical conservatism, and the DO plus HAVE and HAVE *got* forms as innovations within the standard language.

One pattern emerges with striking regularity from the data of Tables 6.3–6.5: the use of HAVE *got* is very much more a feature of ICE-GB than of either of the ICE-Ireland corpora. In both negative and affirmative declaratives, tokens of HAVE with *got* in ICE-GB are almost exactly three times the number of tokens in ICE-Ireland. Although the proportion of forms with *got* in ICE-GB is lower in interrogatives than in negative declaratives, ICE-GB usage of HAVE *got* far outpaces that in ICE-Ireland for both categories. It is possible that close examination of the ICE corpora gives us some insight into the direction of language change in Ireland: if the use of HAVE *got* is increasing, it may be that it is doing so first through its use in interrogatives, before being incorporated into the system of affirmative declaratives. This generalization would be compatible with the strong evidence of a converse retention of the simple [HAVE S NP] pattern without *do* or *got* in the interrogatives of ICE-Ireland.

We should note, however, that while there is a fundamental difference in practice between ICE-Ireland and ICE-GB on the use of HAVE with DO and *got*, our evidence of differences within Ireland is more equivocal. Table 6.4 shows affirmative interrogatives with *DO* roughly twice as frequently in ICE (ROI) as in ICE (NI), while a similar pattern also holds for the simple [HAVE S NP] pattern. Conversely, though the use of HAVE *got* is very low in ICE-Ireland compared to its use in ICE-GB, ICE (NI) more closely resembles ICE (ROI) than ICE-GB on the frequency of this realization. The low frequency of affirmative interrogatives in ICE (NI) relative to the other corpora, however, tempers our ability to draw a conclusive generalization from this pattern. In fact, the data of Table 6.5, where ICE (ROI) aligns more closely than ICE (NI) to ICE (GB) for the use of HAVE *got*, calls out for further data analysis before reaching a definitive view on intra-island similarities or differences.

With regard to negation, we focus here on two aspects of a complex system: patterns in the distribution of *hasn't*, and a combination of syntactic and semantic features seen in the distribution of *never* as a negator. Table 6.6 examines patterns in the use of *hasn't* in the ICE Face-to-face conversation text files. Under consideration here is not only *hasn't* used with noun phrases, as discussed above, but *hasn't* as a true auxiliary preceding a main verb and *hasn't* as part of a tag question. Table 6.6 shows that although the frequency of occurrence of *hasn't* in the ICE-Ireland corpus appears to be uniform across the subcorpora, the distribution of functions is far from uniform. For the ICE (NI) corpus, *hasn't* functions mainly as an Auxiliary, with no tag question usage and minimal distribution on some other functions. ICE (ROI), however, shows only 50 per cent usage of auxiliary *hasn't*, and a wider distribution across other types. With regard to auxiliary usage, the ICE (ROI) corpus is thus virtually identical with ICE-GB, though it does not share the high frequency of tag question usage in the British corpus.

In terms of our investigative hypotheses, Table 6.6 gives some support to the single-island hypothesis, in showing a reduced use of auxiliary *hasn't* in both ICE-Ireland corpora relative to ICE-GB. A tendency to favour the simple past tense over the perfect has long been attributed to Irish English (see Hayden and Hartog, 1909, p. 937; Henry, 1957, p. 19; Harris, 1984, p. 317; and Milroy, 1984, p. 21), and while the lexical search here does not test this possibility directly, it may offer a partial island-wide confirmation of it. The relatively low use of *hasn't* in canonical tag questions in ICE-Ireland may reflect the use of constructions (including those shared with Scots) that have the discourse functions of tag questions but do not involve subject–auxiliary inversion. These forms (seen in tags such as *That's delicious, **so it is***) do not show up in the same searches as those which give rise to Table 6.6, and so call for a

Table 6.6 Constraints and patterns for *hasn't* in ICE Face-to-face conversations

	Distribution of tokens			
	ICE (NI)	**ICE (ROI)**	**ICE-Ireland**	**ICE-GB**
S hasn't NP	1	1	2	3
S hasn't got NP	–	2	2	8
S hasn't VP	5	4	9	22
Tag question	–	1	1	10
F *hasn't*/1,000	0.1	0.1	0.1	0.2
Auxiliary *hasn't* %	83	50	64	51
Tag question *hasn't* %	0	12	7	22

Forms
Well he *hasn't* a good job (S hasn't NP)
Met Peter Kavanagh that *hasn't got* a bit of grammar in his head (S hasn't got NP)
He *hasn't* changed much (S hasn't VP) [auxiliary *hasn't*]
Tom has a quare bike *hasn't* he (tag question)

fuller investigation of sentence tags within ICE corpora generally. Following the approach seen in Kirk *et al.* (2003), Tables 6.6 and 6.7 show not only the raw frequency of occurrence for each of the relevant forms, but the frequency of occurrence of the form per thousand words of ICE text (F/1,000).

Negation with *never* is different from many other forms of negation in English, in that it cannot be contracted or cliticized with a subject or auxiliary, and so does not show morphological variability. Unlike negation with *not*, a speaker must either negate with full *never* or choose some other negative marker. The semantic constraints on *never* are complex and go beyond the scope of this chapter: for discussion see Miller (1993, p. 115; 2003, p. 88; 2004, p. 51), Görlach (2002, p. 105) and Beal (2004, pp. 125–6). The basic question which faces us here is whether *never* is used with a bare past tense verb form (favouring a punctual interpretation of *never*, as in *I waited but he never came*), or whether it is used with perfective *have* (favouring durative reference and often accompanied by durative adverbials, as in *He has never been to see me*). Although we cannot posit a strictly analogous correlation between punctual reference and the use of *never* with bare verbs and durative reference with the use of *never* and auxiliaries, we do suggest that a corpus with a high percentage of *never* and bare verbs (the first two realizational categories of Table 6.7) implies a high proportion of *never* used with punctual reference. With this tendency in mind, we

Table 6.7 Constraints and patterns for *never* in ICE Face-to-face conversations

	Distribution of tokens			
	ICE (NI)	**ICE (ROI)**	**ICE-Ireland**	**ICE-GB**
S BE never X	5	1	6	7
S never VP (Main verb)	57	26	**83**	**47**
S AUX never VP (Auxiliary)	41	26	67	74
#Never	10	6	16	23
Other *never* (not analysed)	8	2	10	20
Total analysed *never*	113	59	172	151
F analysed *never*/1000	1.3	0.7	1.0	0.9
Never with copula, main verb %	55	46	**52**	**36**
Auxiliary *never* %	36	**44**	39	**49**

Forms
He *was* never poor [implies punctual reference] (S BE never X)
I never *heard* a sound and I went to bed [implies punctual reference] (S never VP: main verb)
I've never seen the guy *in my life* [implies durative reference] (S AUX never VP: auxiliary)
Never do anything you can get away with not doing (#Never)

understand the data of Table 6.7, in which the two ICE-Ireland corpora show considerably greater use of *never* with main verbs relative to that found in ICE-GB, to show a continuum for this feature. ICE (NI) appears well in advance in the use of *never* with main verbs, with ICE (ROI) in an intermediate position, and ICE-GB showing proportionately more usage of *never* with auxiliaries and in other patterns that are not analysed here. Table 6.7 invites comparisons with the use of punctual *never* in Scotland and points us in the direction of the dialectal–historical hypothesis to account for the observed patterns of difference, without ignoring the presence of punctual *never* in ICE (ROI).

3.7 'Standard' syntax: ICE-Ireland and subordinate clauses

Finally we come to an area of potential linguistic variation which lies well beyond the realm of governmental policy or, as far as we know, any prescriptive grammatical practice in Ireland: the use of different subordinate clause types. Because of the abstract and pervasive nature of this aspect of linguistic structure, we consider this area to offer a particularly good chance to test the default hypothesis which predicts similarity across ICE corpora as a reflex of the standardization process in general. For this purpose, we have investigated 25,148 words of ICE-Ireland, taking from each subcorpus one text of Popular publication, Learned publication, Social letters, Unscripted speeches, Broadcast discussion and Face-to-face conversation. This sample is designed to match the distribution of text categories found in the 89,051 words of ICE-GB investigated by Greenbaum *et al.* (1996). Our continuing analysis of all 1,564 subordinate clauses in this sample of ICE-Ireland involves the following distinctions: ICE (NI) versus ICE (ROI); spoken texts versus written texts; levels of formality in both spoken and written text categories; finite versus non-finite verbs in subordinate clauses; and the use of complement clauses, adverbial clauses, restrictive relative clauses, non-restrictive relative clauses, nominal relatives, comparative clauses, degree-intensifying clauses and some other infrequent types. A detailed presentation of results would lie outside the scope of this chapter, and again we can do no more than sample results and demonstrate the potential for deeper analysis. We demonstrate two aspects of relative clause distribution here: Table 6.8 shows the distribution of subordinate clause types across ICE-Ireland and ICE-GB, while Table 6.9 shows the frequency of finite and non-finite complement clauses in speech versus writing across the different corpus samples.

Table 6.8 analyses the subordinate clauses of our sample in terms of four main functional categories: (a) complement clauses (*I couldn't believe that she was going to let me jump* – ICE (NI)), (b) adverbial clauses (*She died a year later when she was almost 112 years old* – ICE (ROI)), (c) restrictive relative clauses (*It's the highest compliment I can pay him* – ICE (ROI)), and (d) others, primarily nominal relatives, such as *I've just divided them up into what I've described as fundamental factors, genetic*

Table 6.8 Distribution of subordinate clauses (ICE sample)

	Clause type (%)				
Corpus	**Complement**	**Adverbial**	**Restrictive relative**	**Other**	**Total (%)**
ICE (NI)	49.7	23.4	26.6	0.3	100
ICE (ROI)	46.0	26.7	25.2	2.1	100
ICE-GB	40.2	26.8	23.5	9.6	100

Table 6.9 Frequency of finite and non-finite complement clauses in speech and writing

			Frequency of complement clause per 1,000 words	
Corpus	**Mode**	**No-of words**	**Finite**	**Non-finite**
ICE (NI)	Written	6,604	12.6	12.9
	Spoken	5,927	**25.3**	**17.0**
ICE (ROI)	Written	6,432	14.6	13.3
	Spoken	6,185	**15.7**	**17.3**
ICE-GB	Written	25,286	9.0	12.4
	Spoken	63,765	**17.5**	**7.3**

influences ... or early learning practices – ICE (NI), and non-restrictive relative clauses, as in *You have five readings which are evenly spread* – ICE (ROI). Table 6.8 shows that, apart from a relatively high frequency for complement clauses in ICE (NI) and for 'other' clause types in ICE-GB (which may be partly attributable to methodological considerations), the frequencies across the two Irish subcorpora and ICE-GB are highly similar. These similarities may be taken as evidence in support of our default hypothesis.

While Table 6.8 shows a relatively strong degree of congruence across the ICE samples under consideration, Table 6.9 shows that whereas finite complement clauses are approximately twice as frequent in spoken language relative to written language in both ICE (NI) and ICE-GB, the distribution between speech and writing in ICE (ROI) is much more evenly balanced. On the other hand, Table 6.9 also shows that with non-finite complement clauses, the two subcorpora of ICE-Ireland are very similar but are at odds with ICE-GB, where the frequency of spoken non-finite clauses is nearly half that for written clauses.

4 Conclusion: ICE-Ireland – past, present and future

With the completion of the task of collecting data for ICE-Ireland and the conversion of transcribed material into a machine-readable database following ICE principles, we are, as discussed in this chapter, in a position to examine a wide range of topics in the development of Standard English in Ireland and elsewhere. ICE-Ireland is very much dependent on the understandings which govern ICE projects generally: it is not an ideal place to find information on questions of dialectology or variation in vernacular English in Ireland, nor on the effects which historical and contemporary bilingualism with Irish have had on the development of Irish English, nor on the interactions between Standard Irish English and Ulster Scots. Even in considering these questions, however, ICE-Ireland does have a significant role to play in demonstrating the degree to which the 'standard' language maintains continuity and points of contact with other types of English as spoken in Ireland and elsewhere. Moreover, ICE-Ireland is well-placed to shed light on the role which has been played by the different governmental structures which exist on a single island with a linguistically complex history.

In generating and evaluating the four hypotheses which we discuss above, we have tried to understand the limits of 'official' language intervention in relation to dialectal history and the global spread of English (on the wider relations between language globalization and the development of vernaculars, see, for example, Meyerhoff and Niedzielski, 2003). We find that there is no single pattern or hypothesis which accounts for all the data we have sampled from the ICE-Ireland corpus. What we propose instead is that the corpora we have considered (and, indeed, other ICE corpora) share a common element of 'Standard' English that is relatively invariant across national divisions. Alongside this common core, we may also identify points of variability that characterize each corpus, no matter how 'standardized' the corpus is. In some cases, variability coincides with national boundaries: the case of lexical uses related to specific state institutions is an obvious case in point. More often in our data, however, variation arises due to differential dialectal and linguistic histories, the differential pace of change in progress, and other aspects of language choice which we are at this point still short of understanding fully. This diversity of results demonstrates the value of the ICE-Ireland corpus in showing the complexity of 'Standard' English, the diversity within it, and the contradictory dynamics which affect the choices made by speakers and writers, even within supposedly standardized language. It is in this array of choices that we find the sources of variation and change in the system and structure of language generally. While the ideology of 'standard' language may predispose some analysts to dismiss the existence of language variation at the level of linguistic standard (or to account for variation by excluding it as non-standard interference in the standard language) we go so far as to argue that the overall picture that emerges in ICE-Ireland, combining common patterns of usage with variation at local and contextual levels, will hold true of other studies of standard Englishes around the world. In short, our investigation of 'Standard' English in Ireland suggests to us that the ICE project, far from collecting a uniform corpus of international English, provides for a structured investigation of what it means to develop local variations on global standards. The understanding of this diversity in world Englishes should also encourage many further investigations of the means by which languages manage diversity, continuity and change.

5 Acknowledgements

No undertaking of this size would be possible without the help of a large number of people who have given generously of their time and helped in other ways to create the ICE-Ireland corpus. We are grateful to the many students from Trinity College Dublin and Queen's University Belfast who assisted in data collection. We wish to note our gratitude as well to others who have been involved in the project at different stages, notably Goodith White, Francisco Gonzalvez Garcia, the late Ciaran Laffey, Tom Norton, Hildegard Tristram, Irene Forsthoff, Marlies Lofing, Mary Pat O'Malley and Margaret Mannion. Our assistants and partners in the AHRB-funded project on the sociolinguistics of Standard English in Ireland, Orla Lowry and Anne Rooney, have been of invaluable assistance to us. Funding from the Arts and Humanities Research Board and from the Royal Irish Academy and the British Council Social Sciences Committee have been essential to the development of this project and is gratefully acknowledged. Finally, of course, special thanks go to the host of speakers, writers and broadcasters who have kindly given permission for their contributions to be included in ICE-Ireland.

Notes

1. ICE-Ireland is not yet available for public dissemination. Pending the outcome of all discussions on copyright and permission for the creation of ICE-Ireland files, the final version of ICE-Ireland which will be made available to academic users may not entirely match the working version of ICE-Ireland which is reported on here. Any final discrepancies between these versions of ICE-Ireland, however, are expected to be quite minor. We are grateful to Anne Rooney and Orla Lowry, research assistants on the ICE-Ireland project, for the text statistics provided in Table 6.1.

References

Adams, G. B. 1958. 'The emergence of Ulster as a distinct dialect area'. *Ulster Folklife* 4:61–73.

Adams, G. B. (ed.). 1964. *Ulster Dialects: An Introductory Symposium*. Cultra Manor: Ulster Folk Museum.

Adams, G. B. 1981. Letter from G. B. Adams in reply to M. V. Barry's article 'Towards a description of a regional standard pronunciation of English in Ulster'. *NISLF Journal* 7:70–7.

Barry, M. V. 1980. 'Towards a description of a regional standard pronunciation of English in Ulster'. *NISLF Journal* 6:43–7.

Barry, M. V. (ed.). 1981a. *Aspects of English Dialects in Ireland, Volume 1*. Belfast: Queen's University of Belfast.

Barry, M. V. 1981b. 'Towards a description of a regional standard pronunciation of English in Ulster'. *Aspects of English Dialects in Ireland, Volume 1*, ed. by M. V. Barry, pp. 47–51. Belfast: Queen's University of Belfast.

Barry, M. V. 1981c. 'The southern boundaries of northern Hiberno-English speech'. *Aspects of English Dialects in Ireland, Volume 1*. ed. By M. V. Barry, pp. 52–95. Belfast: Queen's University of Belfast.

Barry, M. V. and P. Tilling (eds). 1986. *The English Dialects of Ulster: An Anthology of Articles on Ulster Speech by G. B. Adams*. Cultra Manor: Ulster Folk and Transport Museum.

Bauer, L. 1991. 'Who speaks New Zealand English?' Unpublished ICE working paper.

Beal, J. C. 2004. 'English dialects in the North of England: morphology and syntax'. *A Handbook of Varieties of English, Volume 2*, ed. by B. Kortmann, K. Burridge, R. Mesthrie, E. W. Schneider and C. Upton, pp. 114–41. Berlin: Mouton de Gruyter.

Bex, T. and R. J. Watts (eds). 1999. *Standard English: the Widening Debate*. London: Routledge.

Bliss, A. 1972. 'A Synge glossary'. *Sunshine and the Moon's Delight*, ed. by S. B. Bushrui, pp. 297–316. Gerrards Cross and Beirut: Colin Smythe and The American University of Beirut.

Bliss, A. 1979. *Spoken English in Ireland 1600–1740: Twenty-Seven Representative Texts Assembled & Analysed*. Dublin: Dolmen Press.

Bliss, A. 1984. 'English in the south of Ireland'. *Language in the British Isles*, ed. by P. Trudgill, pp. 135–52. Cambridge: Cambridge University Press.

Braidwood, J. 1964. 'Ulster and Elizabethan English'. *Ulster Dialects: An Introductory Symposium*, ed. by G. B. Adams, pp. 5–109. Cultra Manor: Ulster Folk Museum.

Clarke, S. 1997. 'The role of Irish English in the formation of New World Englishes: the case from Newfoundland'. *Focus on Ireland*, ed. by J. L. Kallen, pp. 207–25. Amsterdam: Benjamins.

Collins, A. 1997. 'Diphthongization of (o) in Claddagh Hiberno-English: a network study'. *Focus on Ireland*, ed. by J. L. Kallen, pp. 153–70. Amsterdam: Benjamins.

Corrigan, K. P. 2000a. 'What are 'small clauses' doing in South Armagh English, Irish and Planter English?' *The Celtic Englishes II*, ed. by H. L. C. Tristram, pp. 75–96. Heidelberg: Universitätsverlag Carl Winter.

Corrigan, K. P. 2000b. '"What bees to be maun be": aspects of deontic and epistemic modality in a northern dialect of Irish English'. *English World-Wide* 21:25–62.

Dolan, T. P. 2004. *A Dictionary of Hiberno-English*, 2nd edn. Dublin: Gill & Macmillan.

Eitner, W. H. 1991 [1951]. 'Affirmative "any more" in present-day American English'. *Dialects of English: Studies in Grammatical Variation*, ed. by P. Trudgill and J. K. Chambers, pp. 267–72. London: Longman.

Farr, F. and A. O'Keeffe. 2002. '*Would* as a hedging device in an Irish context: an intra-varietal comparison of institutionalized spoken interaction'. *Using Corpora to Explore Linguistic Variation*, ed. by R. Reppen, S. Fitzmaurice and D. Biber, pp. 25–48. Amsterdam: Benjamins.

Fenton, J. 2000. *The Hamely Tongue: A Personal Record of Ulster-Scots in County Antrim*. Revised and expanded edn. [N.p.]: The Ullans Press.

Fiess, A. 2000. 'Age-group differentiation in the spoken language of rural East Galway?' *The Celtic Englishes II*, ed. by H. L. C. Tristram, pp. 188–209. Heidelberg: Universitätsverlag Carl Winter.

Filppula, M. 1986. *Some Aspects of Hiberno-English in a Functional Sentence Perspective*. Joensuu: University of Joensuu.

Filppula, M. 1997. 'The influence of Irish on perfect marking in Hiberno-English: the case of the "Extended-now" perfect'. *Focus on Ireland*, ed. by J. L. Kallen, pp. 51–71. Amsterdam: Benjamins.

Filppula, M. 1999. *The Grammar of Irish English: Language in Hibernian Style*. London: Routledge.

Filppula, M. 2001. 'Irish influence in Hiberno-English: some problems of argumentation'. *Language Links: The Languages of Scotland and Ireland*, ed. by J. M. Kirk. and D. P. Ó Baoill, pp. 23–42. Belfast: Cló Ollscoil na Banríona.

Filppula, M. 2004. 'Irish English: morphology and syntax'. *A Handbook of Varieties of English, Volume 2*, ed. by B. Kortmann, K. Burridge, R. Mesthrie, E. W. Schneider and C. Upton, pp. 73–101. Berlin: Mouton de Gruyter.

Görlach, M. 1995. 'Irish English and Irish culture in dictionaries of English'. *More Englishes*, ed. by M. Görlach, pp. 164–91. Amsterdam: Benjamins.

Görlach, M. 2002. *A Textual History of Scots*. Heidelberg: Universitätsverlag C. Winter.

Greenbaum, S. 1988. 'A proposal for an International Corpus of English'. *World Englishes* 7:315.

Greenbaum, S. (ed.). 1996a. *Comparing English Worldwide: The International Corpus of English*. Oxford: Clarendon Press.

Greenbaum, S. 1996b. 'Introducing ICE'. *Comparing English Worldwide: The International Corpus of English*, ed. by S. Greenbaum, pp. 3–12. Oxford: Clarendon Press.

Greenbaum, S., G. Nelson and M. Weitzman. 1996. 'Complement clauses in English'. *Using Corpora for Language Research*, ed. by J. Thomas and M. Short, pp. 76–91. London: Longman.

Gregg, R. J. 1972. 'The Scotch–Irish dialect boundaries in Ulster'. *Patterns in the Folk Speech of the British Isles*, ed. by M. F. Wakelin, pp. 109–39. London: Athlone Press.

Harris, J. 1983. 'The Hiberno-English "I've it eaten" construction: what is it and where does it come from?' *Teanga* 3:30–43. (Reprinted in Ó Baoill, D. P. (ed.) 1985. *Papers on Irish English*. Dublin: Irish Association for Applied Linguistics.)

Harris, J. 1984. 'Syntactic variation and dialect divergence'. *Journal of Linguistics* 20:303–27.

Harris, J. 1985. *The Polylectal Grammar Stops Here*. CLCS Occasional Paper, 13. Dublin: Centre for Language and Communication Studies, University of Dublin, Trinity College.

Harris, J. 1993. 'The grammar of Irish English'. *Real English: The Grammar of English Dialects in the British Isles*, ed. by J. Milroy and L. Milroy, pp. 139–86. London: Longman.

Hayden, M. and M. Hartog. 1909. 'The Irish dialect of English: its origins and vocabulary'. *The Fortnightly Review* New ser. 85:775–85, 933–47.

Henry, A. 1995. *Belfast English and Standard English: Dialect Variation and Parameter Setting*. Oxford: Oxford University Press.

Henry, P. L. 1957. *An Anglo-Irish Dialect of North Roscommon*. Dublin: Department of English, University College Dublin.

Henry, P. L. 1958. 'A linguistic survey of Ireland: preliminary report'. *Lochlann* 1:49–208.

Hickey, R. 1997. 'Arguments for creolisation in Irish English'. *Language History and Linguistic Modelling: A Festschrift for Jacek Fisiak on his 60th Birthday*, ed. by R. Hickey and S. Puppel, pp. 969–1038. Berlin: Mouton de Gruyter.

Hickey, R. 1999. 'Dublin English: current changes and their motivation'. *Urban Voices: Accent Studies in the British Isles*. ed. by P. Foulkes and G. Docherty, pp. 265–81. London: Arnold.

Hickey, R. 2000. 'Models for describing aspect in Irish English'. *The Celtic Englishes II*, ed. by H. L. C. Tristram, pp. 97–116. Heidelberg: Universitätsverlag Carl Winter.

Hickey, R. 2001. 'The south-east of Ireland: a neglected region of dialect study'. *Language Links: The Languages of Scotland and Ireland*, ed. by J. M. Kirk. and D. P. Ó Baoill, pp. 1–22. Belfast: Cló Ollscoil na Banríona.

Hogan, J. 1927. *The English Language in Ireland*. Dublin: The Educational Company of Ireland.

Holmes, J. 1996. 'The New Zealand spoken component of ICE: some methodological challenges'. *Comparing English Worldwide: The International Corpus of English*, ed. by S. Greenbaum, pp. 163–81. Oxford: Clarendon Press.

Hume, A. 1858. 'The Irish dialect of the English language'. *The Ulster Journal of Archaeology* 6:47–56.

Hume, A. 1877–78. 'Remarks on the Irish dialect of the English language'. *Transactions of the Historic Society of Lancashire and Cheshire*, 3rd ser., 6:93–140.

ICE-GB. 1998. *ICE-GB: The International Corpus of English: The British component*. CD-ROM. London: Survey of English Usage.

Joyce, P. W. 1910. *English as we Speak it in Ireland*. Dublin: Gill. (Reprinted Dublin: Wolfhound Press, 1979, 1988.)

Kallen, J. L. 1989. 'Tense and aspect categories in Irish English'. *English World-Wide* 10:1–39.

Kallen, J. L. 1990. 'The Hiberno-English perfect: grammaticalization revisited'. *Irish University Review* 20(1):120–36.

Kallen, J. L. 1991. 'Sociolinguistic variation and methodology: *after* as a Dublin variable'. *English around the World: Sociolinguistic Perspectives*, ed. by J. Cheshire, pp. 61–74. Cambridge: Cambridge University Press.

Kallen, J. L. 1996. 'Entering lexical fields in Irish English'. *Speech Past and Present: Studies in English Dialectology in Memory of Ossi Ihalainen*, ed. by J. Klemola, M. Kytö and M. Rissanen, pp. 101–29. Frankfurt am Main: Peter Lang.

Kallen, J. L. 1997. 'Irish English and World English: lexical perspectives'. *Englishes around the World: Studies in Honour of Manfred Görlach*, ed. by E. W. Schneider, pp. 139–57. Amsterdam: Benjamins.

Kallen, J. L. 1999. 'Irish English and the Ulster Scots controversy'. *Ulster Folklife* 45:70–85.

Kallen, J. L. 2000. 'Two languages, two borders, one island: some linguistic and political borders in Ireland'. *International Journal of the Sociology of Language* 145:29–63.

Kallen, J. L. 2005. 'Internal and external factors in phonological convergence: the case of English /t/ lenition'. *Dialect Change: Convergence and Divergence in European Languages*, ed. by P. Auer, F. Hinskens and P. Kerswill, pp. 51–80. Cambridge: Cambridge University Press.

Kallen, J. L. and J. M. Kirk. 2001. 'Aspects of the verb phrase in Standard Irish English: a corpus-based approach'. *Language Links: The Languages of Scotland and Ireland*, ed. by J. M. Kirk and D. P. Ó Baoill, pp. 59–79. Belfast: Cló Ollscoil na Banríona.

Kirk, J. M. 1991 [1990]. *Northern Ireland Transcribed Corpus of Speech. OCP-compatible Electronic Text.* Revised version. Colchester: Economic and Social Research Council Data Archive, University of Essex.

Kirk, J. M. 1992. 'The Northern Ireland Transcribed Corpus of Speech'. *New Directions in English Language Corpora*, ed. by G. Leitner, pp. 65–73. Berlin: Mouton de Gruyter.

Kirk, J. M. 1997. 'Subordinate clauses in English'. *Journal of English Linguistics* 25:349–364.

Kirk, J. M. 1999. 'The dialect vocabulary of Ulster'. *Cuadernos de Filología Inglesa* 8:305–34

Kirk, J. M., J. L. Kallen, O. Lowry and A. Rooney. 2003. 'Sociolinguistics of standardization of English in Ireland: some insights from negation'. Queen's University Belfast School of English Research Seminar, December 2003.

Kirk, J. M., J. L. Kallen, O. Lowry and A. Rooney. 2004a. 'Issues arising from the compilation of ICE-Ireland'. *Belfast Working Papers in Language and Linguistics* 16:23–41.

Kirk, J. M., J. L. Kallen, O. Lowry and A. Rooney. 2004b. 'Standard Irish English: the four hypotheses'. Paper presented at the ICAME 25 Conference, Verona. 19–23 May.

Kirk, J. M., J. L. Kallen, O. Lowry and A. Rooney. 2005. 'The ICE-Ireland Corpus and the PPD corpus'. Paper presented at Queen's University, Belfast.

Labov, W. 1991 [1973]. 'The boundaries of grammar: inter-dialectal reactions to positive *anymore*'. *Dialects of English: Studies in Grammatical Variation*, ed. by P. Trudgill and J. K. Chambers, pp. 273–88. London: Longman.

Lass, R. 1990. 'Early mainland residues in southern Hiberno-English'. *Irish University Review* 20(1):137–48.

Macafee, C. I. (ed.). 1996. *Concise Ulster Dictionary*. Oxford: Oxford University Press.

Mair, C. [n. d.]. 'Problems in the compilation of a corpus of standard Caribbean English: a pilot study'. Unpublished ICE working paper.

Mallory, J. P. (ed.). 1999. *Language in Ulster/Ulster Folklife*: Special Issue, *Ulster Folklife* 45.

McCafferty, K. 1999a. '"I'll be after telling dee de raison …": *Be after V-ing* as a future gram in Irish English, 1601–1750'. Paper presented at the Celtic Englishes conference, Potsdam, 1999.

McCafferty, K. 1999b. '(London)Derry: between Ulster and local speech – class, ethnicity and language change'. *Urban Voices: Accent Studies in the British Isles*, ed. by P. Foulkes and G. Docherty, pp. 246–64. London: Arnold.

McCafferty, K. 2001. *Ethnicity and Language Change: English in (London)Derry, Northern Ireland*. Amsterdam: Benjamins.

McCafferty, K. 2004. '*Be after V-ing* on the past grammaticalization path: how far is it after coming?' Paper presented at the Celtic Englishes conference, Potsdam, 2004.

Meyerhoff, M. and N. Niedzielski. 2003. 'The globalization of vernacular variation'. *Journal of Sociolinguistics* 7:534–55.

Miller, J. 1993. 'The grammar of Scottish English'. *Real English: The Grammar of English Dialects in the British Isles*, ed. by J. Milroy and L. Milroy, pp. 99–138. London: Longman.

Miller, J. 2003. 'Syntax and discourse in modern Scots'. *The Edinburgh Companion to Scots*, ed. by J. Corbett, J. D. McClure and J. Stuart-Smith, pp. 72–109. Edinburgh: Edinburgh University Press.

Miller, J. 2004. 'Scottish English: morphology and syntax'. *A Handbook of Varieties of English, Volume 2*, ed. by B. Kortmann, K. Burridge, R. Mesthrie, E. W. Schneider and C. Upton, pp. 47–72. Berlin: Mouton de Gruyter.

Milroy, J. and L. Milroy. 1985. 'Linguistic change, social network and speaker innovation'. *Journal of Linguistics* 21:339–84.

Milroy, J. and L. Milroy. 1999. *Authority in Language: Investigating Standard English*, 3rd edn. London: Routledge.

Milroy, L. 1984. 'Comprehension and context: successful communication and communicative breakdown'. *Applied Sociolinguistics*, ed. by P. Trudgill, pp. 7–31. London: Academic Press.

Milroy, L. 1987 [1980]. *Language and Social Networks*, 2nd edn. Oxford: Basil Blackwell.

Montgomery, M. 1989. 'Exploring the roots of Appalachian English'. *English World-Wide* 10:227–78.

Montgomery, M. 1993. 'The lexicography of Hiberno-English'. *Working Papers in Irish Studies* 93(3):20–35.

Montgomery, M. 2000. 'The Celtic element in American English'. *The Celtic Englishes II*, ed. by H. L. C. Tristram, pp. 231–64. Heidelberg: Universitätsverlag C. Winter.

Montgomery, M. 2001. 'On the trail of early Ulster emigrant letters'. *Atlantic Crossroads: Historical Connections between Scotland, Ulster, and North America*, ed. by P. Fitzgerald and S. Ickringill, pp. 13–26. Newtownards: Colourpoint Books.

Montgomery, M. and P. Robinson. 1996. 'Ulster English as Janus: language contact across the Irish Sea and across the North Atlantic'. *Language Contact across the North Atlantic*, ed. by P. Sture Ureland and Iain Clarkson, pp. 411–26. Tübingen: Max Niemeyer.

Moylan, S. 1996. *The Language of Kilkenny: Lexicon, Semantics, Structures*. Dublin: Geography Publications.

Nelson, G. 1996a. 'The design of the corpus'. *Comparing English Worldwide: The International Corpus of English*, ed. by S. Greenbaum, pp. 27–35. Oxford: Clarendon Press.

Nelson, G. 1996b. 'Markup systems'. *Comparing English Worldwide: The International Corpus of English*, ed. by S. Greenbaum, pp. 36–53. Oxford: Clarendon Press.

Nelson, G., S. Wallis and B. Aarts. 2002. *Exploring Natural Language: Working with the British Component of the International Corpus of English*. Amsterdam: Benjamins.

Ní Ghallchóir, C. 1981. 'Aspects of bilingualism in Northwest Donegal'. *Aspects of English Dialects in Ireland, Volume 1*, ed. by M. V. Barry, pp. 142–70. Belfast: Queen's University of Belfast.

Ó Baoill, D. P. 1997. 'The emerging Irish phonological substratum in Irish English'. *Focus on Ireland*, ed. by J. L. Kallen, pp. 73–87. Amsterdam: Benjamins.

Ó Cuív, B. 1951. *Irish Dialects and Irish-Speaking Districts*. Dublin: Dublin Institute for Advanced Studies.

Odlin, T. 1995. *Causation in Language Contact: A Devilish Problem*. CLCS Occasional Paper 41. Dublin: Centre for Language and Communication Studies, University of Dublin, Trinity College.

Ó Muirithe, D. 1996. *A Dictionary of Anglo-Irish*. Dublin: Four Courts Press.

O'Rahilly, T. F. 1932. *Irish Dialects: Past and Present*. Dublin: Browne and Nolan.

Sammon, P. 2002. *Greenspeak: Ireland in Her Own Words*. Dublin: Townhouse.

Share, B. 2001. *Naming Names: Who, What, Where in Irish Nomenclature*. Dublin: Gill & Macmillan.

Share, B. 2003. *Slanguage: A Dictionary of Irish Slang*, 2nd edn. Dublin: Gill & Macmillan.

Tilling, P. M. 1985. 'A tape-recorded survey of Hiberno-English in its context'. *Papers on Irish English*, ed. by D. P. Ó Baoill, pp. 16–26. Dublin: Irish Association for Applied Linguistics.

Todd, L. 1989. *The Language of Irish Literature*. London: Macmillan Education.

Todd, L. 1990. *Words Apart: A Dictionary of Northern Ireland English*. Gerrards Cross: Colin Smythe.

Traynor, M. 1953. *The English Dialect of Donegal: A Glossary*. Dublin: Royal Irish Academy.

Trudgill, P. 1984. 'Standard English in England'. *Language in the British Isles*, ed. by P. Trudgill, pp. 32–44. Cambridge: Cambridge University Press.

Trudgill, P. 1999. 'Standard English: what it isn't'. *Standard English: The Widening Debate*, ed. by T. Bex and R. J. Watts, pp. 117–28. London: Routledge.

Upton, C., D. Parry and J. D. A. Widdowson (eds). 1994. *Survey of English Dialects: The Dictionary and Grammar*. London: Routledge.

van Hamel, A. G. 1912. 'On Anglo-Irish syntax'. *Englische Studien* 45:272–92.

Visser, F. Th. 1969–73. *An Historical Syntax of the English Language*. Revised edn. 3 parts. Leiden: Brill.

Wagner, H. 1958. *Linguistic Atlas and Survey of Irish Dialects*. 4 vols. Dublin: Dublin Institute for Advanced Studies.

Wall, R. 1990. 'Dialect in Irish literature: the hermetic core'. *Irish University Review* 20(1):8–18.

Wall, R. 2001. *An Irish Literary Dictionary and Glossary*. Gerrards Cross: Colin Smythe.

Wright, J. (ed.). 1898–1905. *The English Dialect Dictionary*. 6 vols. Oxford: Henry Frowde.

Younge, K. E. 1923–24. 'Irish idioms in English speech'. *The Gaelic Churchman* 5:155, 167, 214–15, 225, 241, 257–8, 266–7, 286–7.

Zwickl, S. 2002. *Language Attitudes, Ethnic Identity and Dialect Use across the Northern Ireland Border: Armagh and Monaghan*. Belfast: Cló Ollscoil na Banríona.

Websites

Centre for Linguistic Research. 'The influence of the languages of Ireland and Scotland on linguistic varieties in northern England'. Conference, 28 June 2004 (accessed 18 August 2004): http://www.abdn.ac.uk/langling/resources/sympprog.html

ICE East Africa website. The East African Component of the International Corpus of English home page (accessed 18 August 2004): http://www.tu-chemnitz.de/phil/english/chairs/linguist/real/independent/ eafrica/corpus.htm

ICE website. International Corpus of English home page (accessed 18 August 2004): http://www.ucl.ac.uk/english-usage/ice/index.htm

7
The TalkBank Project

Brian MacWhinney

1 Introduction

Recent years have seen a phenomenal growth in computer power and connectivity. The computer on the desktop of the average academic researcher now has the power of room-size supercomputers of the 1980s. Using the internet, we can connect in seconds to the other side of the world and transfer huge amounts of text, programs, audio and video. Our computers are equipped with programs that allow us to view, link and modify this material without even having to think about programming. Nearly all of the major journals are now available in electronic form and the very nature of journals and publication is undergoing radical change.

These new trends have led to dramatic advances in the methodology of science and engineering. However, the social and behavioural sciences have not shared fully in these advances. In large part, this is because the data used in the social sciences are not well-structured patterns of DNA sequences or atomic collisions in supercolliders. Much of our data is based on the messy, ill-structured behaviours of humans as they participate in social interactions. Categorizing and coding these behaviours is an enormous task in itself. Moving on to the next step of constructing a comprehensive database of human interactions in multimedia format is a goal that few of us have even dared to consider. However, recent innovations in internet and database technology provide excellent methods for building this new facility. Unlike the structured databases of relational database programs like Excel or Access, the new database formats are designed specifically to handle messy, ill-structured data, such as that found in human communication. XML tools developed by the World Wide Web Consortium or

W3C (http://w3c.org) can be applied to represent language data. The interlocking framework of XML programs and protocols allows us to build new systems for accessing and sharing spoken language data. At the same time, improvements in computer speed, disk storage, removable storage and connectivity are making it easier and easier for users with only a modest investment in equipment to share in this revolution.

Among the many fields studying human communication, there are two that have already begun to make use of these new opportunities. One of these fields is the child language acquisition community. Beginning in 1984, with help from the MacArthur Foundation, and later National Institute of Health and National Science Foundation, MacWhinney and Snow (1985) developed a system for sharing language-learning data called the Child Language Data Exchange System (CHILDES). This system has been used extensively and forms the backbone of much of the research in child language of the last 15 years. A second field in which data-sharing has become the norm is the area of speech technology. There, with support from Defense Advanced Research Projects Agency (DARPA) and a consortium of businesses and universities, Mark Liberman and Steven Bird have organized the Linguistic Data Consortium (LDC). The corpora of the LDC now also function as the backbone for the development and evaluation of technologies for automatic speech recognition and generation.

Recognizing the positive role of data-sharing in these two fields, and the need for improvement in infrastructure for the social sciences (http://vis.sdsc.edu/sbe/), the National Science Foundation provided funding for a new project called TalkBank (http://talkbank.org). The goal of the project is to support data-sharing and direct, community-wide access to naturalistic recordings and transcripts of human and animal communication. TalkBank has identified these seven shared needs:

1. Guidelines for ethical sharing of data
2. Metadata and infrastructure for identifying available data
3. Common, well-specified formats for text, audio and video
4. Tools for time-aligned transcription and annotation
5. A common interchange format for annotations
6. Network-based infrastructure to support efficient (real time) collaboration
7. Education of researchers to the existence of shared data, tools, standards and best practices.

In order to understand where the TalkBank Project is heading, we need to step back a bit to take a look at how students of human behaviour and communication have been analysing their data up to now.

2 Transcription

The focus of TalkBank is on the study of all forms of spoken or signed interactions, although written interactions are also of occasional interest. Whatever the specific format, each communicative interaction produces a complex pattern of linguistic, motoric and autonomic behaviour. In order to study these patterns, scientists produce transcripts that are designed to capture the raw behaviour in terms of patterns of words and other codes. The construction of these transcripts is a difficult process that faces three major obstacles.

2.1 Lack of coding standards

The first major obstacle is the lack of established coding standards that can be quickly and reliably entered into computer files. The most complex set of codes are those devised by linguists. For transcribing sounds, linguists rely on systems such as the International Phonetic Alphabet (International Phonetic Association, 1999). However, until very recently, there have been no standard ways of entering phonetic codes into the computer. For words, we all use the standard orthographic forms of our language. However, the match between the standard word and the actual forms in colloquial usage is often inexact and misleading. To code morphology and syntax, dozens of coding systems have been devised and none has yet emerged as standard, since the underlying theory in these areas continues to change. Similarly, in areas such as speech act analysis or intentional analysis, there are many detailed systems for coding, but no single standard. The superficial display form of a transcript and the way in which that form emphasizes certain aspects of the interaction is also a topic of much discussion (Ochs, 1979; Edwards and Lampert, 1993).

2.2 Indeterminacy

The second major problem that transcribers face is the difficulty of knowing exactly what people are saying. Anyone who has done transcription work understands that it is virtually impossible to produce a perfect transcription. When we re-transcribe a passage we almost always find minor errors in our original transcription. Sometimes we mishear a word. In other cases, we may miss a pause or a retrace. Often we have to guess at the status of a word, particularly when it is mumbled or incomplete. Child language interactions present a particularly serious challenge, because it is often difficult to know what to count as an utterance or sentence. All of these issues in transcription have been discussed in detail in the CHILDES Manual (MacWhinney, 2000), but it is important to realize that some of these problems simply cannot be resolved. This means that we must accept a certain level of indeterminacy in all transcription.

2.3 Tedium

The third problem that transcribers face is related to the second. Researchers often find that it takes over ten hours to produce a useable transcript of a single hour of interaction. Transcribing passages of babbling or conversations with high amounts of overlap can take up to 20 hours per hour or more. The time commitment involved here is considerable and can easily detract from other important academic goals. Sometimes, when teaching researchers how to use the transcription format of the CHILDES system, I am asked whether these programs will automatically generate a transcript. Would that life were so easy! The truth is that automatic speech recognition programs still struggle with the task of recognizing the words in the clear and non-overlapped speech of broadcast news. As soon as we start working with spontaneous speech in real conditions, any hope for automatic recognition is gone. It will be still several decades before we can achieve truly automatic transcription of natural dialogues.

Tedium also arises during the final phases of transcription and the process of data analysis. During these stages, researchers need to check their transcriptions and codes against the original audio or videotapes. The problem is that doing this involves a tedious process of rewinding the tape, trying to locate a specific passage, word or action. Consider the example of a researcher, such as Adolph (1995), who is interested in observing and coding the ways a child learns to crawl up a steep incline. When the child tries to crawl or walk up an incline that is too steep, they may begin to fall. Adolph's theory makes a crucial distinction between careful falling and careless falling. The assignment of particular behaviours to one of these categories is based on examination in videotapes of a set of movement properties, including arm-flailing, head-turning, body posture and verbalization. As Adolph progresses with her analyses, she often finds that additional indicators need to be added to assign behaviours to categories. However, access to the full video database involves rewinding hours of tape to access and reevaluate each episode during which the child begins to fall. This process is facilitated by Adolph's use of Vertical Interval Time Code (VITC) time markers, as well as by the use of high-end playback units that use time markers to access segments of the videotape. But, even with these tools, the access to data and annotations is so slow and indirect that the investigator avoids more than one or two passes through the data. For audio tapes, researchers rely on foot pedals to rewind the tape, so that small stretches of speech can be repeated for transcription. This legacy technology is extremely fragile, cumbersome and unreliable.

2.4 A direct solution

There is now an effective way of dealing with the three-headed monster of indeterminacy, tedium and lack of standards in transcription. The solution is to use programs that link transcripts and codes directly to the original audio or video data. The idea here is extremely simple. It involves an 'end run' around the core problems in transcription. Since transcriptions and codes will never fully capture the reality of the original interaction, the best way for researchers to keep in contact with the data is to replay the audio or video after reading each utterance in the transcript. In the era of VHS video and cassette-based audio, this solution was possible in principle, but extremely difficult in practice. However, linking of transcripts to audio and video is now extremely simple, once one learns the basics (http://talkbank.org/da).

The first step in linking transcripts to video is to digitize the media. All one needs is a computer, a sound card, digitizing software such as SoundEdit or CoolEdit, and the proper cable connections. Once several hours of sound have been digitized, the output can be written from the hard disk to a recordable CD-ROM for storage and later transcription.

For video, the process is similar, but a bit more time-consuming and costly. An excellent current digital format is mini-DV. However, for data from older studies, we first have to convert VHS video to digital format. The JVC SR-VS10 dual-deck system provides a great way of both converting VHS to mini-DV, as well as providing smooth access to the computer through the IEEE or FireWire port. Digitization can be done within a variety of programs on both Macintosh and Windows computers. However, we are currently using iMovie for digitization and Media Cleaner with the Sorenson codec for compression (http://talkbank.org/dv). All of this technology is rapidly changing with new options continually becoming available. What is important is the fact that all of the pieces for solving this problem are now in place for consumer-level machines at reasonable prices.

For certain types of interaction, researchers may feel that video is crucially necessary. If the researcher wants to pay close attention to the positions of the speakers, their gestures and facial expressions, and their use of external objects, then video is indispensable. Both digital audio and digital video are excellent solutions to the core problems in transcription. Audio is easier to produce, but video is preferable for microanalytic studies of the details of interactions.

2.5 Linking

Once the recording has been digitized, we are ready to begin transcription. This process relies on special software that allows the transcriber to link while transcribing. The three pieces of software that can control this two-pass transcription process are TransAna (http://transana.org), Transcriber (http://www.ldc.upenn.edu/mirror/Transcriber/) and Computerized language analysis (CLAN) (http://childes.psy.cmu.edu). These three systems work in the same basic way, but I will describe the process for CLAN (see also Chapter 5).

To begin the first pass of this process, you open a new blank file in CLAN, insert a @Begin line and a @Participants line for the speakers in the file. You then use the F5 key to locate a sound or video file. The sound or video file begins to play and you press the space bar at the end of each utterance. This automatically inserts a new line for the preceding utterance along with a bullet that contains the time codes that link each line of the transcript to a segment of the digitized audio or video. You listen through the whole digitized file completely, pressing the space bar at the end of each utterance. You will often encounter problems deciding when an utterance has ended, but try not to stop the process. You can correct these problems in the second pass. This first takes only one hour to segment one hour of dialogue, since this is done in real time. Once you are finished with this first pass, you can display and then rehide the time marks using ESC+A.

In the second pass, you use the bullets you entered as a way of replaying the audio or video. CLAN provides additional keys for several functions. You can replay a sound using CTRL-click or command-click at the bullet. There are keys for moving up and down from bullets. You can use the keys in the Tiers menu to insert speaker codes. You use the normal text editor functions to transcribe the utterance. If you need to change the borders of the demarcated sound, there are keys for adjusting the front or the end of the sound segment. Using these new transcription methods, transcription time can be reduced by at least 40 per cent from older approaches.

2.6 Linking the existing database

By linking transcripts to the original recordings, we have lifted a burden off of the shoulders of transcription. Without linkage, transcription is forced to fully represent all of the important details of the original interaction. With linkage, transcription serves as a key into the original recording that allows each researcher to add or modify codes as needed. If a phonetician does not agree with the transcription of a segment of babbling, then it is easy to provide an alternative transcription.

The linkage of transcripts to recordings opens up a whole new way of thinking about corpora and the process of data-sharing. In the previous model, we could only share the computerized transcripts themselves. For some important child language corpora, such as the Brown corpus, the original recordings have been lost. For others, however, we have been able to locate the original reel-to-reel recordings and convert them to digital files that we then link to the transcripts. We have done this for older corpora from Bates, Bernstein, Deuchar, Feldman, Hall, Korman, MacWhinney, Ornat, Peters, Sachs and Snow. Other new corpora, such as those from Forrester, Brent-Siskind, Miyata, Ishii, Thai and French Learner Language Oral Corpora (FLLOC), as well as virtually all of the corpora in the TalkBank database, have been contributed in already linked form.

All of the child language corpora mentioned above, along with about 100 additional corpora, are available from http://childes.psy.cmu.edu. Full documentation with references can be downloaded in the form of an individual electronic manual from http://childes.psy.cmu.edu/manuals. The TalkBank corpora from adults and school-age children are available from http://talkbank.org and the electronic manual for these data sets is available from that site too. Examples of major new TalkBank corpora include the Santa Barbara Corpus of Spoken American English (SBCSAE) and the SCOTUS corpus that includes 50 years of oral arguments at the Supreme Court of the United States.

3 Collaborative commentary

An important side effect of the availability of corpora linked to media is the opening of new opportunities for collaborative commentary. The idea of providing alternative views of a single target is at the core of many areas of historical analysis and literary criticism. However, these fields deal with written discourse, rather than spoken discourse. The works of Shakespeare, Joyce and others have now been digitized and it is easy to refer to specific passages directly. But this was easy to do even in the period before the advent of computers. In the area of spoken discourse, direct reference to a corpus is far more difficult. However, there is now a precedent for this in the field of classroom discourse. This groundbreaking work was contained in a Special Issue in 1999 of *Discourse Processes*, edited by Tim Koschmann (1999), which analysed a five-minute video of an interaction in a problem-based learning (PBL) classroom for medical education. The six students in the class were attempting to diagnose the aetiology of a case of an apraxic, amnesic, dysnomic. This interaction was digitized into MPEG format and included at the back of the Special Issue as a CD-ROM, along with a transcript in conversation analysis (CA) format. However, the transcript was not linked to the video and the five commentary articles made reference to the video only indirectly through the transcript. Despite these limitations, this Special Issue established a model in which researchers from differing theoretical positions could provide alternative views of the same piece of data. In a further refinement of this process, Sfard and McClain (2002) edited a Special Issue of the *Journal of the Learning Sciences* based on a video segment linked to a CLAN transcript. The focus of the commentary in this Special Issue was on students' understanding of graphic representations of numerical data. The CD-ROM included with the Special Issue include copies of the articles in HTML format with links that directly play video segments through QuickTime and a browser.

These two initial experiments in collaborative commentary begin to illustrate the ways in which shared, linked, digitized data can reshape the process of scientific investigation. Consider the application of this technology to the study of child language acquisition. One model relies on small clips from a larger transcript as the basis of commentary. For example, Ann Peters has contributed a set of illustrations of her subject Seth's use of fillers. Currently, these examples are provided as illustrations, rather than as evidence in support of a particular theory. However, it is clear that some of the examples could be subjected to multiple interpretations. For example, it appears that one of Seth's fillers may be simply a reduced form of the progressive <ing>. If a reader of the CHILDES home pages wishes to add this observation to Ann's commentary, we will need to have a mechanism in the HTML pages for comment insertion.

Another approach relies not on small clips, but on larger collections of files or whole corpora. For example, researchers in childhood bilingualism are currently debating the extent to which there may be interlanguage effects in two- and three-year-old bilinguals. Examples of transfer between languages (Hulk and van der Linden, 1998; Döpke, 2000) can also be interpreted as due to errors or incomplete learning of one of the languages. In order to resolve such issues, it would be very helpful to have complete access to all of the data involved, along with direct HTML links illustrating specific claims regarding examples of transfer. If the data were made available in this way, it would be possible to directly compare alternative accounts in terms of both qualitative and quantitative claims.

A third model for collaborative commentary involves even deeper coding and analysis of data. Currently, the CLAN programs provide only a limited set of tools for transcript coding. The main tool in this area is Coder's Editor, which allows the researcher to construct a set of codes that are then applied in lock-step fashion to each utterance in a transcript. Workers in the tradition of 'qualitative analysis' have developed more sophisticated programs such as *NUDIST and NVivo (http://www.qsrinternational.com/) which give the analyst more dynamic control over both the coding scheme and the way in which it is linked to transcripts. As we move toward a fuller understanding of the process of collaborative commentary, it will be necessary for us to support more powerful approaches of this type.

In order to expose the CHILDES and TalkBank corpora to collaborative commentary over the Web, we developed a series of new computational structures. First, we worked for several years to formulate a consistent XML schema for all of the current corpora. This new schema was created by extending the CHAT format (MacWhinney, 2000) to include additional conventions from CA, SALT, Discourse Transcription and other coding systems, all focused on extracting a single, coherent underlying set of meaningful coding categories. We then reformatted all of the CHILDES and TalkBank corpora to match the new standard. Then we built tools for checking the accuracy of the XML by converting CHAT to XML and then back to CHAT to verify accuracy by requiring a complete match across the round trip. We then created HTML from this verified XML. For media, we produced hinted streaming QuickTime movies available on our servers. Then, we built a Java Webstart program (http://childes.psy.cmu.edumanuals/) that could browse the transcript database. Currently, we are working to adapt this viewer tool to support collaborative commentary.

4 A community of disciplines

TalkBank seeks to provide a common framework for data-sharing and analysis for each of the many disciplines that studies conversational interactions. The disciplines involved include Psychology, Linguistics,

Speech and Hearing, Education, Philosophy, Computer Science, Business, Communication, Modern Languages, Sociology, Ethology, Anthropology and Psychiatry. Within each of these larger traditional disciplines, there are subdisciplines that concern themselves specifically with conversational interactions. For example, within the larger discipline of Education, there is the subdiscipline of Educational Psychology that studies classroom discourse. We have identified 16 such subdisciplines that are specifically concerned with the same basic issues in transcription and analysis that we have faced in child language. We have organized meetings of researchers in seven of these subdisciplines to collect a better understanding of their specific needs for transcription software and systems for data- sharing. These meetings included groups in classroom discourse, animal communication, field linguistics, aphasia, child phonology, gesture and computational analysis. Let us consider some of the current database needs in these fields.

4.1 Classroom discourse

Researchers in educational psychology have a long history of relying on videotape to study classroom interactions. It is clear that the technology we are developing will have a major impact on this field and there are now twelve new projects relying on new TalkBank technology. Despite this immense positive interest, it has been difficult to develop a system for data-sharing in the area of classroom discourse. The major problem involves securing permission from children and teachers to open video recordings to scientific analysis. In some cases, teachers are concerned that they will be subject to unfair criticism and even job discrimination or litigation. In other cases, parents are unwilling to have their children filmed for fear that their learning will be criticized. Dealing with these problems will require the creation of special systems for data protection that I will discuss later. Classroom discourse also requires extremely detailed use of ethnographic methods for linking types of data relevant to instructional episodes. These data may include notebooks, room layouts, songs, graphs, diaries, homework and a wide variety of other materials. TalkBank is committed to providing ways of digitizing records for all of these formats. Workers in classroom discourse make use of a wide variety of display methods for their data. These include the standard transcript format of CHAT and CA, left-to-right viewers such as SyncWRiter, and spreadsheet formats with both columns and rows. By relying on XML for data storage, it will be relatively easy for TalkBank to display a core set of data in each of these alternative display forms as desired by the researcher.

4.2 Animal communication

The concept of data-sharing would seem to be natural for the area of animal communication. There is already an archive for birdsong at the Cornell Laboratory of Ornithology (http://www.birds.cornell.edu/). However, researchers in this field had not yet considered the possibility of developing a generally available archive of data from a wide variety of species. The major problems facing data-sharing in this area are technical. First, researchers need to adapt a standard format for audio and video recordings and the linkage of these data to annotations. Most data in this field are best represented in spreadsheet format with rows indicating successive sounds ordered in time and columns representing changing aspects of the environment. We have already built three simple tools for entering data in this area. They have been designed specifically for meerkats, vervets and dolphins. These systems are essentially alternative data-entry systems, since all the data are stored in a common underlying XML-based format. The second major problem facing this field is the fact that the data files are often huge. The problem is not one of storage, since disk space is now extremely inexpensive. Rather, the problem is one of transmitting huge files across the internet. To deal with this, we have to rely on complete access to all files through XML-based tools. Currently, TalkBank has developed data sets of this type for bird song, vervet calls (Seyfarth and Cheney, 1999) and meerkat calls. Other data sets will eventually be added.

4.3 Field linguistics

Linguists have always been concerned with studying the great diversity of languages that exists on our planet. However, many of the languages spoken by small groups of people are now under great pressure and will become extinct by the end of the twenty-first century. One of the major goals of TalkBank is to develop effective tools for storing transcribed data from these many endangered languages, as well as the hundreds of other diverse languages that will survive into the next century. The community that studies these languages has already made important steps toward beginning a process of data-sharing. One initiative, sponsored by a variety of groups summarized at http://www.ldc.upenn.edu/atlas involves the construction of a set of metadata descriptors that will allow researchers to locate data on the internet on specific languages. However, once these data are located, researchers will currently be faced with a diversity of formats and programs for data access and analysis. To overcome this problem, TalkBank will provide users and database developers with a uniform set of XML-based tools for constructing transcripts linked to audio, lexical databases and grammars linked to examples.

4.4 Conversation analysis

Conversation analysis (CA) is a methodological and intellectual tradition stimulated by the ethnographic work of Garfinkel (1967) and systematized by Sacks *et al.* (1974) and others. Recently, workers in this field and the related field of text and discourse have begun to publish fragments of their transcripts over the internet. However, this effort has not yet benefited from the alignment, networking and database technology to be used in TalkBank. The CHILDES project has begun the process of integrating with this community. Working with Johannes Wagner (http://www.conversation-analysis.net), I have developed support for CA transcription within CHILDES. Wagner plans to use this tool as the basis for a growing database of CA interactions studied by researchers in Northern Europe.

4.5 Gesture and sign

Researchers studying gestures have developed sophisticated schemes for coding the relations between language and gesture. For example, David McNeill and his students have shown how gesture and language can provide non-overlapping views of thought and learning processes. A number of laboratories have large databases of video recording of gestures and the introduction of data-sharing could lead to major advances in this field. There are also several major groups studying the acquisition of signed languages. One group uses the CHAT-based Berkeley System of Transcription. Other researchers use either the SignStream system developed by Carol Neidle or the Media Tagger system developed by Sotaru Kita. Other groups use adaptations of CHAT and SALT. Because each of these groups is heavily committed to its own current approach, it may be difficult to find a common method for data-sharing. However, by relying on XML as an interlingua, it should be possible to store data from all of these formats in a way that will permit movement back and forth between systems. However, the details of this will need to be worked out in a meeting with the various groups involved.

4.6 Second language learning and bilingualism

Annotated video plays two important roles in the field of second-language learning. On the one hand, naturalistic studies of second-language learners can help us understand the learning process.

Secondly, the use of video in second-language learning is for the support of instructional technology. By watching authentic interactions between native speakers, learners can develop skills on the lexical, phonological, grammatical and interactional levels simultaneously. TalkBank will work to create a process of data-sharing that will address both of these problems. The database now has major corpora from learners of French, Czech, German, English, Japanese and Spanish. In addition to these new corpora from older second-language learners, there are several extensive new video studies of bilingual development in young children. Finally, there are six corpora documenting dual-language interaction and code-switching in adult bilinguals.

4.7 Aphasia

The facilities provided by TalkBank are also relevant to the study of language disorders. We have now created a password-protected database of 15 corpora of conversations with aphasic patients. As we move to expand this initial database in the context of the AphasiaBank project, we will establish a standardized protocol that will maximize our ability to conduct comparative analyses across patients.

4.8 First-language acquisition

The most fully developed component of TalkBank is the CHILDES database. There are now 100 CHILDES corpora and over 1,500 published studies of first-language acquisition that have relied on the use of the CHILDES database. This work extends across the areas of phonology, morphology, syntax, lexicon, narrative, literacy and discourse. Although CHILDES has been a great success in its current format, workers in this field are becoming increasingly aware of the need for a facility to link transcripts to audio and video. By providing this facility, TalkBank will open up new avenues for child language research. As we progress with developments in TalkBank, it will be necessary to maintain ongoing communication with the child language community to make sure that the new TalkBank software properly addresses its needs.

The second major new facility for child language researchers is the PHON program (http://childes.psy.cmu.edu/phon) developed by Yvan Rose and Greg Hedlund within the TalkBank framework. This program will allow students of child phonology to analyse segmental and prosodic patterns in great detail within and across languages.

4.9 Cultural anthropology

The interests of cultural anthropologists often overlap those of field linguists. However, the two groups use rather different methodologies. In particular, at the turn of the twentieth century, ethnographers pioneered the use of film documentaries to record the lives of non-Western peoples. Modern-day anthropology has continued its reliance on film and video to record aspects of other cultures. For this reason, we believe that the use of multimedia in TalkBank could be of particular interest to cultural anthropologists, as long as concern is taken to preserve the rights of the peoples being recorded and the ethnographers doing the fieldwork. Currently, the only major system for data-sharing in this field is the Human Relations Area Files (HRAF, http://www.yale.edu/hraf/). However, this system is largely devoted to the archiving of field notes, rather than actual recordings of interactions.

4.10 Psychiatry, conflict resolution

Psychiatrists such as Horowitz (1988) have been leaders in the exploration of transcript analysis and annotation. Because of privacy concerns, it is impossible to have open access to videotapes of clinical interviews. However, the application of the technology being developed here could provide a major boost to studies of clinical interactions. Moreover, data could be shared over the internet with password protection for academic users who have signed releases. A related use of annotated multimodal data occurs in work on conflict resolution within Ethics. Currently, there are no systems for data-sharing in these fields.

4.11 Human-computer interaction

Computer scientists are becoming more and more interested in constructing computational agents that can interact in human ways with human computer users. Some laboratories are building animated faces and bodies that express human gestures and facial expressions. These researchers also need to trace the responses of computer users to these new agents. Computer scientists are also interested in constructing automatic representations of ongoing discourse to facilitate the accuracy of speech recognition. Workers in the area of data-mining are interested in extending their techniques to spoken interactions as well as written language. As video data become increasingly available on the Web (http://www.informedia.cs.cmu.edu), new techniques for data-mining will need to build methods for automatic face and scene recognition. All of these computational challenges can be furthered by the construction of the various TalkBank databases. Moreover, computer scientists themselves can often contribute data that they are collecting.

5 The next steps

In this section, I will outline plans for further developments in TalkBank. We have already discussed the construction of the TalkBank Viewer and the system for collaborative commentary. In addition to this new tool, we hope to eventually construct several additional systems.

5.1 Coder

One of the first tools we propose to create is a flexible tool for qualitative data analysis called Coder. Functioning much like *Nudist or NVivo, Coder will allow the user to create and modify a coding framework which can then be applied to various segments of the transcript. Because the underlying data will be represented in XML, we can view Coder as an XML editor in which tags are created on the fly. These tags will be represented in the X-Schema representation of the data. Users will not need to know anything about XML or X-Schema. What they will see is something much like a standard editor window with a separate window that displays the coding system. There will be extensive facilities for comments and linkages to programs for finding and tabulating codes.

5.2 Alternative displays

A major limitation of the current CLAN programs is the lack of good facilities for building alternate displays of data. CLAN has a method for repressing dependent tiers, a program for adding line numbers called LINES, and two old and seldom used programs for formatting called COLUMNS and SLIDE. These last two have not been rewritten since the days of MS-DOS and 80-column windows. A major goal of our new initiative is the creation of flexible ways of displaying data. One method uses a sliding window, as in SignStream, Media Tagger and SyncWriter. Another method uses columns as in MacShapa, Excel, or other home grown systems. For each of these display methods, users will want additional features, such as control of colours, scroll bars and so on. In our new XML framework, developing these new features will be easier and will generalize better across platforms.

5.3 Profiles and queries

With the current CLAN system, the construction of developmental profiles requires several steps. One has to select a group of files, impose a set of filters, run analysis programs and ship the results off to statistical analysis. There are tools for doing all of this, but the options are opaque and the interface is difficult for a novice. New versions of the SALT program do a better job of allowing the user to filter data and compare against a standardized age-matched data set. We need to implement a similar, checklist approach to data analysis within the new TalkBank tools. This facility should be linked to an increasingly powerful method for querying the database.

5.4 Teaching

The increased availability of TalkBank data will have important consequences for teaching. By providing examples of specific types of language phenomena, we can directly introduce students to the study of language behaviour and analysis. TalkBank will make available materials on gesture–speech mismatch, fillers, code-switching, referential communication, learning of L2 prosody, vervet communication, parrot problem-solving, tonal patterns in African languages, prosody in motherese, phonological processes in SLI, persuasion in small groups, conflict resolution processes, breakdowns in intercultural communication and a myriad of other topics in the social sciences. Together, this rich database of interaction will help us teach students how to think about communication and will provide us with a dramatic way of communicating our research to the broader public.

5.5 Community control

Currently, the construction of CHILDES, the LDC database and TalkBank are very much in the hands of a few individuals. Over the next few years, it is important that this system of control be given back to the community. One solution here is technical. By providing methods for setting up local TalkBank databases, we can distribute control over the system across many research groups. In addition, we need to establish links between professional societies and the databases. For example, in child language, there could be a committee of the International Association for the Study of Child Language (IASCL) that supervises additions to the database. In the field of discourse studies, this committee could be associated with the Society for Text and Discourse. Societies such as the Linguistic Society of America (LSA) or Society for Research in Child Development (SRCD) could form similar groups. These groups would recommend corpora for addition and solicit contributions. They could also be responsible for giving awards for excellent contributions to the database and excellent empirical publications. Finally, they could work with journal editors and granting agencies to maximize contributions of new data to the shared database.

6 Conclusion

The advent of new computational opportunities makes it possible to build a system that we could have only dreamed about ten years ago. We can build on the lessons and successes of the CHILDES and LDC projects to build a new system that will lead to a qualitative improvement in social science research on communicative interactions. It is important to begin this project now, before the ongoing proliferation of alternative formats and computational frameworks blocks the possibility of effective collaboration across disciplinary boundaries.

References

Adolph, K. 1995. 'Psychophysical assessment of toddlers' ability to cope with slopes'. *Journal of Experimental Psychology* 21:734–50.

Döpke, S. (ed.). 2000. *Cross-linguistic Structures in Simultaneous Bilingualism*. Philadelphia, Pa: John Benjamins.

Edwards, J. and M. Lampert (eds). 1993. *Talking Data: Transcription and Coding in Discourse Research*. Hillsdale, NJ: Erlbaum.

Garfinkel, H. 1967. *Studies in Ethnomethodology*. Englewood Cliffs, NJ: Prentice-Hall.

Horowitz, M. (ed.). 1988. *Psychodynamics and Cognition*. Chicago: University of Chicago Press.

Hulk, A. C. J. and E. van der Linden. 1998. 'Evidence for transfer in bilingual children?' *Bilingualism: Language and Cognition* 1(3):177–80.

International Phonetic Association. 1999. *Handbook of the International Phonetic Association*. Cambridge: Cambridge University Press.

Koschmann, T. (ed.). 1999. Special Issue on 'Meaning making'. *Discourse Processes* 27(2):98–167.

MacWhinney, B. 2000. *The CHILDES Project: Tools for Analyzing Talk*. Mahwah, NJ: Erlbaum.

MacWhinney, B. and C. Snow. 1985. 'The Child Language Data Exchange System'. *Journal of Child Language* 12:271–95.

Ochs, E. 1979. 'Transcription as theory'. *Developmental pragmatics*, ed. by E. Ochs and B. Schieffelin, pp. 43–72. New York: Academic.

Sacks, H., E. Schegloff and G. Jefferson. 1974. 'A simplest systematics for the organization of turn-taking for conversation'. *Language* 50:696–735.

Seyfarth, R. and D. Cheney. 1999. 'Production, usage, and response in non-human primate vocal development'. *Neural Mechanisms of Communication*, ed. by M. Hauser and M. Konishi, pp. 57–83. Cambridge, Mass.: MIT Press.
Sfard, A. and K. McClain (eds). 2002. Special Issue on 'Analyzing tools: perspective on the role of designed artifacts in mathematics learning'. *Journal of the Learning Sciences* 11:153–388.

Websites

http://childes.psy.cmu.edu
http://talkbank.org
http://vis.sdsc.edu/sbe/
http://www.birds.cornell.edu/
http://www.conversation-analysis.net
http://www.etca.fr/CTA/Projects/Transcriber/
http://www.informedia.cs.cmu.edu
http://www.ldc.upenn.edu/atlas
Human Relations Area Files (HRAF): http://www.yale.edu/hraf/)
NVivo: http://www.qsrinternational.com/
PHON program: http://childes.psy.cmu.edu/phon
TransAna: http://transana.org
Transcriber: http://www.ldc.upenn.edu/mirror/Transcriber/
World Wide Web Consortium or W3C: http://w3c.org

8
Developing and Using a Corpus of Written Creole

Mark Sebba and Susan Dray

1 Introduction

Jamaican Creole, sometimes characterized as a 'dialect' of English, is the vernacular language of Jamaica and the first language of most Jamaicans. It is also understood and used by many people in Britain. Because of its origins, its historical relationship with Standard English (the language of administration and education) and the absence of standardization, it shows a high degree of variation in lexis, grammar and phonology. In writing, this variability extends to orthography. Most Creole, whether spoken or written, contains a mixture of forms: some approximating Standard English, others closer to the broad or 'basilectal' creole.[1]

This variability has, for several decades, provided a special point of interest for linguists. 'Creole studies' has become a laboratory for all sorts of ideas about language origins, variation and change. Surely too, it presents an interesting challenge to the corpus linguist, who is faced with all sorts of tricky (and highly theoretical) decisions about what constitutes a language and what, as a consequence, does or does not belong to the corpus.

In this chapter we present our experiences of developing two computerized Creole corpora at Lancaster University. The corpora we will be discussing are:

- the Corpus of Written British Creole (CWBC), a collection of texts which aims to be representative of the use of Creole in writing in the British context;
- the Corpus of Written Jamaican Creole (CWJC), a collection of texts of diverse types written by Jamaicans in Jamaica.

The CWBC was set up as an experiment, to study the potential and problems of corpora of unstandardized written language. The CWJC was established for a specific research purpose, to study the writing practices of Jamaicans. As a result of the different purposes, the annotation systems differ, although the fundamental issues involved in designing the annotation systems are similar.

We discuss issues which arose when setting up the corpora, in particular the practical issue of the identification of texts for inclusion. Even deciding on a suitable definition of 'text' can be problematic for a language where much of the writing which exists is a representation of oral forms (for example, song lyrics, dialogue). Some problems are specific to English-lexicon Creoles, for example: some texts which contain Creole features seem to be *intended* as Standard English texts by their creators. Should they be included in the corpus? Other texts contain a principled mixture of Creole and Standard English, for example novels where the narration is in Standard English and the dialogue in Creole. How should the corpus deal with such 'mixed' texts?

We then outline our annotation system and discuss some potentially complex linguistic questions to do with the detail of annotation: for example, to what extent do graphological features, such as punctuation, layout and the use of upper- and lower-case letters in a text, need to be included in the corpus? Such features have traditionally been disregarded in corpora, but in the case of an unstandardized language they may play a significant part in how readers interpret the message.

We end with some remarks on the potential of these corpora as a research tool in order to illustrate the application of the annotation method, and an example of how corpus data could be used to distinguish 'real' from 'hoax' Creole. Linguistic items and their orthographic representations can be compared and contrasted with variables such as demographic information (about writers or voices within texts), country, text type and social context. This could provide information, for example, not only on orthographic variations within or across texts, but also on how writing practices may vary according to social, cultural, generational and educational factors as well as over time.

2 'Creole' and 'English' in the Caribbean and Britain

Jamaican Creole may be characterized as an English-lexicon creole, with its origins in the period of plantation slavery. As such it has characteristics in common with other creoles spoken in the Caribbean region, though these creoles all differ somewhat from each other due to the varied geographical, historical, social and linguistic factors that were present in the different environments in which they evolved. Jamaican Creole differs from Standard English (SE) in phonology, lexis and, perhaps most strikingly, syntax (Cassidy, 1961; Bailey, 1966; Cassidy and Le Page, 1980; Patrick, 1999).

In Britain, Jamaicans were numerically and culturally dominant in the first generation of migrants from the Caribbean. Local varieties of Jamaican Creole, influenced by local Englishes, for example 'London Jamaican' in the London area (Sebba, 1993), have come to be used in Britain by second- and third-generation Caribbeans (whether or not of Jamaican ancestry themselves). 'British Creole' is used here as a cover term for these local varieties.

In the 'Anglophone' Caribbean, where Standard English (SE) is the official medium of education at all levels, as well as the language of administration and most publishing and broadcasting, Creole vernaculars have traditionally been low-status varieties considered unacceptable in all prestigious domains, in a situation resembling the classical description of diglossia (Ferguson, 1959). However, the picture is complicated by the fact that Creole shares the majority of its vocabulary with Standard English, allowing it to be viewed as 'bad English' rather than as a separate language of lower status. Furthermore, since all schooling is, at least in theory, through the medium of Standard English, most people have some degree of exposure to the prestige variety and may treat it as a target even if they often are unable to get near it. As a result it has been observed that most Jamaicans speak neither the 'pure' or *basilectal* Creole (defined by maximum difference from the norms of SE) nor the local Standard English (or *acrolect*), but something in between, characterized by a high degree of variability. This is viewed by some researchers as a 'post-Creole continuum' (De Camp, 1961, 1971) and by others as diglossia (see Mühleisen, 2002, for a discussion).

In the last decade, the prestige of Jamaican Creole in Jamaica has increased somewhat and negative attitudes have lessened as it comes to be seen more as a language in its own right (Mühleisen, 2002); in addition, the education system has recently recognized the existence of Creole although the educational goal is still to ensure that the child learns to use Standard English. In Britain, Creole has low overt prestige and is excluded almost totally from the education system, but it is highly valued as an identity marker for British Caribbeans and has a degree of prestige, within the wider community in Britain, connected with the increasing influence of Jamaican music in the international music industry over the past 40 years. Creole lexis (and, to some extent, grammar) is widely used and recognized by adolescents who have no personal contact with Creole speakers (Hewitt, 1986; Rampton, 1995; Sebba, 2003). Second- and third-generation Caribbeans in Britain can mostly be characterized as first-language speakers of local varieties of English who, in addition, have a form of Jamaican Creole as a 'heritage language'. Their active competence in this language is very variable, but when two second- or third-generation Caribbeans are in conversation with each other, code-switching between English and Creole may take place. Exclusively Creole conversations would be rare.

Although, like many vernaculars, Jamaican Creole is primarily a spoken language, it is not the case that it is *exclusively* spoken. In Jamaica and in Britain, predominantly oral art forms, such as performance poems and song lyrics, are often published, sometimes as record album sleeves or CD inserts in Britain, and frequently in the daily press or in pirated 'song books' in Jamaica. Occasionally, they are published as books, either self-published or by relatively specialized presses. In more recent years, websites dedicated to Jamaican music have encouraged the postings of the most popular song lyrics. In Britain, novels by Caribbean-heritage authors with mainly Caribbean protagonists in British settings emerged in the 1990s. These included a genre of 'yardie' (Jamaican gangster) crime fiction largely published by one publisher, X-press. Most of these books have third-person narration in Standard English; however, much of the dialogue is usually in Creole, or in mixtures of Creole and English which reflect the language of British-born, Caribbean-heritage characters. In a minority, there is a Creole-speaking narrator.

There is an increasing amount of work published by Jamaican authors (novelists, poets and playwrights) who write in Creole. In Jamaica there is a genre of 'humorous' writing (first-person accounts, typically gossip or opinion columns in the daily press) which lends itself to writing in Creole. In addition there are products of vernacular literacy such as signs, notices and graffiti, as well as commercial advertising which are sometimes in Creole, especially in Jamaica. There is also an unknown amount of personal writing such as private letters and emails between Creole users; in such letters the target is sometimes Standard English and (we assume) sometimes Creole.[2]

The amount of publicly available written Creole in Britain, though a tiny fraction of the written universe in Standard English, thus grew from almost nothing around 1980 to an 'analysable' size in the 1990s.

The arrival of the internet seems to have led to increased use of Creole in Jamaican and international contexts in emails (Hinrichs, 2003, 2004; Mair, 2003), chat rooms and websites; it is not clear to what extent British Creole users have adopted these practices.[3] Of course, it is often impossible to know the origins or identity of internet users anyway.

3 The goals of the corpora

The appearance of a 'critical mass' of written British Creole (BC) presented itself as an opportunity for research into the development and exploitation of corpora of unstandardized language. A corpus of written Creole could potentially be of interest to several types of researcher:

- creolists interested in Caribbean Creole and its development, especially its development outside the Caribbean;
- corpus linguists, as an opportunity to explore the problems associated with unstandardized, and highly variable, data sets;
- historical sociolinguists, for whom this could be a rare opportunity to document an unstandardized language developing written forms and functions.

The Corpus of Written British Creole was thus set up as an experiment, to study the potential and problems of corpora of unstandardized written language. It was compiled at Lancaster University with financial support from the British Academy.[4] The main research interest of the grant holder (Sebba) at the time was in orthography and its development through time. Most of the searching for texts, permission clearance and inputting work was carried out by Sally Kedge in 1995. In 1998, additional work, including additional tagging and checking for errors, was done by Susan Dray. At the time it was set up, it was hoped that the corpus would encompass all, or almost all, Creole texts actually *published* in Britain (there being relatively few), along with a large selection of unpublished ones. In practice, this goal was unattainable: mainly for reasons of copyright (in the case of published work) and lack of access to unpublished material. Furthermore, a simple lack of resources prevented the transcription and tagging of all the material we *did* obtain. Nevertheless the corpus has a range of text types and is sufficiently large to be able to make some generalizations.

The Corpus of Written Jamaican Creole was established in 2000–01 by Susan Dray for her doctoral thesis. It is not currently available for public use, for ethical reasons. The corpus was created to aid analysis of the non-standard writing strategies employed by Jamaicans in order to complement ethnographic research on literacy practices. The overall goal of the project was to investigate the relationship between power and written language and, as a consequence of this, the annotation method developed for this corpus is project-specific.

Despite the different motivations for setting up these two corpora and the resulting difference in the tagging systems, the fundamental issues encountered when designing the annotation systems were similar because of the linguistic similarities of the data (see section 6).

4 The compilation of the corpora

At the time the original proposal for the Corpus of Written British Creole was formulated, we believed that because of the relatively small volume of texts being produced in Creole in Britain, it was theoretically possible to collect *every* text of that description and still have a corpus of a manageable size. We knew that in practice that would not be possible, and, in the event, things were even more difficult than we had expected. This was partly because of the volume of informal writing (unpublished, and never intended to be published) which was simply not accessible: for example, personal letters written from one Creole speaker to another. It was also in part because of the ethical and legal requirements of copyright and permission. We contacted some authors directly and publishers in other cases. A very few authors refused our requests on ideological or economic grounds; much more commonly, we simply did not get a response to our letters or calls and had no time to chase up authors too busy to deal with us. In either case it meant that even where we had physical possession of a text, it could not be included in the corpus in machine-readable form. With the concept of a corpus being barely understood outside the world of linguistics at the time, it was also uncertain in some cases where consent was given that it was really 'informed consent'.

In fact we were able to collect many more texts than have been placed in the corpus (here we are using 'corpus' to mean the collection of machine-readable and annotated texts, rather than the whole collection of books, pamphlets and other pieces of writing which we have built up). These texts exist on paper but are not available in machine-readable format. As already mentioned, in some cases this was due to lack of permission to use a text in copyright. Like the compilers of the Corpus of Early English Correspondence (Raumolin-Brunberg and Nevalainen, Volume 2, p. 157), we felt that it was a high priority to make as much of the corpus as possible accessible to other researchers on a reasonable timescale. Their solution was to create a sampler corpus of 450,000 words, containing all collections free of copyright restrictions. In our case, we simply concentrated on preparing and tagging the texts which we knew were not problematic from the copyright point of view.

Lack of time and resources has been the other main factor preventing the expansion of the corpus. Inputting the texts (transferring them from paper to machine-readable form) is in itself a time-consuming task. Tagging the texts with spelling, grammatical and discourse information has required even more time and effort.

The Corpus of Written British Creole is very small in corpus-linguistic terms (around 28,000 words; even the early 'small' computer corpora contained 1 million words). This raises the question of how 'representative' the Corpus of Written British Creole is. Corpus linguists typically concern themselves with the question of 'representativeness' of a corpus: in other words, how well the sample of texts in the corpus reflects the language found in a particular 'universe' of texts (that is, the totality of texts in that language).[5] The representativeness of a corpus is not easy to determine, partly because, as Rieger (1979, p. 66) points out, 'a sample ... can only be characterized as representative when so much is known about the universe from which it comes that the construction of this sample is no longer necessary'.

In the case of the Creole corpus, there are additional complicating factors. Exactly what should count as the 'universe' is not very clear, as Creole does not exist in a separate world from Standard English. Mixing of the two is very common. Therefore, should the 'universe' include all texts which contain both Standard English and Creole, as well as all texts purely in Creole?

A less demanding requirement which can be made of a corpus is that it be *exemplary*. According to Bungarten (1979, pp. 42–3), 'A corpus is exemplary, when its representativeness is not proven, but less formal arguments, like evident cohesiveness, linguistic judgments of a competent researcher, professional consensus, textual and pragmatic indicators, argue that the corpus may reasonably function as representative.'[6]

Because of the limitations mentioned above, the best that we could hope to establish is an exemplary corpus of written British Creole, which according to the 'linguistic judgments of a competent researcher' (Bungarten, 1979, p. 43) is sufficiently wide-ranging and yet sufficiently cohesive that it could be considered representative of the language in its current state. Yet even that is not an easy goal. There are substantial difficulties entailed in determining what may reasonably be taken to 'represent' an unstandardized language where the boundaries between it and its related standard (Standard English in this case) are so fuzzy.[7] It is not clear that any researcher is really competent to make this linguistic judgement at the present time, given the theoretical complexity of the issues.

The size of the electronic Corpus of Written Jamaican Creole is currently 70,000 words. Like the Corpus of Written British Creole, the number of paper texts collected by far exceeds the size of the electronic corpus, and is estimated to be between 100,000 and 200,000 words. The main body of texts included in the electronic corpus were selected because they had been written by participants in the research project. Thus, in its entirety, the Corpus of Written Jamaican Creole is not representative, nor necessarily exemplary of the current writing strategies within Jamaica. However, included in the corpus is a subcorpus of 'outdoor' texts (for example, road signs, posters, advertisements, graffiti etc.) which, although small in terms of words (4,500) is exemplary of the types of non-standard written texts that could be publicly viewed outdoors (mostly along the roadside) between 1999 and 2002. This subcorpus consists of over 300 short texts, which were recorded by field notes and photographs. Many of these texts were handwritten or handpainted and included images and symbols that raised issues at the transcription stage (see section 6.2).

5 Issues to do with selection of data

Since the intention behind the Corpus of Written British Creole was that it should document the emerging *British* variety of Creole, it was decided to include in the corpus only texts which met the following criteria:

1. That the texts have been written and/or published in Britain;
2. That all or part of the text is a written representation of English-lexicon Caribbean Creole (variously also called Patois/Patwa/Nation Language);
3. That the writer had been born or had spent their formative years in Britain.[8]

Identifying Creole was not particularly problematic as there are several reliable descriptions available and it was generally clear which parts of a text contained Creole and which did not. The requirement that texts be written and/or published in Britain was in practice much more problematic. Where a text was published in Britain this was usually easy to determine, but some of the writing we obtained was unpublished. Also, some texts were published in Britain, but by writers known to have spent much of their lives in the Caribbean. Though the text would technically be 'British' its language might well reflect Caribbean rather than British usage. Should these be included? And what of the cases where we had no biographical information at all about the writer? In a small corpus, like this, the potential for producing a skewed sample is high. In the end we were sometimes forced to make arbitrary judgements. We concentrated on including writers who are known either to be British-born or to have spent most of their formative years in Britain. Even then, we have not been able to exclude, with certainty, texts which do not relate to Britain, for example where the speech styles reported are in a Caribbean context.

Deciding how much of a text to include was also a problem. Many of the texts which met our criteria contained a mixture of Standard English and Creole. Typically, novels would have their narration in Standard English only, while dialogue (reported speech) would be partly in Standard English or a local variety of English and partly in Creole. Including the complete novel would have involved an amount of work which would quickly have used up our modest resources, and furthermore would have produced a corpus mainly of British Standard English with a marginal amount of Creole in it. A possible decision in this case would have been to have included all and only reported speech (that is, everything between sets of quotation marks) making this part of the corpus a reflection of representations of reported speech, including possible code-switching. In the event, we did not do this; we decided instead to aim to include complete paragraphs or stanzas, the criterion for inclusion being that *some part* of the extract was in Creole. The result is that we have included only fragments of the novels themselves, but that we have samples which contain relatively high proportions of Creole and are representative of the Creole contained in the book as a whole. Since many of the extracts include both Standard English and Creole, the corpus could be used to study how these languages interact with each other at a local level.

In the Corpus of Written Jamaican Creole, the proviso for including a text was that it should contain non-standard elements. Such texts have been included in their entirety irrespective of the ratio of standard to non-standard elements. This decision was made because in this Jamaican corpus it was less common to find texts in which English and Creole could be so easily distinguished. A further complication with the Jamaican corpus was whether or how to tag Creole items that were also considered to be Standard Jamaican English.

A text written by Pollard exemplifies this difference (Figure 8.1 below). The narration in Pollard's novel draws mostly on Standard English (SE), with Creole tending to be used to represent reported speech. However on several occasions in the English narrative, Creole lexical or grammatical items are present, and it is not always clear whether they should be regarded as Creole or Standard (Jamaican) English (SJE).

Most of post–op is bound up in one tight ball of total pain. And helplessness. For true now you came on your own two feet to beg them disable you. And that they do very effectively and leave you unable to perform the most elementary services without help. (Pollard, 1999, p.11)

Figure 8.1 Example from a novel using Creole

In this extract *beg them disable you* is a Creole structure, but *for true now*, though clearly Creole in its idiom, would be acceptable (as a 'folk expression') in an otherwise wholly SJE text. Its presence therefore does not help to characterize the text as one code or the other.

We had also to make decisions about the types of text which would be included in the two corpora. For both it was decided that, in principle, no genre would be excluded. However, it was very obvious that it would be impossible to obtain a balance of genres, as in more conventional types of corpus-building.[9] The range of genres using written Creole is narrow compared to the range available in a standardized language like English. Furthermore, to obtain samples of some genres mere 'collection' is not enough: fieldwork is necessary, for example, to obtain examples of advertisements and graffiti. At the time the corpora were built, there was very little available in electronic form; now there is somewhat more.

The corpora currently contain texts of the following types:

CWBC

- Poems
- Extracts from novels and other fiction
- Plays
- Miscellaneous, including advertisements and graffiti

CWJC

- Poems
- Song lyrics (folk and reggae/dancehall)
- Plays
- Novels
- Research papers and articles
- Phrase book
- Opinion columns, gossip columns, press editorials and journalism
- Political press cartoons
- Letters, cards and emails
- Outdoor texts (subcorpus)

The decision to limit the Corpus of Written British Creole to include writers who 'either are known to be British-born or to have spent most of their formative years in Britain' was taken on two grounds. One was the desire to be as representative as possible of one particular emergent variety of Creole. The other reason for limiting the corpus to writers with a strong British connection was the feeling that a distinctive British tradition of writing Creole might be emerging. This may well have turned out to be wrong, as it involves the implicit assumption of a break in the tradition of writing Creole between the Caribbean and Britain. In fact, since many published authors have lived in both places and, to some extent, texts published in the Caribbean are also available in Britain and vice versa, it is more reasonable to think of an unbroken tradition of Creole writing which unites the Caribbean with Britain (particularly since many Creole writers in the Caribbean look to Europe to get published).[10,11] On the other hand, it may well be that differences will emerge over time. It is hoped that the corpus will grow over time as new texts are added to it. Each extract in the corpus contains a tag <year=xxxx> containing the year of publication or writing, so that it will be possible to track spelling, lexical or grammatical changes by comparing the dates associated with the different usages; the corpus thus has built into it the capability of being a 'monitor corpus', allowing for research into language change over time. While we anticipate that there would be methodological problems for a researcher wanting to use such a small corpus in this way, we felt it was important to allow for the possibility of using it to look at language change. This was especially the case because one of our research questions concerned whether a de facto standardization was taking place (outside any formal or official framework) and if so how that process might be operating.

Although, at present, the Corpus of Written Jamaican Creole is not publicly available, with more time and resources we hope to continue to build the electronic corpus with a view to gaining ethical clearance from writers and making the corpus available for general use. It is likely that as the Jamaican corpus develops, the tagging system will focus on tags providing contextual and orthographic information, with less focus on the grammatical functions of elements. Some of the reasons for this decision are discussed in the following section.

6 Tagging

6.1 Principles of tagging

The Corpus of Written British Creole was set up on the understanding that it would be a resource for researchers who have different methodologies, theoretical orientations and research questions in mind. We set out to increase the usefulness of the corpus by tagging the items within it according to a set of explicit principles.

The choice of which elements to tag and what tags to use was one of the most difficult issues facing the compilers of the corpus. While the ideal might be to create a set of 'theory-neutral' and 'application-neutral' tags, in practice the tag set and the principles behind its application rest on a theory about the nature of the data *and* reflect the interests of the corpus compilers. In corpora of unstandardized language forms like those under consideration here, we need to start from very basic theoretical questions about what language variety(ies) is/are represented in the data. Should it be assumed that there is just one linguistic code present in the data, or two, or several? If there is more than one, should they all be treated in the same way for tagging purposes, or should they be marked in different ways?

Tagging is a developing area of corpus linguistics (see, for example, McEnery *et al.*, 2005). Given that in a well-studied standard language like written Standard English where the grammatical classes of words are not too controversial in themselves, much of the current research in this area is devoted to developing *automatic* tagging.[12] For the Creole corpora the problem is a much more basic one, of simply deciding what should be tagged and how. All tagging is manual.

In a typical 'monolingual' tagged corpus, each individual word in the corpus would be tagged with one or more tags relating to the grammatical, semantic or other properties of the word. We felt that tagging like this was not practical for these two corpora. First, as all tagging would have to be manual it was simply beyond our resources. Second, there was not yet a sufficiently well-developed descriptive grammar for Creole to make the assignment of tags straightforward. The main existing grammar, Bailey (1966), is a description of selective aspects of grammar using a transformational grammar framework; other works mainly contain grammatical notes by way of background to other topics. Jamaican Creole is at the moment far from having a comprehensive reference grammar, even if that were possible given the variability of the spoken language. Third, it was not obvious that this type of tagging would be of much use to researchers. In fact, it was more likely that a detailed descriptive grammar would develop *out of* the Corpus of Written British Creole, using it as a resource, rather than the other way around.

For the CWBC, we decided to use a set of contrastive tags which would mark differences in spelling, lexis, and discoursal and grammatical structure between Standard English and the language of the corpus texts. In other words, tags have mainly been used only where the word or structure encountered would not be expected in a text which was in Standard English. This greatly simplified the work of tagging the corpus, though at a cost: the tagging appears to focus on the language of the corpus as a variety of English, rather than as a language in its own right. It would be very unfortunate if anyone took this to imply either that Creole is in some way inferior to English, or that the purpose of the corpus is to draw attention to 'mistakes' or 'deviant' grammar. That is absolutely not the intention, and would go against the drift of both Creole Studies and Linguistics in general over the last half-century. Indeed, the intention behind the CWBC is not to provide a contrastive grammar of Jamaican Creole and Standard English, but to provide a resource for studying Jamaican Creole in its own right. We hope that users of the corpus will understand this. The general rule for tagging in the CWBC is: where a form (word, structure, meaning and so on) is identical to an acceptable Standard English form, no tag has been added. Where the form is different from that expected in Standard English, a tag has been added which flags the nature of that difference.

So, for example, extract 20 from text 1 in the corpus is tagged as shown in Figure 8.2. In this extract, we can see that an entire sentence,

Joseph switched to business, has no tags at all. This is because it is indistinguishable from written Standard English. Several words in the other sentences of the extract, for example, *I, have, room, load, so,* are also untagged, for the same reason. However, most of the other words are tagged, to signal spelling differences (weh<sp=where>), grammar differences (deh<gr=de-cop>), lexical (yah<lex=yah>) or discoursal features (man<disc=man>) which characterize Creole in opposition to Standard English.

'I have one<gr=art> room in yah<lex=yah><sp=especially> for you, man<disc=man>. 'Joseph switched to business. 'So is weh<sp=where> de<sp=the> load deh<gr=de-cop><gr=cleft><gr-queststr>, sah<sp=sir>?'<bookid=01><speakerid =joseph><year=1992><extractid=20><pageno=9>

Figure 8.2 Example of tagged text

The same general rule for tagging was applied to the CWJC. Additional tags in the header were developed to include contextual information about the text, both geographical and visual. Such tags indicated where the text was seen or found, the materials that had been used to make it, whether it had been produced by hand or printed, whether images were also part of the text and whether standard punctuation and use of upper and lower case had been used. A significant tag was that which indicated whether speech was explicitly represented in the text (for example, through punctuation, speech bubbles, or images of the speaker). Each word was also tagged according to how it was spelled. A typology of spelling strategies was developed for this purpose.

For example, the tagged text of one of the images (Image 3) in section 6.2 is as shown in Figure 8.3 below. The tag <form= > indicates the spelling strategy. In this example the word *here-so* is tagged as using standard spelling conventions (form=a). The punctuation is tagged as non-standard (punc=ns) at the point in the text where it occurs as well as in the header. This was an attempt to indicate in the electronic form that the layout of this text is not conventional. However, it is not entirely satisfactory because it does not indicate the nature of the text's layout. Perhaps the only way to achieve this would be to include the image in the corpus. This brings us to a related issue, the relationship between types and tokens in the corpus.

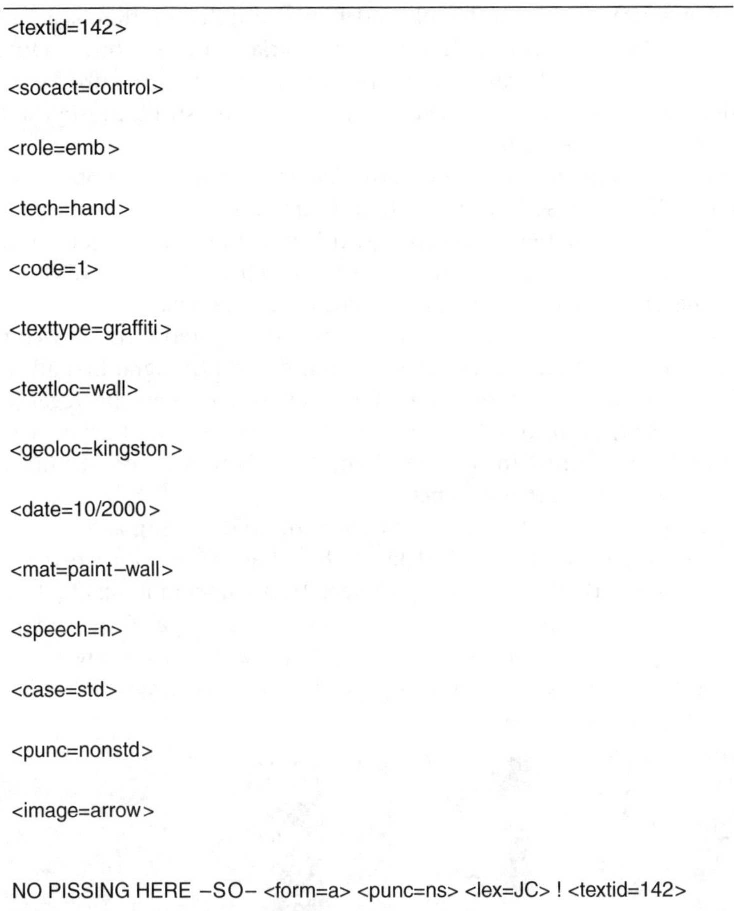

<textid=142>

<socact=control>

<role=emb>

<tech=hand>

<code=1>

<texttype=graffiti>

<textloc=wall>

<geoloc=kingston>

<date=10/2000>

<mat=paint–wall>

<speech=n>

<case=std>

<punc=nonstd>

<image=arrow>

NO PISSING HERE –SO– <form=a> <punc=ns> <lex=JC> ! <textid=142>

Figure 8.3 Example of tagged text from an image

6.2 Issues to do with the type–token relationship

In a standardized written language the type–token relationship seems to be a relatively unproblematic one for corpus linguists. In particular, the standardizing processes which apply to printed language usually make it clear which tokens should be assigned to a given type. For example, orthographic conventions regulate the distribution of capital and lower-case letters so that we know that table, Table, TABLE and *table* are all tokens of the type <table>. For most purposes we would probably not need to treat Table and TABLE as different; they will most likely be treated as 'mere' graphological variants of each other. Other forms such as taBlE are deviant from the normal conventions and might warrant a tag to indicate this, but they are still unmistakeably tokens of the type <table>.[13]

In an unstandardized language the relationship is more problematic, especially in a case like this, where there is a complex relationship between the varieties in the corpus. It is much less clear what should count as a type, and whether a type which could be 'English' or 'Creole' should count as a separate type in each language.

For example, an expression meaning 'here' (Creole *yaso*) is commonly found in graffiti. Susan Dray found and photographed all the images shown in Figure 8.4 in Jamaica: should these be regarded as tokens (a) all of one type, <yaso> (b) of two different types, with (1) and (2) assigned to the same type and (3) to a different 'mixed' type, or (c) three different types?

The question is relevant to transcription and tagging as well as at this more abstract theoretical level. To what extent can we reduce items such as the three above, produced by an 'unstandardizing' technology (that is hand-lettered) to a standardized type? Can we transcribe (1) and (2) both as *yaso* but tag them as shown in Figure 8.5, or is this adding unnecessarily to the corpus tagger's burden?

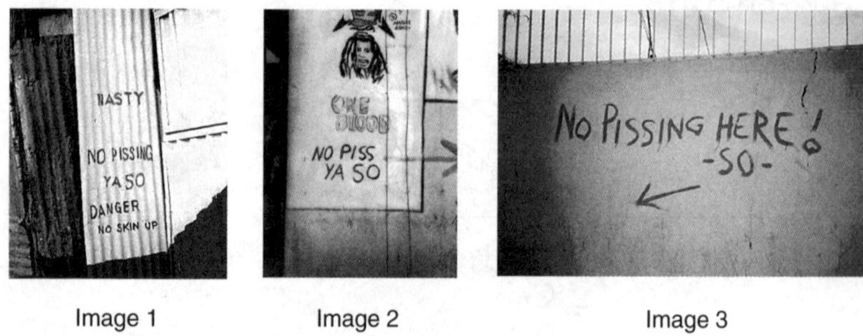

Figure 8.4 Examples of graffiti in Jamaica

yaso<capitals><hand lettered>

yaso<capitals><separate words><hand lettered>

Figure 8.5 Example of text tagging

And then what about (3)? Can we treat *HERE* as an instance of its Creole cognate *ya*, but tagged as having a more 'Standard English' form? And how do we account then for the positioning of *so*? Or should we not bother?

This issue recurs at different levels of analysis. At the grammatical level, are the following two instances of *is* (both taken from the same novel: *Yardie* by Victor Headley, 1993, and both direct speech of characters) to be treated as different types, or two tokens of the same type?

```
(1) But this is not the way, D. <bookid=01><extractid =73>
(2) we know say you is a top soldier down ah Yard
<bookid=01><extractid=11>
    'We know that you are a top soldier back home (in
Jamaica)'
```

Though both on the surface appear to be instances of *is*, a part of the verb *to be*, one could argue that this is true only for the first of the two. The second could be argued, in line with the grammar of Jamaican Creole, to be an invariant (that is unconjugated) copula form and thus only superficially similar (in appearance and in function) to the English *is*.[14]

So do we need to annotate more than one type of *is*? As Cornips and Corrigan (2005, p. 100) point out, there is a fairly intractable problem with the notion of 'synonymy' in sociolinguistic studies of variation at the morphosyntactic level.[15] It is difficult, some would say impossible, to establish criteria by which two (morpho)syntactic forms can be treated as 'variants' of one underlying form or construction: 'issues relating to pragmatic and semantic conditioning' (Cornips and Corrigan, 2005, p. 100) frequently intervene. Even where the forms are apparently the same, as in the example above, this is no guarantee that they occupy the same position within the grammatical system(s) of which they are part. In the CWBC, it was decided that *is* would not be tagged, no matter where it occurred (that is, it is treated as though it were a standard form, a token of the Standard English *is*), whereas *ah* is given the tag `<gr=a-cop>`, but we are not confident that this was the correct decision to make.

To summarize, the type–token relationship is problematic and impacts on decisions relating to transcription and tagging. It also raises questions of the type of data formats and data structures which are appropriate for a corpus such as this; so, for example, should the aim be to store an image of the original text (for example, a photograph or photocopy) and, if so, is this necessary or desirable for all texts or just for those which are not produced by conventional print technology?

6.3 Issues to do with meanings in the texts

Some of the texts in the corpora draw on non-verbal resources to enhance the meaning of the text. Published poetry, for example, may be creatively positioned on a page in a non-conventional way in order to suggest a particular rhythm or movement. On many of the outdoor texts found in Jamaica, images accompanied the text and often provided contextualization cues to the meaning of the text. These images could not be incorporated into the electronic corpus and the concern was that decontextualizing the written text in this way could easily lead to misinterpretation by those using the corpus. For example, the images painted above the text requesting people to refrain from urinating against the wall of a shop near a market in Papine, Kingston (Jamaica) (Image 2 in Figure 8.4) depict people of significance in the Rastafarian faith. These, along with the phrase *one blood* (a respectful Rastafarian/Jamaican salutation signifying brotherhood), mitigate the command *no piss ya so* which, standing alone, could be interpreted as the work of an angry, aggressive writer. Instead, it appears as if the writer was almost apologetic for having to write the sign.[16]

7 Applications of the corpus

The small size of the corpora make them of limited use for traditional corpus-linguistic applications, such as producing descriptive grammars. Some relatively infrequent syntactic constructions are unrepresented, or barely represented, in the CWBC.[17] Nevertheless, the corpora can be used for a variety of purposes; for example, the CWBC has been used for a small-scale study of future modality (Facchinetti, 1998) and for a study of orthographic practices (Sebba, 1998a, 1998b). In this section we give one detailed example of how we ourselves have used the corpus.

Late in 1999 a row erupted in the United States over a pamphlet published by the Department of Housing and Urban Development (HUD) on *Resident Rights and Responsibilities*. Among many translations of the pamphlet into different languages, the 'Creole' version (Rezedents Rights & Rispansabilities) drew media attention because it seemed, on the surface, to be a parodic written representation of English-lexicon Creole speech. The debate which followed in the internet columns of the *Chicago Reader*, on the CREOList email bulletin board and elsewhere enabled linguists to engage to some extent with the public on the subject of 'Creole' as a written language. While the question of whether the pamphlet was a racially motivated hoax or the product of well-intentioned ignorance was never resolved, the discussion may have served to raise awareness of issues such as attitudes to non-standard language varieties, the responsibilities of public bodies to different language communities, and the way translating services are delivered.[18,19]

Even to us, as linguists used to dealing with creoles, the HUD text was odd. It did not look like other examples of written creole which we had seen.[20] In spite of there being no written standard for any of the Caribbean English-lexicon Creoles, something about this document seemed to be different from other examples of written creole whose authenticity was beyond doubt. A method of deciding the genuineness of the HUD text suggested itself: to compare it in terms of its linguistic features with a corpus of written creole texts of known provenance. For this purpose, we used a subcorpus of the CWBC.

Within the CWBC five main areas have been identified which distinguish written Creole from written Standard English (SE): orthography, lexis, grammar, semantics and discourse. Features in each of these categories are tagged within the corpus (Sebba *et al.*, 1999). We considered each of them as a basis on which to compare the CWBC and the HUD pamphlet. Discourse markers seemed an inappropriate basis on which to compare texts of this genre.[21] Word-level semantic differences are common in the CWBC but we found none at all in the HUD text. This fact may well be significant but it makes it impossible to do an interesting comparison.[22] Similarly, we found over 200 specifically Creole lexical items in the CWBC subcorpus but none in the HUD text.[23] We therefore decided to concentrate on looking at grammar and orthography.

A strategy that emerges from the CWBC (and our selected subcorpus) is that writers tend to achieve differing 'depths' of Creole through the use of spelling and grammar conventions which are closely linked. There is a strong relationship (correlation significant at the 0.05 level) between the number of Creole grammar features and the number of non-standard spellings found within an individual text. In other words, as the frequency of Creole grammar items increases, there is a tendency for non-standard spellings also to occur more frequently.

This model derived from the CWBC does not, however, describe the relationship found within the HUD document. Using this model, given the high proportion of non-standard spellings in the pamphlet, we would expect there also to be a high proportion of Creole grammar constructions, but in fact the opposite is true. The HUD document contains only 77 instances of Creole grammar constructions. The model predicts that there should be 471 (expected number based on the presence of 635 non-standard spellings). The HUD text actually only contains eight Creole grammar construction types compared to 35 tagged in the CWBC subcorpus.

The high frequency of non-standard spellings suggests that the translator of the HUD pamphlet was aiming to produce a basilectal form of Creole (it would make little sense to translate an SE text into an acrolectal Creole if the purpose of the translation was to reach 'non-English' speakers). But in that case, there is an uncharacteristic lack of Creole grammar forms. In fact, we argue that the HUD text is basically a Standard English text with Creole influences, and that this fact has been disguised by the use of non-standard orthographic strategies. Orthographically it is characterized by an unusually high proportion of non-standard spellings, as compared with the reference corpus of authentic written Creole. Some of these respellings are phonologically motivated, but others are not. This combination of a small number of Creole structures in what is fundamentally a Standard English text, together with respellings of a large number of words, is what creates the impression of parody. As a serious translation of the housing rights document, *Rezedents Rights & Rispansabilities* is a failure.

The fact that it is possible to be 'unsuccessful' when writing a language that has no standard suggests that there is in fact a conventional way to write that language despite a lack of codification. Written Jamaican Creole may be unstandardized, but this does not mean to say that all representations are equally acceptable. This comparative study enabled us to find patterns and trends that are beginning to emerge from written Creole and which can perhaps help to begin explaining how this is coming about. Thus, in spite of its small size, the CWBC has been useful as a tool for distinguishing 'Creole' from 'non-Creole' texts and for studying trends of standardization.

The corpora we have discussed in this chapter are unusual in that they consist of texts in language varieties that are unstandardized, largely thought of as 'unwritten', and which have very fuzzy boundaries separating them from a closely related, high-prestige standard language. As a result, problems of text selection, annotation and tagging arise; some of these (for example, trying to decide whether a text counts as 'British') are specific to these corpora, but others, such as needing a principled basis for deciding what count as tokens of one type, are much broader-ranging. Although our corpora are tiny by modern standards and mainly experimental, they have nonetheless been a source of many usefully interesting challenges.

Notes

1. Here and elsewhere in this chapter, 'Creole' is used as a cover term to mean Jamaican Creole, as used in Britain as well as Jamaica, but no other creoles.
2. In Britain, for example, it has come to light that prisoners of Caribbean origin sometimes write letters in Creole, possibly using it as a sort of code to avoid censorship.
3. The only research on the use of Creole in British-based computer-mediated communication is research by Sebba (2003), but this relates to the use of a 'made-up' creole by largely non-Caribbean adolescents.
4. British Academy Small Personal Research Grant no. 05-012-4670: grant holder Mark Sebba.
5. For a discussion of 'representativeness' of a corpus, see Sebba (1989); also Bungarten (1979) and Rieger (1979).
6. Translation by Mark Sebba. Original text: 'Ein Korpus ist exemplarisch, wenn seine Repraesentativitaet nicht nachgewiesen ist, andererseits weniger formale Argumente, wie evidenter Zusammenhang, linguistische Urteile des kompetenten Forschers, fachlicher Konsensus, textuelle und pragmatische Indikatoren, für eine sinnvolle Vertreterfunktion des Korpus plaedieren.'
7. A similar problem faces the compilers of the Scottish Corpus (Anderson *et al.*, this volume, p. 18): 'Speakers employ features of Broad Scots and Scottish Standard English to different degrees, often depending on context, so that, rather than regarding them as two distinct varieties, it is more accurate to talk about a linguistic continuum running from Scottish English at one end to Broad Scots at the other.'
8. The criterion 'resident in Britain', while desirable from our point of view, was unrealistic; we could not ascertain where authors were currently living or had lived, and some of them lived partly in Britain and partly in the Caribbean.
9. For example, in the Brown and LOB corpora, two early 1,000,000 word corpora, which included a wide range of different genres in an attempt to represent written Standard English as a whole.
10. This is similar to the 'speaker demographic issue' facing the compilers of the ICE-Ireland corpus (Kallen and Kirk, this volume) which means that it is necessary to take account of cross-border movement and communication; the difference being, of course, that Northern and Southern Ireland are contiguous territories. This geographical fact might turn out to be relatively unimportant, however.
11. Dray (2004) interviewed several Creole writers in Jamaica who perceived the reading of fiction and poetry to be a more European practice and felt that foreign publishers looked more favourably on vernacular texts than local publishers.
12. See, for example, Aston and Burnard (1998) on the development of the automatic tagging of the British National Corpus (BNC). For a counter argument to automatic tagging see Sinclair (2004).
13. Research on the written language of youth cultures has addressed this issue. See, for example, Androutsopoulos's (2000) work on the non-standard spellings of German fanzines and Thurlow's (2003) discussion of types found in British text messages.

14. In Jamaican Creole the copula has sociolectal variants *is* and *a*, where *a* is considered to be the more basilectal (Creole) form, for example: *Ah just foolishness really* <bookid=01> <extractid=63> '(It) is just foolishness really'
15. See their discussion for further details and references on this much-discussed issue.
16. See also Devonish (1996) for an interpretation of a similar, if not the same, sign.
17. Infrequency of morphosyntactic constructions in corpora is a general problem, though 'not insoluble' according to Cornips and Corrigan (2005, p. 100).
18. Yet another explanation (not suggested as far as we know) would be that the pamphlet was intended as industrial sabotage, that is, to undermine the good name of the HUD or of the translation company.
19. These issues do not, of course, arise solely in connection with Creole, but potentially in any situation where two related language varieties, one with high and one with low status, are in use. Any attempt to 'dignify' the low variety by using it in public domains or in writing may backfire, being misinterpreted as a joke or a parody. Similar issues, for example, are currently being raised in connection with Ulster Scots (see Kirk, 2003).
20. In order to show the difference between the look of the HUD text and the look of the written Creole texts in the corpora, we have given below an extract from the HUD text, (1), and two equivalent translations in Jamaican Creole, (2) and (3). (We are grateful to Nicholas Pearson and Anthony Greaves for their help with this.) We have used a non-standardized English-based orthography, typical of many of the texts in our corpus, for (2) and (3):

    (1) 'Yuh as a rezedent, ave di rights ahn di rispansabilities to elp mek yuh HUD-asisted owzing ah behta owme fi yuh ahn yuh fambily.'

    (2) Since you a live in a di HUD-scheme, you haffi chip een fi help mek tings better fi you an you family dem.

    Or, in an even 'stronger' Creole version,

    (3) Since unu live roun yaso ina disya HUD-scheme ya, all a unu haffi clean up di place an mek i look gud fi evribadi roun ya.

21. A small, closed set of specific discourse markers is tagged in the CWBC.
22. In the CWBC, the tag <sem=> has been used to indicate that the meaning of the tagged word differs from the Standard English meaning of the same item, for example *babylon*<sem=babylon> indicates that *babylon* here has a Creole-specific meaning ('the police' in this case).
23. For example, the typically Jamaican word *yaad* 'home', which might be considered a key term in a document like this, is conspicuously absent.

References

Androutsopoulos, J. K. 2000. 'Non-standard spellings in media texts: the case of German fanzines'. *Journal of Sociolinguistics* 4(4):514–33.

Aston, G. and L. Burnard. 1998. *The BNC Handbook: Exploring the British National Corpus with SARA*. Edinburgh: Edinburgh University Press.

Bailey, B. L. 1966. *Jamaican Creole Syntax: A Transformational Approach.* Cambridge: Cambridge University Press.

Bungarten, T. 1979. 'Das Korpus als empirische Grundlage in der Linguistik und Literaturwissenschaft'. *Empirische Textwissenschaft* ed. by Bergenholtz, H. and B. Schaeder, pp. 28–51. Königstein im Taunus: Scriptor.

Cassidy, F. G. 1961. *Jamaica Talk.* London: Macmillan.

Cassidy, F. G. and R. B. Le Page. 1967 / 1980. *Dictionary of Jamaican English.* Cambridge: Cambridge University Press.

Cornips, L. and K. P. Corrigan. 2005. 'Convergence and divergence in grammar'. *Dialect Change: Convergence and Divergence in European Languages,* ed. by P. Auer, F. Hinskens and P. Kerswill, pp. 96–134. Cambridge: Cambridge University Press.

De Camp, D. 1961. 'Social and geographical factors in Jamaican dialects'. *Creole Studies II: Proceedings of the Conference on Creole Language Studies,* ed. by R. B. Le Page, pp. 61–84. London: Macmillan.

De Camp, D. 1971. 'Towards a generative analysis of a post-creole speech continuum'. *Pidginization and Creolization of Languages: Proceedings of a Conference held at the University of the West Indies, Mona, Jamaica, April 1968,* ed. by D. Hymes, pp. 349–70. Cambridge: Cambridge University Press.

Devonish, H. 1996. 'Vernacular languages and writing technology transfer'. *Caribbean Language Issues: Old and New,* ed. by P. Christie, pp. 101–11. Kingston: University Press of the West Indies.

Dray, S. 2004. '(W)rites of passage: exploring non-standard texts, writing practices and power in the context of Jamaica'. Unpublished PhD dissertation, Lancaster University.

Facchinetti, R. 1998. 'Expressions of futurity in British Caribbean Creole'. *ICAME Journal* 22:7–22.

Ferguson, C. A. 1959. 'Diglossia'. *Word* 15:325–40.

Headley, V. 1993. *Yardie.* London: Pan Macmillan.

Hewitt, R. 1986. *White Talk, Black Talk.* Cambridge: Cambridge University Press.

Hinrichs, L. 2003. 'The discourse-analysis of computer-mediated communication: language alternation phenomena in Jamaican e-mail'. Paper presented at the Georgetown University Round Table on Languages and Linguistics, 15–17 February 2003.

Hinrichs, L. 2004. 'Emerging orthographic conventions in written Creole: computer-mediated communication in Jamaica'. *Arbeiten aus Anglistik und Amerikanistik* 29(1):81–109.

Kirk, J. M. 2003. 'Archipelagic glotto-politics: the Scotstacht'. *The Celtic Englishes III,* ed. by H. L. C. Tristram, pp. 339–56. Heidelberg: Carl Winter.

Mair, C. 2003. 'Language, code, and symbol: the changing roles of Jamaican Creole in diaspora communities'. *Arbeiten aus Anglistik und Amerikanistik* 28(2):231–48.

McEnery, A. M., Z. Xiao and Y. Tono. 2005. *Corpus-based Language Studies.* London: Routledge.

Mühleisen, S. 2002. *Creole Discourse: Exploring Prestige Formation and Change Across Caribbean–English-lexicon Creoles.* Amsterdam: John Benjamins.

Patrick, P. L. 1999. *Urban Jamaican Creole: Variation in the Mesolect.* (Varieties of English Around the World G17). Amsterdam: John Benjamins.

Pollard, V. 1999. *Hospital Hyster(ia).* Seminario de Literatura Postcolonial, literatura caribeña contemporánea. Oviedo: Universidad de Oviedo.

Rampton, B. 1995. *Crossing: Language and Ethnicity among Adolescents*. London: Longman.

Raumolin-Brunberg, H. and T. Nevalainen. 2007. 'Historical sociolinguistics: the Corpus of Early English Correspondence'. *Creating and Digitizing Language Corpora: Diachronic Databases (Volume 2)*, ed by J. C. Beal, K. P. Corrigan and H. L. Moisl, pp. 148–71. Basingstoke: Palgrave Macmillan.

Rieger, B. 1979. 'Repräsentativität: von der Unangemessenheit eines Begriffs zur Kennzeichnung eines Problems linguistischer Korpusbildung'. *Empirische Textwissenschaft*, ed. by H. Bergenholtz and B. Schaeder, pp. 52–70. Königstein im Taunus: Scriptor.

Sebba, M. 1989. 'The adequacy of corpora'. Unpublished MSc dissertation, University of Manchester Institute of Science and Technology (UMIST).

Sebba, M. 1993. *London Jamaican: Language Systems in Interaction*. London: Longman.

Sebba, M. 1998a. 'Meaningful choices in Creole orthography: "experts" and users'. *Making Meaningful Choices in English: On Dimensions, Perspectives, Methodology and Evidence*, ed. by R. Schulze, pp. 223–34. Tübingen: Gunter Narr.

Sebba, M. 1998b. 'Phonology meets ideology: the meaning of orthographic practices in British Creole'. *Language Problems and Language Planning* 22(1):19–47.

Sebba, M. 2003. 'Will the real impersonator please stand up? Language and identity in the Ali G websites'. *Arbeiten aus Anglistik und Amerikanistik* 28(2):279–304.

Sebba, M., S. Kedge and S. Dray. 1999. *The Corpus of Written British Creole: A User's Guide*: http://www.ling.lancs.ac.uk/staff/mark/cwbc/cwbcman.htm

Sinclair, J. 2004. 'Intuition and annotation – the discussion continues'. *Advances in Corpus Linguistics: Papers from ICAME 23*, ed. by K. Aijmer and B. Altenberg, pp. 39–59. Amsterdam and New York: Rodopi.

Thurlow, C. 2003. 'Generation txt? The sociolinguistics of young people's text-messaging'. *Discourse Analysis Online*, 1(1) (see http://www. faculty.washington. edu/thurlow/publications. html).

9

Representing Real Language: Consistency, Trade-Offs and Thinking Ahead!

Sali A. Tagliamonte

1 Introduction

When faced with a collection of dozens upon dozens of audio tapes, minidiscs or other recorded media, what do you do next? How can you make the invaluable data contained within maximally accessible and useful? A number of procedures have developed over the years for turning audio-taped vernacular speech materials into efficient, user-friendly computerized data. In these volumes you will find discussion of many corpus creation projects similar to the ones I report here, all with their own strategies (for example, Anderwald and Wagner, this volume, and both Allen *et al.*, and Taylor, Volume 2). Since data sources and type of data as well as researchers' own goals differ, there are wide-ranging differences among them. In this chapter, I focus on 'tried and true' procedures from my own experience. I build on the foundations of earlier corpus-building projects (see Poplack, 1989; Poplack and Tagliamonte, 1991) that I have been involved in, although my main focus is on data arising from recent large-scale fieldwork conducted in Northern Ireland and Britain between 1995 and 2001 (Tagliamonte, 1996–98, 1999–2000, 2000–01, 2001–03).

2 Foundations of a corpus construction project

The fundamental parts of a corpus construction project are listed in Figure 9.1. The basic substance of a language corpus is the data. Most of my corpora have been collected on audio tapes and represent one to two hours of conversation between a single interviewer and an informant. These audio tapes are catalogued (minimally) by number, date and name of the speaker. Each audio tape has a corresponding 'interview report', a document which provides a record of anthropological information and

a.	Recording media, audio tapes (analogue) or other
b.	Interview reports (hard copies)
c.	Transcription files (ASCII, WORD, TXT)
d.	A transcription protocol (hard copy and soft)
e.	A database of information (FileMaker)
f.	Analysis files (GoldVarb files, TOKEN, CEL, CND and RES)

Figure 9.1 Components of a synchronic dialect corpus

observations about the speaker and the interview context. The 'transcription files' are the soft-copy data files in which these conversations have been transcribed. The 'transcription protocol' is a document that details the precise method by which the conversations have been transcribed. The 'database of information' is a relational database on computer in which all the information from the interview reports is recorded (such as speaker codes and numbers, and so on), as well as ongoing information about the linguistic data. Finally, the 'analysis files' are the many different computer files that are produced when a particular linguistic feature is subjected to a fully fledged study. In my own work, analyses of these corpora produce innumerable data files from processing with the Variable Rule Program, the key tool of variationist sociolinguistics (Sankoff and Labov, 1979; Rand and Sankoff, 1990).

In what follows, I provide an account of the principles of database management that I have employed, as well as an overview of the mechanics of corpus-building that have evolved over the years. This information should be of interest to readers who are looking for ideas about how to create and manage their own unconventional corpora. In particular, I discuss the pros and cons of representing non-standard phonological and morphosyntactic features. I have chosen examples from my archive of British dialects to illustrate the points made. These are also intended to provide readers with a 'flavour' of the language data.

3 Strategies for organizing a corpus

Perhaps the most important strategy for corpus-building is to have a strict procedure in place for transcribing the data, maintaining consistency and identifying each of the components of a corpus and linking them together. The analyst must be able to access the required materials easily and efficiently, in other words, to have the data at your fingertips.

3.1 Labelling

The most basic organizational tool is simple: copious 'labelling'. First, each speaker must have a pseudonym. This is, of course, standard ethical practice as well. It ensures that the speakers' identities are entirely anonymous. My own strategy for this is to use the speaker's own initials, but replace these with new, ethnically consistent names, as in Figure 9.2.

a.	Susan Smith	=	Sarah Small
b.	David Patterson	=	Darrel Peters

Figure 9.2 Protocol for pseudonyms

Each speaker is also provided with an informant number and, critically, a single-digit speaker identification code for use in coding his or her data for analysis. Each of the audio tapes or minidiscs, the interview report and the transcription files are all labelled with the same information.

a.	Corpus/community, e.g. YORK [YRK]
	Informant pseudonym, *Elise Burritt* [EB]
	Tape #, 003
	Informant #, 002
	Speaker identification code, b*
b.	Corpus/community, e.g. YORK [YRK]
	Informant pseudonym, *Sophie Ball* [SB]
	Tape #, 079
	Informant #, 049
	Speaker identification code, W

Figure 9.3 Protocol for identification

Note:

* The single digit symbols (speaker identification codes) are unique for each individual and encompass both upper- and lower-case letters as well as symbols. The Courier keyboard offers sufficient symbols for this purpose, although as corpora expand, speakers will inevitably be assigned the same symbol. In such cases they can be differentiated by their community or corpus code.

This may be observed in Figure 9.3 above, which shows these details for two speakers from the York English corpus (Tagliamonte, 1996–98).

The unique identification codes and numbers for each speaker across all the components of a corpus enable the data associated with the individual speakers to be permanently traceable back to their source: the audio record. As we shall see, even with considerable effort invested in transcribing corpora effectively, it is still absolutely necessary to have easy access to the original data source.

An identifying string is always placed at the beginning of the transcription file, as in Figure 9.4. Here, as well, are indicators of speaker age, 82 in (a) and 23 in (b), the interviewer(s) who conducted the interview, in this case Clare and/or Angela, and the speaker numbers that have been assigned to them, interviewer numbers 1 and 2 respectively. In addition, transcriptions must identify the number of the audio tape, as well as the side of the audio tape, if applicable (for example, side A or B).

The speaker's numeric code precedes each segment of their speech in the transcribed interviews. Speakers [002] and [049] are illustrated in the excerpts in Figure 9.5. Participants in the interviews with speaker [002] and speaker [049] are also indicated by numbers in square brackets. Interviewers are typically assigned single-digit numbers, for example 1, 2 or 3; and informants two- or three-digit numbers, for example 001, depending on the total number of speakers in the corpus.[1] The square brackets indicate that the numbers are to be interpreted as speaker changes (rather than numeric data) in later data-processing.

a. [York, Elise Burritt, 82, EB 002, Clare 1, Angela 2, Tape 003]

b. [York, Sophie Ball, 23, SB 049, Clare 1, Informant's mother 7, Tape 079]

Figure 9.4 Protocol for labelling transcription files

a. [1] So where were you born then? Tell me about where you were born. [002] Well the area isn't there now. Actually, it was in Layerthorpe, which you won't know. [1] Right [002] Er, we had a big-ish house where we had all stabling round, because it was horses in those days.

b. [1] Was it one of those black ones? [049] No, it was a white one. Well white plasti-- [1] A soft one? [049] No white plastic one. [1] Yeah, 'cos -I- I had - [049] Hard plastic.

Figure 9.5 Transcription conventions

3.2 Transcribing a corpus

One of the major problems in transcribing conversational data is that the spoken language is not at all like written language. Yet, translation from one medium to the other is required. In fact, recorded conversations of 'real' language present a number of very tricky challenges for transcription to written text. How do you end up with a corpus that provides a maximally usable rendition of the spoken language in an affordable amount of time? A crucial first step is to determine the form that the transcription will take.

Practically speaking, even an interview of one hour might require an investment of anywhere from a day's worth of work to an entire week or more. A standard estimate for a first transcription is 'one hour of recorded data; four hours of transcribing'. However, this estimate varies widely depending on the quality of the sound, the number of speakers in the recording, and the familiarity of the transcriber with the dialect represented on the audio record. Given the time and financial constraints of any project, it is important to keep these practical constraints in mind when balancing between the desired detail of a transcription and the time it takes to complete it. There are inherent and unavoidable limits to any type of transcription. Whenever you transcribe spoken material, it is imperative to keep in mind that 'no score of it can ever be so detailed and precise as to provide for the recreation of the full sound of the tape' (Macaulay, 1991, p. 282, quoting Tedlock, 1983, pp. 5–6). In other words, the audio record will at all times, and in every instance, remain the primary documentation of your data. In light of these considerations, one might think that the most complete, the most detailed transcription would be the best. In fact, this is not the case at all. If you had to represent all the phonetic or even phonological variation in natural speech in writing, it would take an interminable amount of time to transcribe. The fact of the matter is that a good transcription is not the most detailed. Instead, think of transcription (following Pike, 1947) as a process that seeks to establish a satisfactory way of 'reducing languages to writing' (part of the subtitle of Pike's book). The operative words here are *reducing* and *satisfactory*. The transcription process is actually all about deciding, carefully, about what to represent and what not to represent so as to facilitate future research.

A first step in this direction is to decide the *purpose* of the transcription, in other words, what the goals of the research are. Any transcription, no matter how detailed, is going to be an interpretation of what exists on the audio-taped record. Thus, transcribing is necessarily selective. Labov and Fanshel (1977, p. 40) say explicitly, 'we do not attempt to show fine phonetic details in our text'. In the Ottawa–Hull project, one of the largest computerized corpora in the world (three and a half million words), Poplack (1989, p. 430 and the foreword to this volume) notes 'that there's a major trade-off between size of the data base and level of detail of the transcription'. Thus, the goals of a transcription can be encapsulated as the desire for it to be: (a) detailed enough to retain enough information to conduct linguistic analyses in an efficient way, and (b) simple enough to be relatively easily transcribed and easily readable.

Maintaining a workable balance between these two goals is the key component of any corpus construction endeavour.

3.2.1 Procedures for transcription

The first rule of thumb for transcription is that the recorded speech data be represented as faithfully as possible. This means transcribing verbatim what the person said regardless of whether it follows the so-called rules of the standard language. But then how does one represent all the 'weird and wonky' aspects of spoken language consistently? This is perhaps the most important reason for investing in a transcription protocol, particularly when the long-term goal is comparison across a number of different corpora. The transcription protocol is a permanent record that ensures the consistent representation of words, phrases, features of natural discourse and features particular to the data, even if they do not have standard orthographic conventions.

In the first instance, however, what does one do with the normal aspects of speech that are never encountered in written language? Standard orthographic conventions are critical, in order to ensure the utility of automated extraction of individual linguistic items, as well as to make the corpus maximally comprehensible to the wider research community. Take, for example, a writer like Leonard (1984), a poet who has paid particular attention to representing dialect in writing (Macaulay, 1988), as in Figure 9.6.

Yi write doon a wurd, nyi sati yirsell, that's no this way a say it. Nif yi tryti write it doon this way yi say it, yi end up si thi page covered in letter struck thigithir, nwee dots above hof thi letters, in fact yi end up wi wanna they thingz yi needti huv took a course in phonetics ti be able ti read.

Figure 9.6 Leonard's representation of dialect

The problem is that this type of transcription is exceptionally hard to read. As Ochs (1979, p. 44) points out, 'a transcript that is too detailed is difficult to follow and assess. A more useful transcription is a more selective one'. The question then becomes what to select.

3.2.2 Orthographic conventions

Use of standard orthography and standard punctuation are critical for readability and ease of transcription. Indeed, the arguments for using 'normal' orthographic transcription and avoiding semi-phonetic spelling and eye-dialect as far as possible are made quite forcefully by Preston (1985, 2000). This has led me to the following transcription 'rules': (1) spell the word the way it is normally spelled (unless you have just cause to include a different rendition of a word); further, (2) use standard punctuation, that is full stops (periods), question marks, commas and so on, as you would normally use them in writing.

However, natural speech requires even further 'rules' of representation. Because speech is replete with false starts, interrupted words, hesitations, rephrasing, and so on, these must be indicated in a consistent and readable way in the transcription. The practice I have followed is summarized below:

- Use hyphens to represent false starts, as in Figure 9.7.
- Use double hyphens to represent partial words, as in Figure 9.8.
- Audible pauses in the discourse are marked with three dots, as in Figure 9.9 below.

---

a. [002] You got the bull down with *a-* a rope, pulled its head down with a rope…

b. [004] And I just - *didn't-* didn't want to be rotten.

Figure 9.7 False starts

---

a. [002] All around the city walls was cattle pens, and that was where my dad where the *Bar--* Barbican is now, that was a lovely big cattle market.

b. [002] Our Ron, a *lov--* lovely young man.

c. [046] But the *nu--* the nurses on the nights…

Figure 9.8 Partial words

a.	[002] *Er*... wh-- [1] You were saying about Ron.
b.	[002] In them days, you didn't care, but *um*... oh, this is family history now.

Figure 9.9 Pauses or silence

All these protocols facilitate readability of the transcription. Another important thing to keep in mind when transcribing data is the use of hyphenation more generally. This technique can be used as a 'linking' device to associate words with each other so that they are treated together in data-processing at a later stage of research. For example, an informant might have an overwhelming number of forms such as '*that is to say*' throughout his or her discourse. What is its function? Do the words that make it up have equal categorical status to those same words used in other contexts? If not, then it is a good candidate for being a discourse marker of some sort. I will typically hyphenate fixed expressions and exclamations, as in Figure 9.10, as well as tags, as in Figure 9.11. Names of people, places, songs and games are hyphenated, as in Figure 9.12. This procedure ensures that they will be treated uniquely for later retrieval and analysis. It also keeps these constructions separate from other more grammatical uses of the same forms.

Paralinguistic interventions, such as *huh, er, uh, mhm*, and so on, are also indicated in standardized orthography. However, given the frequency of these features and their interdialectal and even idiolectal

a.	god-knows
b.	as-I-say
c.	to-be-honest

Figure 9.10 Formulaic utterances: expressions

a.	and-everthing
b.	do-you-know-what-I-mean?
c.	do-you-know?

Figure 9.11 Formulaic utterances: discourse markers

a.	Foss-Islands-Road
b.	Walmgate-Bar
c.	Barbian-Centre
d.	Santa-Claus
e.	Rosie-and-Jim
f.	Sister-in-law
g.	piggy-in-the-middle

Figure 9.12 Formulaic utterances: people, places, songs, games

differences, it is important not to overly complicate the transcription protocol with innumerable spellings. This will significantly complicate the transcription process as transcribers attempt to judge each time which spelling to employ. I have typically opted to represent the *major* forms of the dialect and abstract away from the innumerable details.

In British dialects I ended up with forms such as <er>, <mm>, and <um>, as in Figures 9.13, 9.14 and 9.15.

Er occurred 128 times in speaker [002]

a.	[1] Was that Maureen? [002] *Er* yes, Maureen was the eldest.
b.	[046] He was *er* extremely lucky

Figure 9.13 Paralinguistic interventions: *er*

Mm occurred 47 times in speaker [002] and three times in speaker [049]

a.	[002] Oh that's lovely, *mm.*
b.	[1] And it happened on the Monday? [049] *Mm.*

Figure 9.14 Paralinguistic interventions: *mm*

Um occurred 24 times in speaker [002] and 52 times with speaker [046]

a. [002] And *um*, er, anyway we got that sorted out, and they were friends again.

b. [046] The blimmin *um*, what-you-call-it.

Figure 9.15 Paralinguistic interventions: *um*

The protocol for what I have referred to as 'legal fillers' from one of our British dialectal corpora is shown in Table 9.1 (Tagliamonte 2000–01).

Laughter, as in Figure 9.16 (a), other noises, and contextual information which aids in interpreting the text, as in Figure 9.16 (b), are marked off from the text with parentheses.

Table 9.1 Legal fillers from the Vernacular Roots Project

Form	Meaning/description
eh?	question (often tag)
euh	expressing distaste
er	
hm?	question
huh	question filler
hum	
mm	1 syllable filler meaning 'yes'
mm-mm	2 syllable filler meaning 'yes'
ooo!	expressing surprise/pain
ouch!	expressing pain
oops!	exclamatory
phew	
shh	as in telling someone to be quiet
uh-huh	2 syllable filler meaning 'yes'
uh-uh	2 syllable filler meaning 'no'
um	
whoa	exclamatory
wow	exclamatory

a. [002] The man never moved so fast in his life! *(laughter)* His language was disgusting, my father'z.

b. [046] There's far too much to do and to see, and- and nobody'd know that i-- *(knocking)*. Hello? Well it's late.

Figure 9.16 Noises and contextual information

Inevitably, some parts of natural speech are entirely incomprehensible. Sometimes this is due to the quality of the recording, sometimes to interference from other noise on the recording, sometimes simply because the transcriber is not sufficiently familiar with the phonology of the dialect. All sections of the discourse that are not understood are indicated, as in Figure 9.17.

Another aspect of natural speech data is that conversations are inherently overlapping. What is to be done with simultaneous speech by two or more interlocutors? A two-tiered transcription significantly complicates the transcription. The practice I have adopted is to record what the first person says, then the second, as in Figure 9.18, despite the fact that much of these interchanges overlaps considerably.

a. [046] You haven't given me my *(inc)*.

b. [002] Before I *(inc)* it will do no good

Figure 9.17 Incomprehensible discourse

[007] Oh aye, aye, I seen that old boy. (laughter) [1] You're laching, you're la-- [007] I'm no laching, I'm jo-- I'm telling you. [1] you've seen it? [007] Scared the life out o me. [1] tell us [009] yeah, tell her about it [1] tell us about it? [007] I was coming- I'm very pally wi a feller called Jim-Steele...(jabbott/007/PVG)*

Figure 9.18 Overlapping conversation

Note:

* Speaker identification strings may include the pseudonym, in this case 'jabbott' is the first initial of the first name, 'j', and the last name, 'abbott'. This is followed by the speaker number, [007], and the corpus identifier, in this case [PVG], which is a corpus collected from the village of Portavogie in Northern Ireland.

3.2.3 Which linguistic phenomena to represent?

I now turn to the linguistic implications of transcribing conversational speech, and the question of what level of linguistic detail to represent.

By the mere fact of being spoken, the language of conversation contains all kinds of natural linguistic processes, things like vowel reduction, consonant elision and so on. At the same time there are literally hundreds of variable processes happening at all levels of the grammar. For example, each word may have a number of different pronunciations in the same discourse and these different pronunciations could be represented in a number of different ways, as you can see in Figure 9.19.

a.	*just* – just, jus'
b.	*going to* – going to, goin' to, gonna, gon
c.	*because* – 'cause, 'cos, beca', etc.
d.	*my* – my, mi

Figure 9.19 Variation in pronunciation

It is necessary to decide which of these variant realizations are meaningful to one's ongoing research interests and which are not. If any of these were meaningful distinctions for future analysis, then they would be worth differentiating. However, I will insert a strong cautionary note here. Each and every one of the distinctions that you decide to represent will complicate the transcription process in terms of having to listen out for and distinguish these items phonologically while transcribing. Further, it will complicate the end product in terms of readability. Thus, it is critical to have a plan in mind that can balance the complexity of transcription with the requirements of the analyses that will follow. Indeed, Labov & Fanshel (1977) emphasize in their transcription methodology that they included just those features that they consider important for their purposes. The following strategies are part of the 'tried and true' protocols I have developed for my own research.

3.2.4 Phonological processes

First, phonological processes are typically not represented in a transcription. This means no commas to indicate dropping of <g>, <t> and <d> deletion, or the like. No abbreviations of things such as <lemme> for <let me>, <wanna> for <want to> and untold others. Many of these phonological processes are quite superficial and result from normal reduction and/or elision processes typical of spoken language. Representing them creates a transcription that is difficult to read, understand and work with, and has few returns linguistically. My strategy is to represent variation resulting from the operation of general phonological processes in standard orthography regardless of the actual pronunciation of the form. In any case, if ever a study on any of these phonological processes was to be undertaken, it would be necessary to go back to the original tape to extract the data. Thus, for example, in a study of variable (t,d) in the York corpus (Tagliamonte and Temple, 2005), we went back to the original recordings in order to extract relevant contexts and code the data. However, with the transcription file available and visible, data retrieval, extraction and coding were greatly facilitated because we could 'see' where the relevant words were coming up in the discourse.

3.2.5 *Morphological processes*

For my own research purposes representation of morphological, syntactic and discourse/pragmatic variation is key. The rule of thumb I use is that morphological alternations that are phonologically marked should be orthographically represented. But the question is: how do you decide on what that representation should be?

3.2.5.1 Variants of the copula. A good example is the variants of copula *is*. When this form of the copula is contracted to another word, it is represented orthographically as an <s> attached to that word by an apostrophe rather than a separate word <is>, as in Figure 9.20 (a).

The issue then becomes how to distinguish the contracted variant and yet be able to identify it as a variant of the full form? Further, is it important to distinguish it from contracted auxiliary *have*? One way to handle this is to create a separate transcription practice for the cliticized forms. In order to ensure that the <s> is treated separately from the pronoun it is attached to, I opted for a practice of leaving a space between the pronoun and the <'s>, as in Figure 9.20 (b). This ensures that automated processing will extract all the instances of apostrophe + <s>, whereas all pronouns will be treated together regardless of whether <s> is attached or not. Notice that two of these forms in Figure 9.20 represent an underlying *is*, while one represents an underlying *has*. In this case, I have left the two contractions identical. It is difficult to imagine an orthographic variant that would not have unnecessarily complicated the transcription. Further, what would be the research return in going to the trouble of doing so? These are the types of trade-offs that go with transcription decisions.

On the other hand, zero copula forms, because of their importance for the study of British dialects, were represented, as in Figure 9.21.[2]

a. He's grown up now, and since the new baby's come along, he's reluctant to leave home. (YRK:x)

b. He 's grown up now, and since the new baby 's come along, he 's reluctant to leave home. (YRK:x)

Figure 9.20 Contracted copula

a.	There ϕ an awful draft. (rwatt/039/CMK)
b.	There ϕ an old chappie come from Aberdeen. (bdonaldson/015/CMK)

Figure 9.21 Zero copula

As anyone who has conducted analyses on corpora knows, unless you mark the zeros somehow, they are impossible to find and extract without re-reading through the transcripts. So this practice enables us to find the zero variants using automated retrieval.

3.2.5.2 Suffixes. In most of my own projects, the research focus has been on morphological and syntactic variation. One of the features of potential interest was the plural suffix *-s*, which I knew was variable in our data before I even started transcribing. Therefore I included in the transcription protocol a specific directive to transcribe every noun that contained a zero plural marker as it was pronounced, as in Figure 9.22.

I note, however, that the decision not to represent the zero contexts overtly has had obvious ramifications for future research. They are not easily retrieved, but must be sought out by reading through the transcription files and checking the context for each noun. Perhaps this is one of the reasons I have never conducted a large-scale study of variable plural marking in British dialects.

Possessive *-s* was assigned the form <z> in order to distinguish it from contracted forms of *is*, *was*, and so on. Verbal *-s*, as in Figure 9.23 (b) below, was left attached to its verb.

In what follows I illustrate a number of additional form/function decisions.

3.2.6 Other key form/function differences

The word *like* has many different uses in English, some of which are currently undergoing change. Thus, there are good reasons to create a

a.	He's four or five *year* ded. (djames/001/PVG)
b.	There's naebody in the last fifty *years* had food poisoning fae fish. (jabbot/007/PVG)
c.	Steamer wa about two *mile* away, outside o us. (jabbot/007/PVG)
d.	They've got an agreement with the traders now to do it for six-*month* to see whether it er improves the situation. (pjackson/031/MPT)

Figure 9.22 Variable zero plural marking

a. Well in my father'*z* young days he would work on farms (jscott/036/CMK)

b. But onyway, away I *goes* to it. (jabbot/007/PVG)

Figure 9.23 Possessive -*s* and verbal -*s*

separate representation for *like*'s different functions. The standard function of *like* is the verb, as in 'I *like* cheese'. However, in many dialects there are numerous, non-standard, other functions, some of which are referred to as 'discourse markers' as in 'I *like* love it'. In order to be able to recuperate from the data all the non-standard uses of *like* simply and efficiently, one has to devise a way to make them extractable separately from the lexical verb *like*, and other standard uses of the form, that is comparatives, 'the moon looks *like* cheese'. One way to do this was to give the non-standard uses a different orthographic representation. My strategy was to transcribe these uses as <lyke> and leave the standard forms as <like>, as in Figure 9.24. This gives the non-standard functions a unique representation.

a. [1] What was it *like* when you were growing up in York then? What- what did it look *like*? [002] Well we were never poor. We never *lyke*- I - I saw people without shoes and things.

b. [049] I was to totally calm *like* this. And I was *lyke*, really really *lyke* surprised at how good I was kind-of-thing, and then he was the one who was *like* that. And then I got out the car, *lyke*, we were sat in there for a while.

c. Well a little silly mistake, *lyke*, a referee, he could cost them millions, *lyke*, millions of pounds *lyke*. (scully/006/PVG)

Figure 9.24 Representing the functions of *like*

At the outset, my thinking was that if this gross distinction was made, it would be recoverable and I would not have to go through the data files painstakingly to separate out those functions that were of interest from those that were not. However, this strategy turned out not to be adequate, as *like* presented a particularly tricky case. As the transcription phase advanced it soon became clear that this feature was in the process of rapid change. Indeed, it was virtually impossible for transcribers (linguistics students in their twenties) to differentiate which *like* uses were standard and which were not! In the end, studies of *like* using these corpora cannot be based on automated extraction alone, but must be conducted by going back through the data files and extracting relevant contexts by hand. Like the study of variable (t,d) however, the most important task has been successfully implemented. All uses of *like* in the materials are recoverable from the transcription files.

Another example of form/function differentiation is the treatment of the collocation *you know*. Most of the time it is an interjection, as in Figure 9.25 (a). The question is whether this should be distinguished from the full verb *know* used with the second-person plural pronoun *you*. The fact that in the interjection the subject–verb association has been bleached (lost) warrants including *you-know* as one word. This ensures that it can be treated as a single lexical entry, with all interjection *you know* forms brought together. This ensures that the interjections can be retrieved separately from instances of the full verb. Similarly, a study of lexical verbs, as in Figure 9.25 (b), will not be 'contaminated' by dozens of interjections.

a. [002] I loved dancing, but he would always be at the door at time, *you-know*, when it was to come home [YRK/x]

b. [049] Do *you know* what I said? [YRK/x]

Figure 9.25 Representing *you know*

There is a wide range of features of this type in English, including *I-mean*, *you-see*, and so on, as in Figure 9.26. What procedure you put in place with respect to these items will depend on whether or not you want to study them at some future time.

All these procedures combine to create a maximally accessible and usable transcription. At the same time, each decision adds to the margin of error in the transcription, since the distinctions amongst forms must be decided upon each time the form is encountered in the data. For example, the comparative *like*, as in Figure 9.24 (b), 'I was totally calm, *like* this', transcribed as *lyke* would be inaccurate. Further, once you decide to represent a particular feature in a certain way, this must be done every single time. If not, the transcription will be unreliable. The problem is that, more often than not, these decisions are not

a. [002] *I-mean* none of us really know what happens in the wars untill you sit and talk about it.

b. [002] But *you-see*, he's grown up now.

c. So the first week was a bit, *you-know*, I was a bit *you-know*, I was a bit lyke-er- in and out, semi *sort-of sort-of* conscious type, an– *I-mean* I- not sleep, but just- because I was taking drugs and that *kind-of-thing* and the state you're in just- feel-

Figure 9.26 Other interjections

transparent and require additional linguistic interpretation. The transcriber must interpret the function of each form before transcribing it. This is the danger of creating variant forms. It adds to the complexity of the transcription process and can lead to errors.

In fact, pre-deciding the way forms will be transcribed is a particularly thorny issue. Most critical is the fact that the function of non-standard forms is often unknown a priori. In most cases, analysis is required to determine what the actual function of a non-standard form is. Furthermore, some forms, as with *like*, are in the process of rapid change. This means that transcribers in one age bracket might not have the same grammaticality judgements as project directors in another age bracket. In my own experience, this can lead to innumerable difficulties. Inconsistencies and errors arising from this type of practical problem can have a major impact on future work on the corpus. In the end, it is often best to opt for the most conservative decision, that is, to transcribe like forms in like manner, and leave the analysis of their (potential) different functions for a later stage in the research process. Indeed, in my view the very best practice for data analysis using machine-readable corpora is to combine automated extraction with the exacting methodological procedures that arise from the principle of accountability and circumscribing of the variable context (see Labov, 1970, 1971; Sankoff, 1980; Sankoff and Thibault, 1980; Wolfram, 1993; Foreword to this volume).

3.2.7 Words that do not exist in (standard) dictionaries

Another challenge for the transcription process is to keep track of the different ways to write the words people use in speech that do not exist in standard dictionaries, or that do appear in dictionaries but have several different orthographies. A decision must be made about how to transcribe these words. The transcription protocol is the place to keep a record of each decision.

Most corpora will inevitably have particular dialect features that are not part of standard English grammar, and which will require a representation. For example, in York the forms <owt> and <nowt> are used for *any-*

a. Oh, I wouldn't know *nowt* about that (rfielding/092/YRK)

b. It's very sad when *owt* like this happens. (csmith/035/YRK)

c. They didn't give us *owt* so I never bothered nae more. (ewilliams/011/MPT)

Figure 9.27 *Nowt* and *owt*

thing and *nothing* respectively, as in Figure 9.27 (a) and (b). Moreover, these same forms are also found in other dialect corpora, for example, Maryport, North-west England, as in Figure 9.27 (c). Thus, the same spelling for this form and function is employed across all dialects in the archive.

Negative constructions are often quite different from Standard English in northern British dialects. I decided on the spelling <nae>, as in Figure 9.28, for cliticized forms and <no>, as in Figure 9.29, for non-cliticized forms. These are entered into the transcription protocol for reference, so that they are consistently represented across all corpora.

a. They would *nae* fall pregnant for another yin. (wburns/037/CMK)

b. I hae *nae* idea where she come from. (djames/001/PVG)

c. And she says this boot come down the stair. Step for step. But there were *nae* boot. (jabbot/007/PVG)

Figure 9.28 Negatives: *nae*

a. It's *no* very long. (djames/001/PVG)

b. Sean's surely *no* getting topsoil? (scully/006/PVG)

Figure 9.29 Negatives: *no*

There are dozens of other dialect words, some of which are shown in Figure 9.30. All of these are recorded in the transcription protocol.

Idiosyncratic spellings can simply be different pronunciations of standard forms, for example <snaw> for <snow>. In dialect materials, I have often opted to represent lexical words in their dialect orthography.

a. *fae = from*

b. *yin = one*

c. *gin = by*

d. *mind = remember*

e. *laal = little*

Figure 9.30 Dialect words

The standard procedure for deciding which dialect spellings to use was straightforward. First, consult the literature (that is, existing dialect dictionaries, online dictionaries and other corpora) and establish form, function and spelling conventions. When different orthographic choices exist, choose the most frequently used one. In the rare case that a word cannot be found, make a reasoned choice regarding its spelling and record it in the transcription protocol for future reference.

3.2.8 Non-standard verbal morphology

Verb forms are notoriously varied in dialect data, as shown in Figure 9.31, illustrating details from transcription records for Ayrshire, south-west Scotland, Northern Ireland and Maryport, North-west England.

a. *Ayrshire:* 'ging' for 'go'
'taen' for 'took / taken'

b. *Maryport:* 'ga' for 'go' ; 'going' is sometimes 'ga'

c. *Northern Ireland:* 'teld' for 'told'
'haen' for 'had' (past participle)
'riz' for 'raise' (preterit)
'quat' : past participle of *quit*

Figure 9.31 Dialectal variation in verb forms

a. Aye, I *hae* a question. (jabbott/007/PVG)

b. There were a jump *riz* ont. (mellis/017/CLB)

c. She *telt* me to clear off. (lfisher/0296/MPT)

d. They're all been *taen* away, they tell me. (abonaldson/016/CMK)

e. They'd *gie* you a penny for it. (fbell/017/CMK)

f. Just because he *knowed* it was there, he could- he could wait ni longer. (rpaisley/008/CLB)

Figure 9.32 Representing dialect forms

I made every effort to represent these unique forms, and record them in our transcription protocol so that they were consistently represented across all corpora. You can see some examples in Figure 9.32.

3.2.9 Slang, local terminology and expressions

Varieties may sometimes have their own unique swear words, as in Figure 9.33, local terminology and expressions, as in Figure 9.34, and formulaic expressions, as in Figure 9.35. All these will require consistent representation across transcriptions or even across a broader set of corpora.

I have found that it is generally best to represent all alternate pronunciations the way they were produced, as long as they result from the operation of linguistic processes rather than from phonological processes or the natural pronunciation aspects of oral speech. However, there are many 'grey areas'. For example, what does the analyst do with phonologically variable pronunciations of *going to* when it is used as a future temporal reference marker? These can be represented orthographically as, <going to>, <gointa>, <goina>, <gonna>, <onna>, and so on. Should these be rendered by identical orthography, namely <going to>, or should they be differentiated? An important factor to consider is that, in the ongoing grammatical change of *going to* as a future temporal reference marker, phonological coalescence of form is an important concomitant of the grammaticalization process (see Poplack and Tagliamonte, 1999). Thus, differentiating phonological forms is implicated in a grammatical process. But is this worth representing in a data transcription? The only way to answer this question is to determine how important the distinctions will be for future research. Do you want to invest the time and attention during the transcription phase, or later on?

3.3 Database management

Concurrent with the corpus construction phase, I always invest a great deal of time in creating a relational database of information using a program called FileMaker. This is where all the information from the interview reports is recorded. Once entered in a relational database, this information can be processed in any number of different ways. For example, at any given time, the corpora in my archive can be searched for females aged 70–75 with minimal education. How many are there? Which community do they live in? Who are they?

blimmin'

frigging (intensifier, 'it was frigging cold')

Figure 9.33 Dialectal swear words

banty: a small, strutting, conceited person; or fowl

caff beds: mattresses filled with chaff

crack: talk, gossip

fadge: type of bread

gulder: shout angrily, grumble

hoke: dig

laghter: a clutch of eggs

prittas: potatoes

tripper: a crude ladder

witchell: wee child, young boy

yam: home

Figure 9.34 Local terminology and expressions

by-golly

boys-a-boys, boys-a-dear, boys-alive, o-boys-oh

roch and ready

Figure 9.35 Formulaic expressions

What are their other characteristics, such as education level, type of employment, and so on? When I search for such individuals in my York English corpus, I get the results in Table 9.2. This type of information is always at my fingertips using the search engine within this program.

A software package like FileMaker can also produce tape labels, informant lists, or data analysis information, all of which are useful administrative aspects of a corpus.

Table 9.2 Automated retrieval of speaker information and characteristics

Speaker #	**Pseudonym**	**Speaker code**	**Sex**	**Age**	**Birthplace**	**Education**
003	Caroline Spence	C	F	70	York, UK	Up to age 14
007	Margaret Brown	g	F	72	York, UK	Up to age 14
016	Jenny Hornsea	p	F	74	York, UK	Up to age 15

3.4 Data-processing

Perhaps most exciting for the corpus-building enterprise is the end product: a database that is capable of automated processing via word lists, indexes and concordances. This opens up an enormous amount of language data for analysis, as automated extraction and data-processing greatly facilitate the extraction and tabulation of linguistic features in preparation for pilot examinations, preliminary distributional analysis, coding and subsequently linguistic analysis.

Once language data has been made machine-readable as transcription files (which are simply ASCII files), they may be imported into any number of programs which can process data automatically. I have always used Concorder (Rand and Patera, 1992). However, there are many others.

One of the most useful procedures in the initial phases of a research project is to do a word list for each speaker. For example, in Figure 9.36 on page 227, automatic processing reveals that the number of words spoken by 'eburritt' is 10,406 words, and her vocabulary is 1,281.

This information can then be entered in the database and used as a baseline for frequency counts of lexical items occurring in the data. For example, simple counts of the non-verbal *like* used by a younger and older female in the York corpus, as in Table 9.3 on page 227, provide a particularly insightful view of this form. Notice the tremendous increase in proportion for the younger speaker. No wonder student transcribers could not tell which uses were standard!

Perhaps the most useful procedure is to create an index. It consists of an alphabetical listing of all the words uttered by the informant in the transcribed interview. Table 9.4 on page 228 shows an excerpt of

```
CatalogueWords ("eburritt.txt",
" eburritt.Cat",
  Liaison(95,202,208),
  ignoreCase,
  passages,
  exclude( ),
  speaker["002"]);
N° of words found...............: 10406
N° of distinct words......: 1281
N° of letters per word: 3.59
N° of entries inserted: 1281
Hours:Min:Sec: 0:00:03
```

Figure 9.36 Speaker vocabulary

Table 9.3 Occurrences and ratio of *like* in the York corpus

Speaker	**Raw number**	**Ratio**
Young female – S Ball [049] age 23	91	1:68
Older female – E Burritt [002] age 82	4	1:3314

the index entries for the alphabetical listing of words from *than* to *three* for EB, speaker 002 in the York English corpus. Notice that even with this small excerpt, clear patterns of linguistic behaviour are apparent. Function words are very frequent compared to lexical words. Compare *the* (n = 294), *thermal* (n = 1) and *thing* (n = 5), for example. Notice also the differential frequencies of certain pronouns, such as *that* (n = 134) versus *this* (n = 42), or *these* (n = 8) versus *those* (n = 17) versus *them* (n = 44), or the distribution of tense forms in the same lexical verb *think*, that is, *think* (27) versus *thought* (8). Such overall distribution patterns can point to potential linguistic features for investigation.

Table 9.4 Excerpt of a word list using Concorder

Word form	Tokens	Word form	Tokens
than	3	things	11
that	134	think	27
the	294	thinking	1
their	7	thirty	5
them	44	this	42
then	58	those	17
there	80	thought	8
thermal	1	thousand	1
these	8	thousands	1
they	126	threatened	2
thing	5	three	10

Another function of some concordance packages is that this same information can be processed, but the program can position each word alphabetically in the context in which it occurred as a centred keyword, as in Figure 9.37, which shows the entry for the form *those.*

THOSE 8

42	round, because it was horses in those days. [1] Uh - huh [002]
48	my Dad had all the um, pub yards those days, with a few pigs in,
49	dealers [1] Yeah. [002] And in those days, if you to go for a
66	because I was having a baby, and in those days you didn 't have
71	1] Uh - huh [002] Which you did those days, and we already had a
92	docks, where you live, through those big gates. And they used
176	scholarship, which was very clever those days, and er, oh my mother
224	who has everything, it was one of those things, but I loved my

Figure 9.37 Excerpt of a concordance using Concorder

These data files are called concordances and are immense. For example, for eburritt's interview, we recorded an hour of audio tape. This produced 24 pages of transcription, double spaced, with a 12-point font size. The concordance, however, is 294 pages long, and takes up 992 kilobytes of computer space.

Perhaps the most useful function, at least in my view, is being able to extract automatically into a text file all instances of a given form in the contexts in which it occurs. For example, in Figures 9.38–9.40, all the instances of *them, these* and *those* have been extracted automatically from eburritt's interview using the index.

31,48	In THEM days, you didn't care, but um... oh, this is
54,34	And nearly all of THEM went down a passage, s
57,87	[002] Er, in there they used to shoot THEM, and
80,64	And all THEM things,
93,25	up to Osbaldwick, all of THEM, hundreds of THEM
93,43	up to Osbaldwick, all of THEM, hundreds of THEM
94,0	THEM, to what you called layeridge, lyke a resting place overnight,
120,76	we must have lived two ot three years with THEM.
138,34	I've two here, of THEM. That's in the church...
152,58	No just leave THEM there, I'll see to THEM.
152,83	No just leave THEM there, I'll see to THEM. I'm a great
164,52	it wasn't worth a lot of money THEM days
227,0	THEM from, and she got a great big book out,
250,35	went to Scarborough, where some of THEM never got a holiday,
283,36	[002] And they couldn't let THEM out when we liberated it
284,36	Typhus you-see, they could speak to THEM through the wires
284,68	and pass THEM a packet of
290,85	[002] And all they could do was give THEM
326,52	[002] Buter, you always made THEM right, but sometimes you had to have
378,8	stopped THEM going in now.
380,81	They saw all those things because I saw that they saw THEM because I
439,27	[002] That- that's THEM yeah, a
500,37	dont't know whether you've heard of THEM, they're ice-cream-parlours in the city,
508,25	all others had gone withTHEM.
541,53	you-know thermal vests and three-quarter sleeves and THEM sort of thing, er,
546,65	she says "Mother if you want THEM, get THEM."
546,75	[she says "Mother if you want THEM." (20.3) And
561,36	they were my mother's but she gave THEM to Glenis, the little girl who died.
562,85	And Glenis was always in and out of hospital, and she used to take all THEM in a
575,31	and I give THEM money, I don't give THEM presents, so they buy what they
575,57	and I give THEM money, I don't give THEM presents, so they buy what they

Figure 9.38 Excerpt of an index using Concorder: *them*

576,20	and I do give THEM money,
578,31	then I would endeavour to give THEM all money.
578,55	I made THEM all the like, you-know, and they all
580,51	and I'll give THEM all a fiver a piece to buy an Easter egg,
601,27	I talk to THEM, they're lovely little dogs
604,66	because my husband bought THEM a pony.
608,0	THEM you-know, within reason.
617,22	the- what do you call THEM little books that they get?
617,76	What's the name of THEM?
619,38	Oh-God, I've been all round edges of THEM when Maureen-
634,9	've read THEM.
636,31	these people, how they collect THEM in, and it mentions all the names.
684,39	Monday at Terry's, 'cos there was jobs THEM days.

Figure 9.38 *Continued*

1.154,80	And of course it's just come out now because THESE things can
1.172,23	funny how they grow up THESE children,
1.379,5	love THESE things myself.
1.404,52	You-know, when we go away we didn't wan to go into THESE big restaurants,
1.493,80	picking potatoes out of the ground in a basket those days, not on THESE machines.
1.629,75	And it was all THESE Irish people who
1.634,0	THESE people, how they collect them in, and it mentions all the names.
1.636,49	Quaker family, they were the families who helped THESE people,

Figure 9.39 Excerpt of an index using Concorder: *these*

This process took seconds. Yet this format provides two noteworthy advantages over the word list. First, the data are immediately put into a form which makes them (practically) ready to import directly into a data-processing program or statistical package such as the variable rule program, GoldVarb 2.0 (Rand and Sankoff, 1990). Second, the patterns

Those	
1.40,82	because it was horses in THOSE days.
1.46,6	yards THOSE days, with a few pigs in, hens,
1.47,67	And in THOSE days, if you to go for a
1.64,22	and in THOSE days you didn't have babies, when
1.69,14	Which you did THOSE days, and we already had a baby.
1.90,52	[002] On the cattle docks, where you live, through THOSE big gates.
1.174,85	Anyway, he passed the scholarship, which was very clever THOSE days,
1.222,34	it was one of THOSE things, but I loved my brother, I loved him dearly,
1.378,40	They saw all THOSE things
1.453,79	chaperoned in THOSE days,
1.455,16	need anybody in THOSE days.
1.463,0	THOSE days, to see to my Mum,
1.479,91	Oh yes, 'cos you died THOSE
1.487,9	remember THOSE days.
1.493,61	picking potatoes out of the ground in a basket THOSE days, not on these machines.
1.556,13	cabinet, all THOSE little pieces,
1.562,0	THOSE pieces were always taken in with her.

Figure 9.40 Excerpt of an index using Concorder: *those*

of use of the forms and particular collocations in the data become exponentially more visible. For example, notice the different functions the forms have. And further, notice the variation between *those* and *them* with certain lexical items, such as *day*. These observations can inform coding strategies for internal linguistic factors. When the data are imported into statistical packages such as GoldVarb, they can be easily coded in preparation for analysis. The data for variable plural demonstratives from speaker 002 in the York corpus, extracted following standard principles of accountability (for example, Labov, 1970) and circumscription of the variable context (for example, Wolfram, 1993), and coded in GoldVarb format are listed in Figure 9.41. These data have been coded for a number of external and internal factors, which are listed in the codes immediately following the open paren-

;eburritt	
(YObP - ID	it was horses in THOSE days.
(YObT - ID	my Dad had all the um, pub yards THOSE days
(YObP - ID	And in THOSE days, if you to go for a
(YObP - ID	and in THOSE days you didn 't have babies ,
(YObT - ID	Which you did THOSE days,
(YObPAI -	through THOSE big gates.
(YObT- ID	which was very clever THOSE days
(YObP- IH	it was one of THOSE things
(YObDQIH	They saw all THOSE things
(YObP - ID	You didn 't need chaperones in THOSE days love.
(YObP - ID	You didn 't need anybody in THOSE days.
(YObT - ID	the midwife it was THOSE days, to see to my Mum,
(YObT - ID	'cos you died THOSE days from percular fever.
(YObT - ID	there were poor people THOSE days.
(YObT - ID	out of the ground in a basket THOSE days,
(YObXBI -	all THOSE little pieces [absolute]
(YObS - I -	THOSE pieces were always
(YEbP - ID	In THEM days, you didn 't care,
(YEbXQIH	And all THEM things [absolute]
(YEbT- ID	it wasn 't worth a lot of money THEM days
(YEbD- C -	three - quarter sleeves and THEM sort of thing,
(YEbDAI -	What do you call THEM little books that they get?
(YEbT - ID	'cos there was jobs THEM days.
(YEbP- ID	In THEM days, you didn 't care,
(YEbXQIH	And all THEM things [absolute]
(YEbT- ID	it wasn 't worth a lot of money THEM days
(YEbD-C-	three - quarter sleeves and THEM sort of thing,
(YEbDAI -	What do you call THEM little books that they get?
(YEbT- ID	'cos there was jobs THEM days.

Figure 9.41 Variable plural demonstratives for 'eburritt', YRK: coded data

thesis in each line. The first column codes the corpus from which the datum comes, in this case YORK, 'Y'. In the second column, the surface form of the plural demonstrative, whether *those*, 'O' or *them*, 'E' is indi-

Name of token file: eburritt
Name of condition file: OD.Cnd

VARIANTS THOSE THEM TOTAL %

----

1 (4) GRAMMATICAL CATEGORY OF THE NOUN

		those	*them*	N	%	
P	N	7	2	9	31	PREPOSITION PHRASE
	%	78	22			e.g. in THEM days ...
T	N	7	4	11	38	TEMPORAL PHRASE WITHOUT PREPOSITION
	%	64	36			e.g. Dad had all the um, pub yards THOSE days
D	N	1	4	5	17	DIRECT OBJECT
	%	20	80			e.g. THEM little pieces
X	N	1	2	3	10	e.g. all THOSE little pieces
	%	33	67			
S	N	1	0	1	3	SUBJECT
	%	100	0			e.g. THOSE pieces were always ...
Total	N	17	12	29		
	%	59	41			

----

2 (5) DETERMINATION ON THE NOUN

		those	*them*	N	%	
-	N	14	8	22	76	BARE DEMONSTRATIVE
	%	64	36			
A	N	1	2	3	10	ADJECTIVE
	%	33	67			
Q	N	1	2	3	10	QUANTIFIER
	%	33	67			
B	N	1	0	1	3	ADJECTIVE/QUANTIFIER
	%	1 00	0			
Total	N	17	12	2 9		
	%	59	41			

Figure 9.42 Variable plural demonstratives for 'eburritt', YRK: statistics

3 (6) ANIMACY OF THE NOUN						
		those	*them*	N	%	
I	N	17	10	27	93	INANIMATE
	%	63	37			
C	N	0	2	2	7	kind of/sort of + INANIMATE
	%	0	100			
Total	N	17	12	29		
	%	59	41			
TOTAL	N	17	12	29		
	%	59	41			

Figure 9.42 Continued

cated. In the third column, the individual speaker is coded, in this case eburritt, speaker identification code 'b'.

Once in this format, the data can be processed statistically very easily. The marginal data, produced by GoldVarb 2.0, for this speaker's data are shown in Figure 9.41. Overall, there are 29 tokens of the demonstrative: 59 per cent are *those*, and 41 per cent *them*. This means that there is robust variation between the standard and non-standard variant. Is there any way to predict one over the other? This is where the coding for internal factors comes into play. These data have been coded for several putative effects. In the fourth column of the listing in Figure 9.42, grammatical category of the noun phrase is coded as follows: prepositional phrase, 'P'; temporal phrase without preposition, 'T'; direct object, 'D'; subject, 'S'; and absolute contexts, 'X'. In column five, determination on the noun phrase is coded as: preceding quantifier, 'Q'; adjective(s) before the noun, 'A'; both quantifier(s) and adjectives(s), 'B'; a preceding partitive, 'P'; numeric quantifier, 'N'; and a bare demonstrative only, '-'. In column six, animacy of the noun is coded as: human, 'H'; animal, 'A'; and inanimate, 'I'. There are also specific codes for *kind* or *sort* with an animate noun, as in *them kind of folk*, 'K', and *kind* or *sort* with an inanimate noun, as in *those kind of shops*, 'C'. Note that the data for this single individual speaker do not contain all of these possible contexts.

While very little can be gleaned from such a small sample, a few observations can be made. First, most of the data are inanimate, at least for this speaker: 93 per cent ($n = 27$). The non-standard variant *them* appears most often as a direct object: 80 per cent of these contexts are encoded with

• CELL CREATION • 1/6/05 • 1: 15 PM ••••••
Name of token file: THEM/THOSE. Tkn
Name of condition file: YRK_OD2. Cnd
VARIANTS THOSE THEM Total%

---

1 (4) GRAMMATICAL CATEGORY OF THE NOUN

		those	*them*	N	%
P	N	157	34	191	66
	%	82	18		
R	N	5	4	9	3
	%	56	44		
I	N	18	1	19	7
	%	95	5		
D	N	22	7	29	10
	%	76	24		
Y	N	4	0	4	1
	%	100	0		
S	N	11	3	14	5
	%	79	21		
X	N	6	1	7	2
	%	86	14		
T	N	10	3	13	4
	%	77	23		
Z	N	2	1	3	1
	%	67	33		
Total	N	285	54	289	
	%	81	19		

---

2 (5) DETERMINATION ON THE NOUN

		those	*them*	N	%
–	N	190	44	234	81
	%	81	19		
N	N	14	3	17	6
	%	82	18		
A	N	5	3	8	3
	%	63	38		
Q	N	13	2	15	5
	%	87	13		
B	N	5	0	5	2
	%	100	0		
P	N	8	2	10	3
	%	80	20		
Total	N	235	54	289	
	%	81	19		

Figure 9.43 Variable plural demonstratives for York English

VARIANTS THOSE THEM Total %

3 (6) ANIMACY OF THE NOUN

		those	*them*	N	%
I	N	210	48	258	89
	%	81	19		
C	N	4	1	5	2
	%	80	20		
H	N	19	5	24	8
	%	79	21		
A	N	1	0	1	0
	%	100	0		
K	N	1	0	1	0
	%	100	0		
Total	N	235	54	289	
	%	81	19		

4 (7)

D	N	126	30	156	54
	%	81	19		
–	N	95	20	115	40
	%	83	17		
Y	N	3	1	4	1
	%	75	25		
P	N	3	0	3	1
	%	100	0		
G	N	0	1	1	0
	%	0	100		
H	N	7	2	9	3
	%	78	22		
C	N	1	0	1	0
	%	100	0		
Total	N	235	54	289	
	%	81	19		

TOTAL	N	235	54	289
	%	81	19	

Figure 9.43 *Continued*

them. The non-standard variant is also more likely to occur in contexts determined by quantifiers and/or adjectives. The non-standard variant *them* appears in four out of five of these contexts, but only in eight out of 22 contexts that have only the demonstrative. An interesting research question then becomes: do these preliminary patterns endure once additional speakers and dialects are considered?

In fact, this excerpt is part of a much larger study on variation in demonstrative use of *them* and *those*. In Figure 9.43, we can take a peek at the same findings, but this time for all 97 speakers of the York corpus. The same codes described above are relevant, although here more categories are represented due to the substantial increase in data.

We are now looking at 289 tokens of the feature under investigation. Most of the data continue to be inanimate (89 per cent of all the data). However, with all the speakers included (who range in age from 17 to 95) the standard variant is in the majority, 81 per cent. Nevertheless, note that, as before, *them* occurs more often with direct objects, 24 per cent of the time ($n = 29$). Further, *them* occurs more often in contexts determined by adjectives, 63 per cent of the time ($n = 8$). However, in both cases, the number of instances is quite small. There are numerous other observations that could be made. The relevant point for this chapter is simply that the machine-readable corpus, along with the additional linguistic work mentioned above, produced this study in a reasonable amount of time (several months). Indeed, the full-scale analysis encompassed not only the York corpus, but also seven other dialect corpora totalling 2,107 tokens of the plural demonstrative in all (Tagliamonte, 2001). Without the machine-readable corpora it might have taken years.

4 Summary

When language materials have been transcribed consistently, as I have outlined here, and the analyst has been successful in anticipating future research interests, then machine-readable corpora will provide innumerable opportunities for research.[3] At the same time, the sheer availability of enormous amounts of data means that there is an increased imperative for caution in linguistic accountability. In particular, it is critical that the form/function relationship is taken into account. Overarching counts of forms only become meaningful if the forms are all representative of the same function in the grammar. Indeed, this is one of the foremost arguments for 'tagging' corpora for grammatical function (see Allen *et al.*, 2007 and Taylor, 2007, Volume 2). Thus, for example, blanket extraction of the form <going> in untagged corpora, such as my own, would mix the progressive verb with the gerund with the future temporal reference marker, among other functions. This can be illustrated effectively with the data on *them* and *those*. The data shown in Figures 9.38–9.40 (above) were produced by an automated procedure that extracted *all* forms of *them* and *those*. However, in order to produce the appropriate data set for an analysis of plural demonstratives it was necessary to narrow these data down to only those forms that were functioning as plural demonstratives. Thus, additional linguistic work was required to produce the data in Figure 9.41.

Another important methodological point is that raw frequencies must be normalized so that they can be meaningfully compared. A count of 1,000 tokens of X is only useful if the denominator from which it has been extracted is known. As more and more corpora are collected, processed and added to the body of materials available for analysis, it will become even more critical to maintain rigorous and replicable standards in method. Further, as analysts begin to move beyond single data sets to broad cross-variety studies it will be important to situate their research both in the context of other corpora and with other findings in the field. Thus, it is imperative that the work and the findings are comparable across the board.

In the end, however, the task of corpus-building is only the first step. Machine-readable corpora and their components do not result in static, finished products, but are actually evolving features in the research enterprise. As more and more research analyses are completed, the details relevant to ongoing work on the corpora evolve as well. The transcription protocol is added to and revised. In this way, it becomes an invaluable reference document that ensures that not only future recurrences of the same phenomenon will be treated consistently, but also previous ones. It also provides a check on the consistency of new corpora and a permanent record of the overall characteristics of each data set. The transcriptions themselves may also continue to evolve as additional details of the language are understood (see Labov and Fanshel, 1977, p.355). Furthermore, as linguistic variables are studied in the corpora, they are entered into the database along with other details that have been discovered along the way. For example, I always keep a running record of interesting examples, new features that I had not noticed before, who says them and how often. This is all part of the ongoing, unpredictable nature of corpus-building: 'Given a body of text, there is almost no way of saying what features will arouse the interest of the analyst, and once he has found a structural point of interest, it is very difficult to say in what direction his interest will carry him' (Labov and Fanshel, 1977, p.350).

Thus, it is important to have transcription files that are maximally flexible. Because my transcription files are basically just text files, they can be processed by just about any concordance software package, any time I want to dip into the data to see what is there. All these procedures become an extremely valuable part of *ongoing* research, not to mention a rich reservoir of ideas that you can use for your own future research.

Notes

1. Other participants who happen to talk during an interview are also assigned single-digit numbers, for example 4 or higher, to distinguish them from the informants of the corpus.
2. The zero copula has long been considered absent from British dialects.
3. Indeed, alongside efficient support documentation, even unanticipated research interests can be realized if there is easy access to the original audio record.

References

Allen, W. H., J. C. Beal, K. P. Corrigan, W. Maguire and Hermann L. Moisl. 2007. 'A linguistic "time capsule": The Newcastle Electronic Corpus of Tyneside English'. *Creating and Digitizing Language Corpora: Diachronic Databases (Volume 2)*, ed. by J. C. Beal, K. P. Corrigan and H. L. Moisl, pp. 16–48. Basingstoke: Palgrave Macmillan.

Anderwald, L. and S. Wagner. 2007. 'FRED: The Freiburg English dialect corpus – applying corpus-linguistic research tools to the analysis of dialect data'. *Creating and Digitizing Language Corpora: Synchronic Databases* (Volume 1), ed. by J. C. Beal, K. P. Corrigan and H. L. Moisl, pp. 35–53. Basingstoke: Palgrave Macmillan.

Labov, W. 1970. 'The study of language in its social context'. *Studium Generale* 23:30–87.

Labov, W. 1971. 'Some principles of linguistic methodology'. *Language in Society* 1:97–120.

Labov, W. and D. Fanshel. 1977. *Therapeutic Discourse; Psychotherapy as Conversation*. San Diego, Caly.: Academic.

Leonard, T. 1984. *Intimate Voices: Selected Works 1965–1983*. Newcastle-upon-Tyne: Galloping Dog.

Macaulay, R. K. S. 1988. 'Urbanity in an urban dialect: the poetry of Tom Leonard'. *Studies in Scottish Literature* 23:150–63.

Macaulay, R. K. S. 1991. '"Coz it izny spelt when they say it": displaying dialect in writing'. *American Speech* 66:280–91.

Ochs, E. 1979. 'Transcription as theory'. *Developmental Pragmatics*, ed. by E. Ochs and B. B. Schieffelin, pp. 43–72. New York: Academic Press.

Pike, K. 1947. *Phonemics: A Technique for Reducing Languages to Writing*. Ann Arbor: University of Michigan Press.

Poplack, S. 1989. 'The care and handling of a megacorpus: the Ottawa–Hull French project'. *Language Change and Variation*, ed. by R. Fasold and D. Schiffrin, pp. 411–51. Amsterdam: Benjamins.

Poplack, S. and S. A. Tagliamonte. 1991. 'African American English in the diaspora: evidence from old-line Nova Scotians'. *Language Variation and Change* 3:301–39.

Poplack, S. and S. A. Tagliamonte. 1999. 'The grammaticalization of *going to* in (African American) English'. *Language Variation and Change* 11:315–42.

Preston, D. 1985. 'The Li'l Abner syndrome: written representations of speech'. *American Speech* 60:328–36.

Preston, D. 2000. '"Mowr and mowr bayud spellin": confessions of a sociolinguist'. *Journal of Sociolinguistics* 4:614–21.

Rand, D. and T. Patera. 1992. *Concorder*, Version 1.1S. Montréal: Centre de recherches mathématiques, Université de Montréal.

Rand, D. and D. Sankoff. 1990. *GoldVarb: A Variable Rule Application for the Macintosh*, Version 2. Montréal: Centre de recherches mathématiques, Université de Montréal.

Sankoff, D. and W. Labov. 1979. 'On the uses of variable rules'. *Language in Society* 8:189–222.

Sankoff, G. 1980. 'A quantitative paradigm for the study of communicative competence'. *The Social Life of Language*, ed. by G. Sankoff, pp. 47–79. Philadelphia: University of Pennsylvania Press.

Sankoff, G. and P. Thibault. 1980. 'The alternation between the auxiliaries *avoir* and *être* in Montréal French'. *The Social Life of Language*, ed. by G. Sankoff, pp. 311–45. Philadelphia: University of Pennsylvania Press.

Tagliamonte, S. A. 1996–98. *Roots of Identity: Variation and Grammaticization in Contemporary British English*. Research Grant R000221842, Economic and Social Sciences Research Council (ESRC) of Great Britain.

Tagliamonte, S. A. 1999–2000. *Grammatical Variation and Change in British English: Perspectives from York*. University of York. Research Grant R000238287, Economic and Social Science Research Council of the United Kingdom.

Tagliamonte, S. A. 2000–01. *Vernacular Roots: A Database of British Dialects*. Research Grant B/RG/AN 6093/APN11081, Arts and Humanities Research Board of the United Kingdom (AHRB).

Tagliamonte, S. A. 2001. 'English dialects ... *and them*: form and function in comparative perspective'. *American Speech* 75:405–9.

Tagliamonte, S. A. 2001–03. *Back to the Roots: The Legacy of British Dialects*. Research Grant R000239097, Economic and Social Research Council of the United Kingdom (ESRC).

Tagliamonte, S. A. and R. Temple. 2005. 'New perspectives on an ol' variable: (t,d) in British English'. *Language Variation and Change* 17(3):281–302.

Taylor, A. 2007. 'The York–Toronto–Helsinki Parsed Corpus of Old English Prose'. *Creating and Digitizing Language Corpora: Diachronic Databases (Volume 2)*, ed. by J. C. Beal, K. P. Corrigan and H. L. Moisl, pp. 196–227. Basingstoke: Palgrave Macmillan.

Wolfram, W. 1993. 'Identifying and interpreting variables'. *American Dialect Research*, ed. by D. Preston, pp. 193–221. Amsterdam and Philadelphia: John Benjamins.

Index